HALTON BOYS

"The aim of apprentice training is to produce a completely reliable man."

Lord Trenchard

HALTON BOYS

TRUE TALES FROM PILOTS AND GROUND CREW
PROUD TO BE CALLED 'TRENCHARD BRATS'

SEAN FEAST

Foreword by The Viscount Trenchard DL
Introduction by Group Captain Min Larkin CBE

GRUB STREET · LONDON

Published by
Grub Street
4 Rainham Close
London SW11 6SS

Copyright © Grub Street 2020
Copyright text © Sean Feast 2020

A CIP record for this title is available from the British library

ISBN-13: 978-1-911621-94-2

Design by Lucy Thorne

Printed and bound in the Czech Republic by Finidr

CONTENTS

AN APPRECIATION

A reliable account of the varied and numerous contributions that the engineering apprentices of the Royal Air Force have made over the years to that service has long been overdue. In 24 fluent chapters the author Sean Feast offers a very well-balanced picture to remedy that omission. His book is not merely about the ground crews that Halton produced, it also captures the spirit of the Halton training school that so strongly guided its graduates in peace, war and even into careers such as politics, high levels of industry, the police service and colonial administration. *Halton Boys* is a most worthy contribution to the broader history of our times and is strongly recommended.

Air Chief Marshal Sir Michael Armitage KCB, CBE (56th Entry)

ACKNOWLEDGEMENTS

This book could not have been written without the full support of Halton's Brats, past and present, for which I owe them an enormous debt of thanks.

To Sir Hugh, for graciously writing the foreword and Sir Michael for his kind appreciation and encouragement throughout. To those who agreed to feature in the story – John Clements, Eugene Borysiuk, Mike Hines, Peter Goodwin, Alan Kidson, Sir Dusty Miller, Wally Epton and Lawrie Haynes – I similarly extend my thanks for their willingness to help at every stage, and in reading their respective chapters and their politeness in correcting my mistakes. So too Francis Hanford of the Trenchard Museum for kindly reading the finished draft and suggesting amendments. Any mistakes that are left are entirely of my own making, and I apologise in advance!

I also offer thanks to all those who provided photographs, many not published before. To Eric Yocum my thanks for his help in creating the chapter on Graham Hulse, and for putting me in touch with James K. Thompson who flew Wing with Graham in Korea, and my friend Ben van Drogenbroek of the Stalag Luft 3 Archives of the Netherlands for use of imagery and his general passion for conserving the memory of those murdered in the Great Escape. My thanks are also extended to Rob Owen, 617 Squadron historian, and fellow Grub Street author Graham Pitchfork for his research on Surtees Elliott. Indeed, my thanks go to the whole of the Grub Street Publishing team for their usual professionalism and good humour. This is now our eighth sortie together since they took their first leap of faith with me more than 15 years' ago and it is always a fun experience. And a good lunch.

Books can never be written as a hobby without the support of others around you, and for that I acknowledge the help and general encouragement of my Gravity team, and especially Iona (yes, she's still there after 18 years), Imogen, Laura and Rob, the best team anyone could wish for. And, of course, no thanks would be complete without mentioning the genius that is my wife, Elaine, and my two boys Matt and James who are now grown-ups (at least in theory).

I would like to reserve my greatest thanks, however, for Min Larkin and his team at the Halton Archive. It has been a genuine pleasure to work with Min on this project for the last 18 months, although the idea of the book has been much longer in discussion. Min's passion for Halton, and for life generally, is infectious and it is a privilege to think that we have become friends. This one is for you, Min.

Sean Feast
December 2019

FOREWORD
THE SPIRIT OF HALTON

I am delighted to have been asked by Sean Feast to write a foreword to his book, *Halton Boys*, which tells the story of the RAF Apprentices' Scheme, located at RAF Halton, better known as 'Trenchard's Brats'.

My grandfather envisaged that the scheme would deliver a cadre of highly trained, highly motivated airmen which would not only help develop a unique Royal Air Force spirit, but would provide the fledgling service with a solid foundation of highly skilled personnel on which to expand rapidly in the event of another world war.

In 1944 he said in the House of Lords:

> "…the Halton-trained men provided the nucleus on which the great expansion of the air force was centred. Surely the efficient maintenance of aircraft has also been one of the outstanding features of the war, and that has been made possible by the Halton training of our men."

Trenchard's Brats made an outstanding contribution to the Second World War, sadly at a great cost in life. Their courage, loyalty and devotion to duty was recognised by the award to former apprentices of over 3,000 decorations for gallantry, including a Victoria Cross and five George Crosses.

My grandfather always wanted the Royal Air Force to recruit the very best people, regardless of background, and to provide them with the opportunity to develop their skills to the best of their ability. In the event, over 100 Halton apprentices attained air rank and over 30 per cent were commissioned.

Many apprentices made outstanding contributions to the country beyond the RAF, including Sir Frank Whittle who gave the world the jet engine. Sean has written about a number of them in this fascinating book which well illustrates the importance of Halton and the apprentices' scheme not only to the Royal Air Force but to the nation as a whole.

The Viscount Trenchard DL
Honorary Air Commodore, 600 (City of London) Squadron
Royal Auxiliary Air Force

INTRODUCTION
AN IDEA IS BORN – GROUP CAPTAIN MIN LARKIN CBE

From the moment the Royal Flying Corps (RFC) was founded in 1912, it suffered from a shortage of trained personnel, and especially air mechanics. In the short term, this was solved by combing through the ranks for skilled artificers among those already in uniform and identifying likely candidates among the many volunteers who were joining the colours. A longer-term solution, however, had to be found.

In January 1917, the Army Council authorised the expansion of the RFC to a total of 106 squadrons – 86 in France – and in July this was almost doubled to 200. But there was a problem: the manufacturers could build the aircraft, but a typical front-line aircraft required a ground crew of a dozen skilled men to keep it in the air, and such men were rather thin on the ground.

To their credit, the authorities recognised that demand could not be met within the existing infrastructure, and that a dedicated training programme was required. Again, a short-term solution was found; training was delivered wherever suitable sites could be found, with air mechanic schools large and small scattered all over the country including one in a converted jam factory.

Under the continuing pressure on manpower another very important decision for the future of the RFC was taken; it was decided to recruit boys. This kind of improvisation, however, could not provide all of the men the RFC needed, and rationalisation of the training machine became an urgent requirement. In June 1917 Major General Sefton Brancker, deputy director general of Military Aeronautics, submitted proposals to centralise the technical training of men, women and boys in a new large school to be located at Halton. The new school was to be under the direct control of the War Office and commanded by Lieutenant Colonel Ian Bonham-Carter.

The first 400 RFC boy mechanics enlisted at Farnborough in May 1917, shortly followed by further intakes at Blandford. These boys moved to Halton in the late summer of 1917 where, by the end of the year, some 2,000 boys were under training as air mechanics, living in spartan conditions in dilapidated wooden huts previously occupied by infantry troops. Although many of the boys were later transferred to Cranwell, where permanent accommodation was available, several thousand remained at Halton undergoing in equal measure, drill, physical training, fatigues and technical training for which only basic facilities were available. The latter improved, however, with the opening of large training workshops in early 1918 which had been rapidly constructed by the Royal Engineers using German POW labour.

The arrival of the first RAF commandant and former naval man, Air Commodore Francis Scarlett CB DSO, in December 1919 heralded many improvements to all aspects of boy training, in particular the tightening of disciplinary standards which had been allowed to slacken after the armistice. The brass 'wheel' badge, worn by all RAF apprentices for some 75 years, to distinguish them from men, had been introduced in April 1919. Now with some 4,000 boys on strength, Scarlett wanted an additional distinguishing feature on their uniforms to facilitate immediate recognition of the sections (later wings) to which an individual belonged. His reason for this was to ensure

A. J. Gooding – the youngest RFC apprentice at 14 years of age at Farnborough Depot.

that boys committing offences both on and off the station could be dealt with expeditiously by the appropriate authority. His recommendation to the Air Ministry of distinctive coloured hatbands was approved in 1920 and this too became a permanent feature of an apprentice's uniform.

In March 1920 No. 1 School of Technical Training was established at Halton, the future home of aircraft apprentice training. Scarlett remained in post until 1924 and oversaw the transformation of a temporary wartime military camp into the beginnings of a permanent RAF station. He had laid firm ground on which Lord Trenchard, the father of the Royal Air Force (as the RFC officially became on 1 April 1918), was able to develop his aircraft apprentice scheme.

In his memorandum, 'Permanent Organisation of the Royal Air Force', which was presented to the House of Commons as a White Paper by Secretary of State Winston Churchill in December 1919, Trenchard placed great emphasis on the importance of training, particularly of skilled ground crew. He argued that the best way to ensure that,

> '... the training of our mechanics in the multiplicity of trades necessitated by a highly technical service [...] is to enlist the bulk of our skilled ranks as boys, and train them ourselves. This has the added advantage that it will undoubtedly foster the Air Force spirit on which so much depends.'

Later in the paper, he continues:

> 'The training of all these boys will eventually be carried out at Halton Park
> [...] The first entry under the scheme will take place early in 1920 at Cran-
> well [...] and move to Halton as soon as permanent accommodation is
> ready.'

He provided more detail about his intentions for the scheme in a letter to Churchill in November 1919, writing:

> 'It is necessary to enlist the bulk of the technical tradesmen of the force as
> boys, because the Royal Air Force cannot hope to compete in the recruit-
> ment of men who have served full apprenticeships and who can command
> high wages in civil life.'

He goes on to say that apprentices were to form 40 per cent of all ground crews in
the Royal Air Force, and 62 per cent of all the skilled tradesmen.

It was clear that Trenchard wanted highly skilled men at a price the service could
afford from its very meagre budget, and men who would foster an 'air force spirit'.
Thus, in late 1919 the Halton Apprentice Scheme was promulgated to local education authorities, and competitive entrance examinations (similar to those for boy
artificers joining the Royal Navy) were held in London and the provinces. Medi-
cally fit potential recruits were offered training in the trade of their choice, or one
the selectors thought most appropriate for them. The rigorous selection procedure
ensured that recruits would be of the highest quality and, because of their resource-
fulness and intelligence, they could be expected to complete their apprenticeships
in three years rather than the five normally served by civilian engineering apprentices. A shorter course meant a cheaper one, which no doubt pleased the Secretary
of State for Air, Winston Churchill!

In February 1920, still known as 'Boy Mechanics', the first intake of 235 was
accepted at Cranwell for a three-year apprenticeship. Indeed, the first four intakes
trained at Cranwell, and it was not until January 1922 that the first cohort arrived
at Halton to become the 5th Entry. This move coincided with the official adoption
of the rank of aircraft apprentice. Two entries a year were planned.

On arrival at Halton, apprentices were signed on for 12 years from the age of
18, allocated accommodation and kitted out. They very soon found their lives
falling into a well-ordered routine governed largely by bugle calls. They were wok-
en with reveille at 06.30 hours, called on colour hoisting parade an hour later and
sent to bed at 21.45 hours. Apprentices were not allowed time to dwell too much
on their personal thoughts, as evenings and most of the weekends were spent in

Carpenter rigger apprentices pictured in 1922.

their 20-man billets and taken up with room cleaning, inspections and parades.

Recreational facilities were available in abundance, including a debating society, aircraft modelling and playing in one of the several apprentice bands, in addition a wide variety of sporting facilities was available. A world-class RAF hospital on the doorstep ensured their medical and dental care were second to none, and spiritual needs were more than well looked after; though few enjoyed the compulsory church parades every other Sunday. In addition to all these privileges they enjoyed six weeks' holiday a year, mid-term breaks, and were paid, albeit a paltry amount (ten shillings and sixpence a week in the first year, with small rises in the second and third).

The cost of running Halton was a contentious issue in the early days. Following a visit by members of a parliamentary select committee in 1923, they reported that they were:

> '[…] of the opinion that the management and training of these boys is conducted in a very efficient manner; they were much struck with the discipline, with the order which was kept, and the arrangement by which they were efficiently taught a trade [and they] receive a payment of 10s. 6d. a week. This payment seems to the committee to be unnecessary. These boys are […] not only extremely well lodged, fed, and clothed, but are

taught […] trades which will be useful to them in after-life. Under these circumstances it would appear that, if any payment is to be made, it should be made by the parents of the boys, and not by the state.'

Fortunately for thousands of apprentices yet to come, this point was not pursued. But the cost issue resurfaced in a Commons debate in 1926 when one MP, Sir Frank Nelson, pointed out that £230, which was the estimated cost of training an apprentice, 'is probably more than it costs a parent to send a boy to any of the four or five leading public schools of England.' He went on to complain that, 'these apprentices at Halton get 1s a day pocket money, which, when they number 3,000, will cost the country £55,000 a year, and even now it costs between £30,000 and £35,000 a year.' But, once again, the point was not pursued.

For the first 50 years of the scheme apprentices were classified as minors and their officers and SNCOs acted in loco parentis. In addition to their responsibilities under the tenets of normal military discipline, each apprentice was issued with a small booklet entitled 'Standing Orders for Apprentices'. This contained a myriad of rules which severely restricted an apprentice's freedom to spend what precious spare time he was allowed as he might wish. 'These rules are necessary for your own benefit', apprentices were often told by their superiors.

Some of the rules were reasonable for boys below the age of 18, such as 'apprentices are to take a bath twice a week' and 'apprentices are prohibited from visiting public houses and consuming alcohol'. One of the oddest rules was, 'Females are not to attend the monthly apprentice dances'. This reflects contemporary society's deeply conservative approach to sex before marriage. Perhaps the rule least respected, especially by older apprentices in their third year of training, was lights out at 21.45 hours, when their former school chums were still out enjoying themselves with their girlfriends.

Despite the harsh standards of discipline, it was virtually a point of honour for apprentices to break as many of the rules as they could, hopefully without getting caught. With an average of 2,000 boys in residence at any one time, the establishment of RAF police at Halton, known as 'Snoops' to apprentices, was higher than normal. The RAF police could often be seen patrolling local towns, especially on Saturday evenings when their chances of nabbing a few apprentices in the local pubs or dance halls were high.

Apprentice flight commanders were always busy during lunch hours hearing charges but never more so than on Mondays when they were usually faced with a crop of alleged offences resulting from apprentices enjoying themselves beyond 'lights out' on Saturday nights. Some apprentices clocked up cricket-type scores in days of 'jankers', but someone had the good sense to rule that punishments awarded for 'youthful' offences were to be erased from apprentice records on graduation. However, many apprentices believe that this anti-establishment activity contributed as much to the development of the famous Halton Spirit as did all of the discipline, communal living, sporting activities, and marching with bands.

Training at Halton was divided into three distinct, but closely co-ordinated departments: trade; academic; and general service training. Initial trade training was carried out in the workshops and on redundant aircraft on the airfield. The trades evolved with the ever-developing advances in aeronautical engineering, but they were principally engines, airframes, armaments, instruments, electrics and wireless. A pass mark in all aspects of his trade training was an absolute for an appren-

Engine fitters learning their trade.

tice to graduate. Until 1951, this mark also governed the rank with which an apprentice graduated.

Their academic training was comparable with that of a good technical college and was to National Certificate level. 'Schools', as it was known by apprentices, was conducted in a purpose-built college building which had a well-stocked library and excellent engineering science laboratories.

All apprentices studied the same mathematics, mechanics and engineering drawing syllabuses, but engineering science was tailored to suit an individual's trade. Included in the syllabus were English and general studies, which covered the history of the RAF in some depth. In the third year of training, all apprentices were required to produce a set task of 5,000 words on a subject of their choice. A National Certificate, or at least a B grade pass in the final school examinations, was sufficient to qualify an apprentice academically for commissioning. A C grade was the minimum requirement for graduation.

General service training was an important part of the curriculum, because, once he entered productive service, an apprentice was expected to gain rapid promotion and command men. From the outset of his training he became a member of a society based on the orderly pattern of RAF life in wings, squadrons and flights, where he learned the give and take of community living and developed a feeling

Lord Mountbatten inspects the apprentices.

for the customs and traditions of the service. Under the guidance of his flight commander and the NCO instructors, he was taught drill, physical training and air force law. Leadership and management experience were provided through resource and initiative training, field exercises at summer camps and the Apprentice NCO scheme.

For the many who were selected for promotion this gave greater responsibility as they progressed through the ranks. The top rank, normally flight sergeant apprentice was, in effect, the head boy of the school. He commanded the whole apprentice population and also enjoyed the privilege of commanding his entry's graduation parade, and parades for visiting VIPs and royalty.

To keep abreast of changes in RAF engineering practice, four different types of apprenticeships were introduced over the lifetime of the scheme. The original aircraft apprentice (AA) training started in 1920 and continued until December 1966, with the graduation of the 106th Entry. This scheme produced single-skill fitters who maintained aircraft and associated equipment and could, if necessary, fashion small replacement parts themselves. Initially, aircraft apprentices graduated as an aircraftman second class (AC2), an aircraftman first class (AC1), or a leading aircraftman, (LAC), depending on their final trade test results. Some who graduated as LACs in the 1920s were given immediate further training at Henlow and took up their first appointments as corporals.

Most pre-war apprentices soon attained LAC rank but, following the Great Depression, from the late 1920s to the start of the Second World War, many did not advance beyond corporal, unless selected for flying training. After the introduction of a new trade structure in 1951, all aircraft apprentices graduated as junior technicians with some gaining accelerated promotion to corporal. Most post-1951 AAs were corporals within a year of graduation.

It was in the earliest days of the aircraft apprentice scheme that the term 'Trenchard (or Halton) Brat' came into vogue, initially as a term of derision used by 'old sweats' who took a rather jaundiced view of these clever young upstarts who were destined for rapid promotion to corporal. However, as time passed and the 'brats' were able to prove their worth, it became a title which all ex-apprentices are proud to claim, even those who attained air rank.

In the late 1950s, a study was initiated into the RAF's youth training requirements. This was undertaken in parallel with another study into the requirements for trade specialisations and resulted in the 1964 Trade Structure, introduced in April that year. The aim of the two studies was to match the growing complexity of aircraft and their systems, particularly those associated with the projected Tactical Strike and Reconnaissance 2 (TSR-2) programme, with ground crew who had the ability to diagnose faults in systems which cut across the traditional trade boundaries.

The RAF's previous reliance on maintenance by repair was being superseded by a new concept of repair by component change. As a result, the single-skill aircraft apprentice was replaced by a new breed, the technician apprentice (TA), who trained in the four trades of airframe, propulsion, electrical and weapons. Technician apprentices were recruited with a minimum of four GCE O levels and more emphasis was placed on their academic training to ensure that most graduated with a National Certificate in Engineering.

The first TA intake (the 107th Entry) started training in October 1964 but, along with many others in the service, they were disappointed to learn in April 1965 that the Wilson government had scrapped the TSR-2 programme. Although the government took options on the purchase of the American F-111 this never came about. The members of Halton's 107th Entry were offered a free discharge or re-mustering to another trade. However, most volunteered to remain on the TA course as the high quality of the training they were receiving was very marketable. Equally attractive was the opportunity to graduate in the rank of corporal with early promotion to substantive sergeant after just two years satisfactory productive service.

With no TSR-2 or F-111 on which to employ these highly skilled graduates, on graduation they were initially added to existing manpower establishments that were based on single trades, but their multi-trade capabilities made them particularly useful as trade supervisors and in the diagnosis and rectification of the more intractable faults in the complex aircraft systems then coming into service. There were also more openings for TAs to be commissioned in the engineering branch as

Cabin pressurisation learning.

many of them eventually were. The TA scheme ended in 1972.

Whilst the TA scheme took care of engineering support for future aircraft and equipment coming into service, there was a continuing need for single-skill fitters. To meet this requirement a two-year craft apprentice (CA) scheme, with a new numbering series starting with the 201st Entry had been introduced concurrently with the start of the TA scheme. The CA scheme was, in effect, a direct replacement for AA training, but required lower academic qualifications on entry. Craft apprentices graduated as junior technicians but without formal academic qualifications, unless taken ex-curriculum. However, this did not prevent CAs from being commissioned, with some attaining air rank and others filling senior appointments in industry. The craft apprentice scheme lasted ten years, ending with the 231st Entry in 1974.

In 1969 a one-year mechanic apprentice course was introduced starting with the 401st Entry. Its trainees graduated as LAC with many of them still less than 17-and-a-half years of age. This was short-lived and the scheme was terminated after ten intakes. Another short-lived course training medical admin apprentices for one year starting with the 301st Entry in 1964 ended in 1969.

By the early 1970s, technical training had reached a crossroads and after considerable debate in the upper echelons of the Engineering Branch it was decided to continue apprentice training with the introduction of the apprentice engineering technician (AET) scheme. The January 1973 Entry, the 123rd, was the first to undertake AET training. The winds of change were now well and truly blowing through Halton. The maximum age for the recruitment of apprentices was raised to 18-and-a-half and, exceptionally, to 21. With many apprentices now older than direct entry airmen, there was no need for many of the 'rules' which governed the lives of their predecessors. Indeed, some AETs were married during training, had children and lived in married quarters.

The standards of behaviour expected of AETs when off-duty were similar to those required from all RAF personnel. Their adult status was recognised by the discontinuance of the NCO ranks and the removal of all apprentice insignia from uniforms. Nevertheless, certain aspects of the original scheme were retained such as the apprentice entry numbering system and AETs were accommodated separately from airmen. However, following a concerted campaign led by the RAF Halton and RAF Cranwell Apprentices Associations, supported by some prominent ex-apprentices serving at air rank (including Air Chief Marshal Sir Michael Armitage and Air Marshal Sir Eric Dunn), NCO apprentice ranks and the wearing of the iconic 'wheel' badge were reinstated in 1982. Ironically, many of the apprentices under training at this time were keen to see these symbols of their past heritage restored.

Air Commodore Mike Evans, one of six former Halton apprentices who returned to command the station[1], recalled:

> 'After the re-introduction of the "wheel" it was paraded for the first time at the graduation of the 134th Entry on 29 September 1982. AET Prevett, the parade commander, was so delighted, that he wore a "wheel" on both arms. We did not charge him with being improperly dressed.'

AETs were trained as dual-trade airframe and propulsion technicians and initially followed the National Certificate curriculum in their academic training as their predecessors had done. This element of the course was replaced in 1977 by the Ordinary Diploma and for most the Higher Certificate awarded by the newly formed Business and Technician Education Council (BTEC). These certificates were awarded for achievement in all aspects of trade and academic training. The AET scheme ended in June 1993 with the graduation of the 155th Entry, which also marked the end of apprentice training in the RAF. AETs enjoyed the highest level of aircraft engineering training during the life of the various apprentice schemes and, unsurprisingly, produced the highest number of commissioning candidates. At the end of 2015, only 65 ex-AETs were still serving, of whom 26 were holding commissions, with several at senior officer level and six with air rank.

Halton was arguably one of the first aeronautical engineering colleges in the world and certainly the first in any air force. The 'Halton Apprentice' label soon became synonymous with aeronautical engineering excellence, a reputation that rapidly gained recognition throughout the aircraft industry and internationally. The Royal New Zealand, Pakistan, Ceylon and Rhodesian Air Forces and the Burmese and Malayan Air Forces all sent boys to Halton to train alongside British apprentices. The Venezuelan Air Force also sent boys to train at Halton in the 1950s.

When the expansion of the RAF began in the mid-1930s, ex-apprentices, as Trenchard had planned, formed about 50 per cent of the trained strength of the service. With recruiting buoyant, the size of Halton intakes ballooned, reaching over 1,000 boys per entry. The 40th Entry, which enlisted in August 1939, was the largest ever with 1,385 boys taking the King's shilling. Coincidentally with the arrival of this large entry, as a war emergency measure the duration of training was gradually shortened, initially to two-and-a-half then to two years.

This reduction in training time reached its nadir with the early graduation of the 39th Entry in April 1940, after only 20 months. Many of this entry were still less than 17-and-a-half, some as young as 16, officially still boys but now serving as airmen on the front line. One of the youngest recruits to join the RAF, at just 15 years and two months, was Apprentice Harry Clack. Sadly, he would also become one of the RAF's youngest casualties on active service (see Chapter Five).

Interestingly, apprentices were the only people who continued to join the wartime RAF; from September 1939 until 1945 all other recruits were enlisted, or commissioned, into the RAFVR.

A large minority of the boys joining the RAF as apprentices saw it as a route via which they might achieve their real ambition, which was to become pilots (see

Malaysian Brats from 104 and 106th Entry with Mohamed Noor.

the stories of John Clements and Wally Epton – Chapters Ten and Twenty). Ever since 1921, airmen had been able to volunteer for training as sergeant pilots and to serve as such for six years before returning to their ground trades, retaining their rank. The idea was to create future leaders of the technical branch with an appreciation of the challenges faced by aircrew. Several hundred ex-apprentices serving on these engagements at the start of hostilities were, however, retained in flying posts. Many were soon commissioned rising quickly to executive positions on operational squadrons.

While many of their colleagues were fighting in the air, thousands of former apprentices were working tirelessly on the ground to ensure their aircraft were in fighting condition. Promotion in the ground branches in the inter-war years had been slow, even non-existent in some trades. With the rapidly growing numbers now joining the service, thousands of ex-apprentices suddenly found themselves racing through the ranks to SNCO and warrant officer, providing a vital source of experienced technical supervisors on front-line squadrons, maintenance units and as instructors for the growing number of technical training schools, just as Trenchard had planned.

Halton apprentices contributed to all of the major air campaigns of the Second World War, both in the air and on the ground. The introduction of the four-engined

Halton prepares for invasion.

Apprentices working on Mosquitos on the Halton airfield.

bombers in 1941 brought an urgent need for an additional crew member, a flight engineer. His role was to assist the pilot to manage the complicated systems in these more advanced aircraft. Former Halton apprentices were ideally suited to this new challenge, and several thousand of them transferred their engineering skills from the ground to the air in this role. Some achieved everlasting fame for their part in the Dams Raid (see Chapter Eight).

By the middle of the 1920s some apprentices were posted after a year or two of productive service to serve on aircraft carriers, then under the control of the Royal Air Force. When control of the Fleet Air Arm passed to the Royal Navy in January 1937 it lacked the facilities for training its own aircraft engineering apprentices. To meet the immediate need for these skills, volunteers were invited from the 35th, 36th and 37th Entries to transfer to the Royal Navy, and 160 of Halton's apprentices answered the call.

Subsequently the Royal Navy sent 400 directly recruited Fleet Air Arm apprentices to train with the 38th to 41st Entries. Halton and the junior service therefore made an important contribution to the foundations on which the carrier force developed into a vital arm of the nation's capability in the Second World War and beyond. Many of the initial Halton transferees were killed in various sea battles during the war; 15 went down with HMS *Glorious* at the end of the Norwegian campaign in 1940.

In 1943 hundreds of boys, mainly orphans and some as young as 14, were driven out of Poland by Hitler and, after a tortuous journey through the Middle East, ended up in the UK. Two hundred of these Polish boys were selected to train at Halton as aircraft apprentices and another 100 at Cranwell. They spent most of their first year in the RAF settling into their new country and learning English. At Halton, they joined the 49th and 50th Entries which eventually graduated in the late 1940s. Although invited to remain in the RAF on a five-year engagement, most opted to leave the service.

The Halton apprentices' loyalty and devotion to duty during the war were recognised by the large number of decorations they received. Bravery, however, was no guarantee of survival, neither was experience. The first to die were killed within hours of war being declared in Europe and never got to fulfil their true potential; the last, believed to be Flight Lieutenant James Sprigge DFM of the 33rd Entry, was killed as a passenger in a transport aircraft a few days prior to the Japanese surrender in the Far East.

The service and achievements of Halton's Boys were also recognised in the memoires and recollections of many senior commanders. Marshal of the Royal Air Force Viscount Portal, for example, recorded:

> 'The consistent technical excellence of the RAF has rested upon the skill and high devotion to duty of those who learned at Halton their trades and first formed their sense of duty. Their success in the air and on the ground pays a finer tribute than any words of mine to the standard of Halton's achievements.'

MRAF Sir Dermot Boyle was even more expansive in his praise: 'Halton throughout the years has made an outstanding contribution not only to the RAF but to the country as a whole.'

Admiral of the Fleet Earl Mountbatten was similarly effusive: 'One thing is absolutely true, the air battles of Burma were won in the classrooms and workshops at Halton; won not just by knowledge and skill of your maintenance crews, it was won by the spirit that Halton produced.'

Air Marshal Sir John Whitworth Jones concluded: 'Halton has given the Royal Air Force not only its hard core of efficient technical NCOs and airmen but also a magnificent core of officers many of whom are in high rank in all branches of the service.'

Lord Trenchard was of course proud of, and took a keen interest in, his apprentices at Halton and visited them often at work and play. He had always intended that the best of each entry should be awarded cadetships to Cranwell, but were he alive today he would be amazed to discover that over 20 per cent were commissioned, with 110 attaining air rank. One of these, MRAF Sir Keith Williamson, a Cranwell apprentice, became chief of Air Staff, and several others served on the Air Force Board, including Sir Michael Armitage who was AMSO in the early 1980s and has been the patron of the RAF Halton Apprentices Association since its foundation in 1980.

Of those apprentices who became Cranwell cadets, 17 won the Sword of Honour, giving credence to Trenchard's vision that the new service should base the selection of its future leaders on ability and merit, and not class and social background. Halton apprentice training gave many a boy from a humble background the chance to aspire to heights not normally expected of him. This very deliberate commissioning from the ranks was an outstanding example of social mobility, uncommon for the time.

Of the Halton apprentices who achieved air rank, 17 were knighted. Another was knighted when Hong Kong was transferred to China after leaving the service as a sergeant after the Second World War and rising to the top ranks of the civil service in the former colony. Thousands of others made senior officer rank. Ongoing research indicates that some 1,000 have been awarded state honours.

Although thousands of former apprentices had very successful careers in the RAF, many did not reach their full potential until life beyond the service. The aircraft industries were naturally the first port of call for many ex-apprentices where they made magnificent contributions on the shop floor, at all levels of management, and in the boardrooms. Many former apprentices who trained as pilots and flight engineers continued to fly with civil airlines and/or made notable contributions to flight safety.

After leaving the RAF, many ex-apprentices turned away from engineering altogether and forged successful second careers in other professions including medicine and the law. Some became top surgeons and a few served on the Crown Court circuit. Considering they were the two professions most apprentices had spent three years trying to avoid at Halton and Cranwell, a surprising number became vicars and policemen. In the latter respect, two Cranwell apprentices excelled, one becoming a bishop and another – Sir Kenneth Newman – followed in Lord Trenchard's footsteps by becoming head of the London Metropolitan Police.

Some former apprentices ended up as BBC TV stars. Most notable of these was Cliff Michelmore who, having graduated from Halton in 1938 (as part of the 32nd Entry), was serving as a squadron leader with a military wireless station in Germany in the mid-1940s when his talent as a broadcaster was recognised. He later hosted *Two-Way Family Favourites*, a radio programme much loved by the UK population in general and especially by personnel serving in Germany in the immediate post-war years.

The most famous of the aircraft apprentice alumni is Air Commodore Sir Frank Whittle who gave the world the jet engine. Whittle initially applied to join the 7th Entry at Halton in January 1923 but failed the medical owing to his lack of height. In an article he wrote for the *Halton Magazine* while in Halton Hospital for a short period in early 1944, Whittle explains the advice he was given by a flight sergeant physical training instructor which enabled him to add three inches to his height, enough to be accepted for the 8th Entry in September 1923. However, because the permanent barrack building programme at Halton had fallen behind schedule, this entry was trained at Cranwell.

Interestingly, at the critical stage of the development of the engine which was to power the first flight of a British jet aircraft, Whittle requested and received the support of four ex-Halton apprentice engine fitters to help out in his workshop at

Working on ejector seats.

Power Jets. Whittle's final examination results along with those of 40,000 other former Halton apprentices are preserved at the Trenchard Museum Archives at Halton.

Trenchard's aim in founding his scheme had been to produce a cadre of well-motivated, highly trained airmen capable of becoming competent supervisors in the direction of work and control of men. Most ex-apprentices did exactly that. They were the true heroes of the piece, becoming SNCOs and warrant officers whose training taught them never to accept second best in keeping our aircraft serviceable and safe. They gave of their best in the inter-war years, during the Second World War, throughout the Cold War and in peacetime, in all theatres, in all circumstances. They rightly earned the sobriquet: 'The Backbone of the Royal Air Force'.

THE FIRST OF THE FRONTIERSMEN

Robert Ellis is one of Halton's most remarkable sons. In the inter-war period, he was awarded the Distinguished Flying Medal (DFM) not once, but twice in two years. It was a feat that was matched by no other in the North-West Frontier campaigns and only one other airman in the whole of the 1918-1939 period. What was particularly remarkable was that Ellis was not a pilot or observer, nor even a full-time air gunner. He volunteered to man the guns, as so many ex-Halton apprentices did, for the chance to fly and add a few extra coppers to his pay.

There was little about Ellis' early life that suggested what was to come in the future. His time at Halton was, by most standards, unremarkable. As part of the 7th Entry, Ellis finished 222nd in the order of merit, a veritable achievement on first glance until it is known that in those days there were likely to be no more than 250 in each group. Perhaps not surprisingly he did not gain promotion, passing out a mere AC2 (aircraftman second class) as a fitter AE, with a particular aptitude towards aircraft engines.

As with most of his contemporaries, Ellis was contented working with the familiar aircraft and engine types of the time, including many that were relics from the First World War. He was also eager for a posting overseas and was delighted when the time came to join 39 Squadron in India. Originally formed in April 1916 as a home defence unit, 39 Squadron was disbanded at the end of hostilities only to be reformed soon after flying DH9A biplanes as a light-bomber unit. This required Ellis to get to grips with the aircraft's 400-hp Liberty engine from the US, cutting-edge technology in its day but by the late 1920s already superseded by more powerful engines, including the 480-hp Bristol Jupiter VIII and VIIIFs that equipped the Westland Wapiti IIAs that replaced the DH9As in early 1929.

The RAF's presence in India at that time was to police the North-West Frontier, an area of supreme importance to the British Empire, forming as it did the boundary between British-owned India and Afghanistan. Ghandi's civil disobedience movement of 1929 received support from one of the diminutive leader's political friends, Abdul Ghaffar Khan, and his Frontier Youth League. Although supposedly peaceful,

The commander-in-chief for RAF India makes an inspection.

the Youth League was a para-military-style force whose members wore a distinctive uniform dyed with brick dust, thus earning them the nickname 'Red Shirts'.

The number of Red Shirts grew significantly in the first few months of 1930, and in April, Khan held a show of force in Peshawar. Arrested for inciting government hatred, his imprisonment served as a rallying call for every malcontent in the region, and as the weeks passed not only did their ranks continue to swell, but the levels of rioting and violence also increased to such levels that the British military was obliged to intervene. Large forces of local tribesmen – known as Lashkar – were particularly targeted as they sought to take advantage of the unrest.

Air Ministry doctrine at that time stated that if the Royal Air Force was called upon to lend support, then its attacks with bombs and machine guns must be 'relentless and unremitting'. This doctrine later evolved to one closer to an air blockade, but the concept of terrorising and demoralising local tribesmen from the air was one that continued throughout, and one of the first to come under attack from aircraft of 39 Squadron were the Mohmands.

The squadron executed its first bombing attack on 12 May 1930 dropping some 56 lbs of bombs in an assault led by the squadron commander, Squadron Leader Stafford 'Bunny' Harris. Harris was no stranger to 'The Grim', as the ex-apprentices used to call the North-West Frontier. He'd won the DFC back in 1922 for operations in

A DH9A of 8 Squadron in flight.

Waziristan, flying DH9As with 27 Squadron. After a spell at Staff College, he'd been the personal assistant to Air Vice-Marshal Sir Geoffrey Salmond, the AOC RAF India, before being promoted to take command of 39 Squadron at Risalpur.

Ellis took part in that first attack on the 12th, as air gunner to Sergeant John Gowing. They were briefed to reconnoitre and bomb an area known to be occupied by the Haji of Turangzai, a man respected as a reformer by his own people but considered a menace by the British. At least five of his followers were killed and a similar number injured.

To give some idea of the flavour of the attacks taking place, a typical raid is reported in the squadron's operations record book appendices for 17 June. It reads:

> 'At 1500 hours a formation of three machines (Pilots: Flight Lieutenant McKeever, Flying Officer Collings, and Sergeant Wren together with LAC Ellis, AC1 Rootes and AC1 Jones) took off and proceeded to point R1870 Map Reference 38 N/11. All nullahs in the vicinity were searched for caves or signs of tribesmen. Nothing was observed. Twelve 112-lb bombs were then dropped on a cave in a nullah in Loe Kwhar. The formation then proceeded to [a position] one mile east and south of Hafiz Kor and searched the area of tribesmen. Three men with one horse were seen by the crew of one machine. These were fired on and the horse was killed, 120 rounds [were] fired.'

History does not record the names either of the air gunner responsible for killing the animal, or the name of the horse.

All of the pilots quoted in this example were among the half a dozen or so officers and NCO pilots Ellis flew with over the next five months on a series of bombing raids, reconnaissance and photographic sorties over various territories as the disturbances moved further north. On more than one occasion he flew three or even four operations in a single day, often in the back of different aircraft. From sunrise to sunset, the squadron was on constant call. On 5 June, for example, he flew three ops in a day with three different pilots, Sergeant James Wren, Sergeant John Gowing and Flying Officer Wheeler. These were in the Utman Khel region. Two days earlier he'd been forced into an early return when his Wapiti IIA (J9484) with Flying Officer Lowry at the controls had a burst oil tank. Another burst oil tank obliged Gowing and Ellis to force-land at Peshawar on 14 June.

In July, Ellis flew at least 12 operations, mostly in Waziristan; in August, he flew 17, including nine ops in three days, against targets in the Tirah. As well as targeting tribesmen with bombs and machine-gun fire, the squadron also dropped bombs and incendiaries to set fire to villages known to support the Haji, partly as 'punishment' but also with the intention of destroying his support network. Many of the attacks were on the villages in the Barah Valley, often with mixed results, with bombing invariably described as 'indifferent'.

It was not only the pilots and aircrew who were working overtime; the ground crews were also flat out, constantly changing bomb racks to accommodate different ordnance, often between raids. The operational records book (ORB) for the time mournfully notes: 'A considerable strain was thus put on all personnel, which could be avoided by the use of a universally adjustable type rack.'

On 5 September, the squadron swapped bombs for supplies, dropping essential food and ammunition to the column of troops tasked with the relief of Chitral, a fortification in the Khyber Pakhtunkhwa that had been the scene of ongoing conflict for more than 40 years. The relief effort was a bi-annual affair; army personnel undertook a two-year stint of frontier guard duties, and the relief column had to march 140 miles through hostile territory to reach their objective. To the local tribesmen, this was open season.

By the end of September, the bombing work of the squadron was all but done, a routine established over the next 12 months of reconnaissance in order to monitor the situation on the ground, particularly in the Mohmand. Crews were briefed to report not only on the movement of tribesmen and their animals, but also the progress of the crops growing in the fields. Three areas of the Tirah were also photographed as part of a vast survey being undertaken to map some of the most remote areas of the British Empire, an exercise that was in itself not without risk.

Ellis and his colleagues also returned to the routine of more peaceful times, taking part in an air display at Delhi on 14 February 1931, that D.W Goffe, another Halton apprentice (11th Entry), described as '…quite a good effort, considering the very limited variety and great antiqueness of the majority of the machines at their disposal'[1].

The day before the display it had rained hard, and the Halton Brats arrived to find that many of the aircraft were axle deep in mud and had to be dragged free. The Wapitis in particular proved to be difficult to budge, and '… persisted in settling down gracefully on their wing skids with every evidence of satisfaction. Only after much coaxing could they be made to resume their normal attitude.'

Valentine's Day, however, proved to be dry and warm, and by the afternoon the aerodrome was serviceable enough for the programme to commence. 'Event 5' was a demonstration of army co-operation involving 39 (B) Squadron and 5 (AC) Squadron and presumed a small British force in an isolated post requiring air supply – a close approximation of the RAF's role in support of the Chitral relief column.

In June of 1931, nine of the pilots and airmen of 39 Squadron were singled out for awards. Among these, 'Bunny' Harris was awarded a Bar to his DFC and Sergeant James Wren and LAC (now corporal) Robert Ellis were awarded the DFM. Sadly, Wren did not live long enough to receive his medal, for he was killed in a crash at Risalpur early into the new year. The citation which appeared in the *London Gazette* adds little to what we already know. It stated simply that it was 'in recognition of gallant and distinguished service rendered in connection with the operations on the North-West Frontier of India between 23 April and 12 September 1930'. The recommendation for 'Bunny' Harris' Bar, however, provides more of an insight into the scale of operations being undertaken:

> 'During the period 23 April to 11 October 1930, this officer has carried out 66 operational flights of which 55 have been bombing raids across the border. His keenness and efficiency as a bombing formation leader have been infectious, and this spirit is clearly reflected by his squadron. His courage and devotion to duty are of a very high order.'

It was by no means the end of Ellis' Indian adventure. Throughout November and December 1931, the squadron at last replaced their ageing Wapitis with the rather more modern Hawker Hart IIs, and the new aircraft were put through their paces in January of the following year. They were the first to reach India (although a Hart had taken place in the air display in February – 'the only really up-to-date machine present'). Pilots were delighted with the Rolls-Royce Kestrel 1B engines which gave them a top speed of more than 180 mph, fast enough to outpace many an RAF fighter at that time and almost 50 miles per hour quicker than the Wapiti. In almost every respect it was better; it was quicker to make height and had a range of 470 miles.

At the end of 1931 and in the new year of 1932, trouble once more stirred after a period of comparative peace. The Red Shirts were again on the move, and daily reconnaissance sorties in the district surrounding Mardan, Swabi and Now-shera were ordered. Working closely with the ground forces, the squadron flew 95 sorties in six weeks, dropping leaflets warning the tribesmen not to incite violence and even dropping small dolls dressed in Red Shirt uniforms. It is not known what, if any, effect these had on the local villagers.

Trouble particularly developed in Dir State and Mohmand Territory. The squad-ron flew 12 reconnaissance flights during the month, including one on 29 January 1932. As reported in the squadron's ORB:

> 'The Commanding Officer [Harris] carried out an armed reconnaissance in Laram-Khongi-Sandal Area. The Laram and Khongi levy posts were burnt out and, at 1600 hours, a gathering of about 500 was observed outside Sandal carrying a number of red and white banners. Sixty men at once opened fire on the aircraft and a number also threw stones. The command-ing officer replied by dropping 8 20-lb bombs and firing 200 rounds of Lewis gun ammunition. Casualties were afterwards reported to be 13 killed and a number wounded.'

The RAF did not have it all their own way; on at least three separate occasions their aircraft were fired upon, sometimes heavily, although the air gunners – Robert Ellis among them – nearly always fired back.

Ellis operated throughout this period and by March was regularly crewed with the squadron commander. On 11 March he flew three trips with Harris on a single day, and three attacks on the home of the Haji of Turangzai at Bagh. On one occa-sion they recorded a direct hit. He went with Harris again the following morning but in the afternoon his seat was taken by Wing Commander de Crespigny[2], the former CO of 39 Squadron and now in command of 2 (India) Wing, who clearly wanted to see things for himself.

The weight of the RAF attacks, and the weapons used, soon took their toll, and ultimately led to the Mahmunds asking for the attacks to stop. In all, 39 Squadron aircraft had dropped more than 20 tons of heavy explosive (HE) bombs and fired off thousands of rounds of ammunition. They had also dropped 20 petrol bombs, 13 of which had been recorded as direct hits.

Robert Ellis had been heavily engaged in the 'war', and was now equally heav-ily engaged in the peace, taking part in 'shows of strength' but not being fired upon. In April he was also involved in escorting the Viceroy and Vicerine of Peshawar from Rawalpindi to Peshawar as recorded in the ORB:

> 'On 16 April three aircraft of A Flight, led by the commanding officer, met

the Avro X over Rawalpindi and escorted it to Attock, where they were joined by the remaining flights (of the squadron). The whole squadron then escorted their Excellencies to Peshawar, flying in squadron formation above and behind the Avro X. The squadron dived in salute as their Excellencies were de-planing at Peshawar.'

In September the following year, Robert Ellis learned that he had been awarded a Bar to his DFM. It was included in the same *London Gazette* that announced the award of a Second Bar to the DFC for 'Bunny' Harris 'in recognition of gallant and distinguished service rendered in connection with the operations on the North-West Frontier of India during the periods 28 January 1932 to 8 February 1932 and 6 March 1932 to 18 March 1932.' Ellis retired from the RAF as a flight lieutenant having added an MBE to his DFM & Bar.

Despite Ellis' achievement, he was not the first of the brats to be awarded a DFM. That honour went to Sergeant Edward Coleman of the 1st Entry. He was recognised for 'gallant and distinguished service rendered in connection with the operations against the Akhwan in the Southern Desert, Iraq, during the period November 1927 to May 1928'. He was commissioned soon after, and in the Second World War joined the Technical Branch, reaching the rank of wing commander. He retired from the RAF as a group captain in 1952 on the grounds of ill health.

His DFM was gazetted alongside that of Colin Reeve, an apprentice from the 5th Entry (and the 1st Entry at Flowerdown³).

Two other notable Old Boys had their DFMs gazetted at the same time that Robert Ellis was awarded his first, and both were in recognition of the same campaign between April and September. The first was Corporal John Lewis (6th Entry and 2nd Entry at Flowerdown). The second was Sergeant Richard Falconer of the 8th Entry (and 5th Entry Cranwell).

Richard Falconer was a member of 60 (B) Squadron in Kohat, North-West Frontier, flying the de Havilland GA and Westland Wapiti. The recommendation made by his commanding officer for his DFM survives, and highlights his role in photographic reconnaissance and the importance attached to aerial surveys at that time:

'I wish to recommend 363944 Sergeant Falconer for the award of the Distinguished Flying Medal for devotion to duty whilst flying on photographic reconnaissance over enemy territory. When operations commenced this year, it was shown that the maps of the country over which aircraft were operating were very inaccurate; it therefore became necessary to prepare very large photographic mosaics with upmost speed.

'Pilot Sergeant Falconer showed a great aptitude for this type of highly skilled work and during operations photographed an area of well over 1,000 square miles with excellent results. Had it not been for the wholehearted manner in which the pilot undertook his task, the actual photography would have taken considerably longer than it did, at considerable extra expense in both flying time and photographic material.

'Also the excellent results which have been attained in bombing can be directly attributed to him in producing accurate photos of the area to be bombed. Pilot Sergeant Falconer did 102 hours 40 minutes flying on these photo flights, in addition he did 29 hours 40 minutes over enemy country. He is an excellent pilot and a zealous worker at all times.'

In his later career, Falconer was commissioned and qualified as an instructor. Among the hundreds of pupils he taught was acting Pilot Officer Gibson, later to become Wing Commander Gibson, VC, DSO & Bar, DFC & Bar, who led the Dambusters raid in 1943. Falconer retired from the RAF in 1953.

2 THE FIRST OF THE MANY

It was on the morning of 3 September 1939, that an uncertain peace at last transcended into a definite war. For two days, since the German Wehrmacht had smashed through the borders of Poland, a Bristol Blenheim of 139 Squadron at RAF Wyton had been standing by to reconnoitre and photograph the German Fleet. A strange and almost perverse gentlemen's agreement had been reached between the warring parties. Whilst Germany's warships were deemed to be legitimate targets, no bombs were to be dropped on shore. Indeed, this very agreement had been conveyed to Bomber Command squadrons as a direct order. The tricky part was in finding those ships.

Forty-eight minutes after war was declared, Flying Officer Andrew McPherson was on the hunt for potential targets. Skill and luck were on his side, for he found what he was looking for: several enemy warships emerging into the Schillig Roads from Wilhelmshaven. Then his luck ran out; radio transmissions failed (the Blenheim was flying at 24,000 ft and most likely his wireless was half frozen) and it was not until after he landed that his message could be relayed. A strike force eventually took off, but bad weather and failing light forced them to return home without success.

At just after 08.30 hours the following morning, McPherson was again in the air, and this time at very low level (and at great danger to himself and his Royal Navy observer) he was able to photograph warships in Brunnsbüttel, at the mouth of the Kiel Canal. Two could be clearly identified: the *Scharnhorst* and the *Gneisenau*, steaming for the open sea. Once more his attempts to broadcast his findings failed, and vital time was wasted before his message could finally reach the ears of those in command.

At 9 Squadron, crews had been waiting patiently for news. They had in fact been standing by and expecting orders since being mobilised on 1 September. Regular squadron pilots and aircrew had been joined by an additional team of four general reconnaissance (GR) observers, to make sure that it was German ships they found and bombed, and not their own.

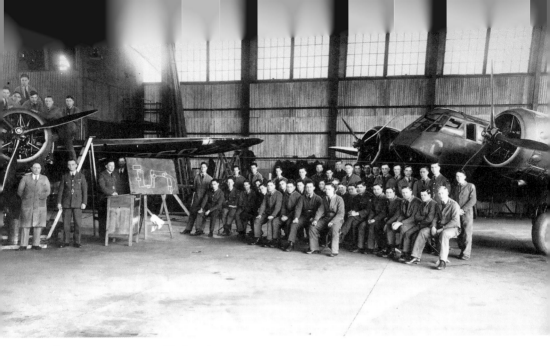

Aerodrome course training on Blenheim Is.

After sterling service in the First World War, largely in a tactical-reconnaissance and artillery-spotting role, the squadron reformed in 1924 purely as a bomber unit. By 1939, the squadron had exchanged lumbering Handley Page Heyfords for the more advanced Vickers Wellington Is, powered by Bristol Pegasus XVIII radial engines. Under the command of the redoubtable Wing Commander Hugh Pughe Lloyd DFC, MC, later to achieve fame in Malta, the squadron moved to Honington in July 1939, just as war seemed inevitable[1].

At 15.00 hours they at last got the news they had been waiting for – operations were 'on'. The squadron was to contribute six Wellingtons out of a total attacking force of 14 aircraft. Elsewhere, a second force of Blenheims was also being deployed. The squadron was to fly in two sections of three aircraft each: One Section, was under the command of a New Zealander, Squadron Leader Lennox Lamb; Four Section was led by Flight Lieutenant Peter Grant.

Lamb and Grant were the only two officers chosen for the task. The four other crews were all led by non-commissioned men. Two of those were Halton Boys – Flight Sergeants Ian Borley and John Turner.

Ian Borley, who'd been educated at Morehall School in Folkestone, had been with the 10th Entry at Halton, finishing 270th in his course and passing out as an AC2 in the role of a fitter (AE). Despite his comparatively unspectacular Halton career, he was selected for pilot training in 1931. By the start of the war, and now living in Somerset with his wife, the 30-year-old was an experienced captain of aircraft, having been with the squadron since June 1933. He was detailed to fly as number two in One Section with his crew comprising Sergeant George Miller (second pilot), Corporal George Park, LAC Harry Dore[2], and AC Robert Henderson.

At 27, John Turner was a little younger than his contemporary, having joined Halton as part of the 16th Entry and passing out similarly as a fitter (AE). Also selected for pilot training, Turner, a former pupil at Portsmouth Junior Technical School, had been with 9 Squadron since June 1936. Within his crew was another Halton Boy, Donald Jarvis, of the 24th Entry and another qualified pilot who had only recently moved to Honington. Jarvis' father had been a naval officer, a commissioned gunner, who'd sent his son to Chatham Technical Junior School. The younger Jarvis came to Halton in September 1931 and qualified as a metal rigger with the rank of AC1. Coincidentally, he'd finished 24th in the 24th Entry.

The rest of their crew comprised Sergeant Bertie Walton, AC Ken Day, and AC George Brocking. They were detailed as number three in One Section.

Four Section was the first to take off, with Flight Lieutenant Grant in the lead. The time was recorded at 15.40 hours, less than an hour after the squadron had at last been given the green light. One Section took off 25 minutes later at 16.05 hours.

What happened next is recorded by the two leaders in their subsequent reports. Flak was intense, the bombers finding themselves a target not only of the ships' own, highly accurate defences, but also various gun emplacements along the shoreline. Great attention to detail had been paid by the ships' designers to their anti-aircraft capabilities – the *Scharnhorst* and *Gneisenau* alone boasting almost 50 37-mm and 20-mm cannon – which were lethal to lower-flying aircraft.

Grant claims to have dropped his bombs in salvo with the two other aircraft in his section at 18.12 hours at a battleship around a mile south of the entrance of the canal and from a height of around 6,000 ft:

> "Immediately after the release [we] were forced to pull up into the cloud owing to the very high concentration of anti-aircraft fire and turned for home without waiting to see the results. Six of eight cruisers were firing at us as well as the battleships. We were hit three times."

One Section was a little later arriving on target, and found danger not only in the flak, but also in German fighter cover which had now arrived in strength: "Towards the end of a fighter attack carried out by nine German fighters at approximately 18.35 hours I jettisoned my three bombs 'live and in a stick' at 400 ft to the south side of the harbour."

Lamb could not be sure he was aiming at anything in particular: "At the moment of bombing I felt sure there was no shipping in the vicinity, but having pressed the bomb release, I saw a merchant ship, approximately 7,000 tons, athwartships [sic]."

Self-preservation, and more importantly, the need to protect his crew, drove Lamb to head for the cover of the clouds:

"I climbed rapidly, still being attacked by fighters, and succeeded in reaching cloud cover. It was necessary for the safety of my crew that these bombs were jettisoned as the decreased load enabled the machine to successfully evade the attack."

One Section had the great misfortune of being intercepted by Bf 109Es of II./JG77 who had been warned of the bombers' approach long before reaching their target. Based at Nordholz, an airfield 12 kilometres south of Cuxhaven and only 45 kilometres north-east of Wilhelmshaven, the fighters were rapidly on the scene, and with plenty of fuel and ammunition to inflict major damage on their enemy. Among their number was a veteran of the Spanish Civil War, Feldwebel Alfred Held, who had had vital experience flying with the Legion Condor.

Scrambled in good time, Held was drawn to the exploding shells of the anti-aircraft guns which told him that the bombers had to be close by. Then he saw his opportunity to attack, as retold to a war correspondent from the *Propaganda Kompanie* (PK) shortly afterwards:

"With my Staffel comrades still relatively far behind me, I already had the Englishman in my sights. Calmly and confidently I fired the first bullets into his aircraft, feeling as hardened to combat as if I had already shot down a dozen Englishmen. However, the bomber's rear gunner wasn't going to allow me any complacency. As I streaked past, he fired one burst after another at me. Despite fiercely concentrating all my senses on the job, I managed to make out clearly every single detail of the Wellington bomber, even its various crew members. Whether that rear gunner was a good shot and had hit me I could not see for the moment. So, unperturbed, every time I had a free field of fire I shot at the enemy aircraft. Was I a better shot than the Englishman? Time and again we rushed each other, machine guns hammering away and engines howling like maddened beasts, and thus twisting about we strayed far out over Jade Bay."

Held said he sensed the bomber was doomed as it dived to escape his lethal cannon and machine-gun fire.

"Lower and lower I forced the Tommy but still he defended himself desperately. Then – I could hardly believe my eyes – a long flame shot from the left side of the bomber. Was this the finale? Already the aircraft seemed to be out of control and wallowing about. A last burst of fire from my guns – and that was enough. The aircraft dropped its nose and fell. I throttled down and circled to follow the Englishman's descent, but already there was just a burning pile in the water and that lasted only a few seconds. Then the waves closed the grave and foaming wavetops glided above as before."

Held was not the only German pilot to claim an enemy bomber as destroyed. Feldwebel Troitsch of the same Gruppe also found himself in a good position to attack, spotting a formation of three Wellingtons at very low level:

"I was flying in the front of our formation so I was the first to fire. Two of the aircraft immediately turned towards the low-hanging clouds and disappeared. The third one was right in front of my guns and I closed to 100 metres to be sure of hitting him. At 50 metres the Englishman's left wing broke off and a flame shot from the fuselage. Shortly before the Englishman had returned my fire, though without hitting my machine. By the time the bomber was engulfed in flames I was only 20 metres behind him. The burning tail fell off and streaked past, just above my machine, so that I had to dive to avoid being swallowed by the flames. I dived away to the right and followed the bomber, which dropped from some 400 metres into the water, where it quickly disappeared, leaving just an oil slick."

Troitsch went on to describe to the war correspondent how he engaged a second bomber:

"At full revs I raced after him and again his rear gunner tried to rake me, but this Tommy had no success either. Unfortunately, I lost the Englishman as we were soon into cloud. But as I curved away, I found myself fired on by the Englishman's front gunner. I dived immediately to follow the bomber, but then realised we were too far out to sea."

Who had claimed the first victory? Historians have argued this point ever since. Held was certainly widely proclaimed in the German press as the first to vanquish a British bomber, though Troitsch may have beaten him to the trigger. The full transcript of Held's account talks of him seeing two bombers already burning in the sea at the time he made his attack, but the records book shows that only two Wellingtons failed to return: L4268 flown by Flight Sergeant Ian Borley; and L4275 with Flight Sergeant John Turner at the controls, and Donald Jarvis in the second pilot's seat. One had certainly been shot down by fighters; a second, perhaps by a fighter, flak, or even a combination of the two. It didn't really matter; the outcome was the same.

The surviving Wellingtons reached home and landed shortly after 21.00 hours, the senior men no doubt chastened by their experiences. Almost all of their pre-war training, mounting daylight raids against the Royal Navy, had been rendered worthless in a stroke. While there were still those who thought the bomber would always get through, with its speed and its defensive armament, wiser minds would soon prevail.

In the debriefing, the aircrew told their stories, and what they had seen. All three aircraft from Four Section had returned safely and Flying Officer Torkington-Leech, a South African in Squadron Leader Lamb's crew, even claimed to have shot one of the German fighters down while manning the front turret. From One Section, only Lamb had made it back, and it was almost immediately clear that the two other aircraft in his section would not be coming home. The author of the squadron's ORB wrote simply: 'First squadron to draw blood.'[3]

In Ian Borley's crew, there were no survivors, nor were any of their bodies recovered. Their names are immortalised on the Runnymede Memorial to those aircrew with no known graves. Harry Dore, a wireless operator/air gunner, was only 19. For the families of John Turner, Donald Jarvis, and Kenneth Day, there was at least the comfort of a grave at which to grieve or give thanks for a death nobly borne.

Thus, the first of the Halton Boys died, fighting against impossible odds and in an attack that achieved nothing of any significance other than learning an expensive lesson. Contemporary newspaper reports described the attack as a total failure, despite a British Ministry of Information communiqué suggesting that 'heavy damage' had been inflicted. Alongside the actual fighting, the propaganda war had also begun, and the first shots fired.

Sadly, the deaths of Ian Borley, John Turner and Donald Jarvis would be the first among many. Alfred Held, also, did not survive long after the battle. Awarded the Iron Cross (Second Class) for his victory, he died two month later in a collision, rammed by one of his own side.

3 CONSPICUOUS GALLANTRY

The Victoria Cross (VC) is a comparatively small, bronze medal which ranks as Britain's highest and most prestigious award for gallantry. Since being introduced in the reign of Queen Victoria, the VC has been awarded 1,358 times to 1,355 recipients, including three remarkable men who were awarded the medal twice – Charles Upham VC & Bar, Noel Chavasse VC & Bar and Arthur Martin-Leake VC & Bar.

To win a Victoria Cross, the recipient needs to have displayed most conspicuous bravery or extreme devotion to duty in the presence of the enemy. To this end it differs from the only medal that serves as its equal, the George Cross (GC), where the presence of the enemy is not a factor in the courage displayed, or the act undertaken.

Halton can boast no fewer than nine recipients of the George Cross, including those men awarded the Albert Medal (AM) and the Empire Gallantry Medal (EGM) which preceded the GC's introduction in 1940. The first was in 1928, when LAC Walter Arnold, a 7th Entry man, was flying as a passenger in an aircraft that crashed at Digby. Despite his injuries, he managed to scramble clear from the burning wreckage and then head back into the fire to free the unconscious pilot, ignoring the fierce flames that threatened to consume him. He was badly burned around the face, neck and hands, but his actions undoubtedly saved the pilot's life for which he was duly recognised with the EGM.

The following year, on 20 June, William Neil McKechnie of the 11th Entry was honoured for a similar feat and with a similar medal when a DH9A tipped over and caught fire landing at Cranwell where he was a cadet. Although the dazed and only semi-conscious pilot managed to get out of the aircraft, he immediately staggered and fell and was surrounded by a pool of aviation fuel that burst into flames. McKechnie, in another aircraft that had just landed, leapt from his machine and sprinted the 200 yards or so across to the injured man, pulling him clear of danger. The citation reads: 'There is no doubt that without McKechnie's assistance, [the pilot] would have been burned to death.'

Both 'Bill' McKechnie and the pilot, another 11th Entry Halton Brat, Cyril Giles[1], were badly burned, the latter being treated by Archie McIndoe. Much of what McIndoe learned from this tragic case was put to good use during the war at his famous burns unit at East Grinstead. Giles later recovered and resumed his RAF career as a stores officer. Bill McKechnie, a keen sportsman and talented rugby player, went on to qualify as a pilot and serve on the North-West Frontier. As an acting group captain and station commander at RAF Metheringham, he was killed on the night of 30 August 1944, when a 106 Squadron Lancaster he was piloting was shot down over Königsberg[2].

Halton Boys appeared to make a habit of rushing in to raging infernos. Out on the North-West Frontier on a summer's afternoon in 1930, LAC Robert Douglas Ewing of the 5th Entry was observing the take-off of a 60 Squadron Westland Wapiti from Kohat with a full load of fuel, bombs and ammunition when the aircraft stalled and crashed at the edge of the airfield. Robert ran to the burning wreckage, and quickly spotted the gunner and fellow LAC laying a few feet from the crash with his clothes on fire. The quick-thinking airman doused the flames with a handheld extinguisher and with the help of a second airman, managed to drag the gunner clear and get him into an ambulance, before rushing back towards the aircraft to rescue the pilot. He was a dozen or so yards short of the Wapiti when one of its bombs exploded, throwing Robert to the ground. A desire to try a second time was thwarted by the explosion of another bomb by which time he realised any further rescue attempt was hopeless. Ewing was awarded the EGM, the citation making specific reference to the grave risk he was taking in approaching an aircraft that contained 'live bombs of a powerful type'.[3]

The only award of an Albert Medal to an apprentice was gazetted in January 1937. The previous year, Corporal Archibald Charles Wood of the 3rd Entry, was flying as a passenger in a 60 (B) Squadron aircraft from RAF Kohat on 8 February when the aircraft, a Westland Wapiti, got into difficulties and crashed near Nidhauli, India. Wood, who was uninjured, but dazed as a result of the crash, re-entered the blazing wreckage in an endeavour to save the pilot. In doing so he received very severe burns as a result of which his left hand had to be amputated. His award is particularly interesting in that it was approved by 'His former Majesty King Edward VIII' who, of course, had subsequently abdicated.

A more recent example of supreme gallantry came after the end of the Second World War, when the full horrors of those held as prisoners of the Japanese became known, and tales of steadfast bravery began to emerge. One of those stories concerned Flight Lieutenant Bertram Gray of the 13th Entry, who before the war had won the Air Force Medal (AFM) for his part in setting a world record for the longest flight by a single-engined aircraft. He had at that time been a member of the RAF's Long-Range Development Flight as a wireless operator/mechanic in one of three Vickers Wellesley bombers that flew non-stop for two days from Egypt to Australia.

When the Japanese declared war on Britain, Gray – who was now commissioned – was part of a group captured after the fall of Hong Kong in December 1941. During his captivity, and despite severe depredation, Gray did all that he could to sustain the morale of his fellow prisoners. He smuggled in much-needed drugs and distributed them to the most seriously ill, and even ran a news service on information gleaned from people outside the camp. Despite being tortured over a period of nearly six months, he refused to divulge the names of his informants and co-conspirators. He was eventually executed by firing squad on 18 December 1943. Two-and-a-half years later, the King was graciously pleased to approve a posthumous award of the George Cross in recognition of most conspicuous gallantry. The award appeared in the *London Gazette* on 19 April 1946.

A particular feature of both the VC and the GC is that they can be granted posthumously, which is perhaps unsurprising given the criteria for which the awards are given. It is not surprising therefore, that the only Victoria Cross awarded to a Halton Boy should be to one who made the ultimate sacrifice. His name was also Gray – Thomas Gray.

It was no accident that Thomas Gray opted for a life in the RAF, or that he chose Halton. From a very early age he was fascinated with flight. Born on 17 May 1914 in the small rural village of Urchfont near Devizes, Thomas was the fourth of seven boys, three of whom went on to become Halton apprentices. Five in all chose the RAF: the eldest brother, Arthur, was in the 17th Entry and trained as a metal rigger. He eventually retired from the service as a flight sergeant; younger brother Reginald joined the 30th Entry and was later commissioned, retiring at the end of the Second World War as a flight lieutenant; brother John arrived at Halton in February 1943, as part of the 46th Entry. Tragically, John was killed in a Lancaster crash at Hullavington in September 1945, along with two other Brats, Herbert Bird (5th Entry) and Roland Meadows (46th Entry). All three had been selected for aircrew and were on an air experience flight with Squadron Leader Roy Reynolds at the controls when their aircraft stalled and crashed. The fifth brother, Robert, enlisted as direct entry aircrew and trained in Canada. He too was later killed when the Wellington he was piloting crashed on take-off.

After secondary school at Warminster, Thomas enlisted as an apprentice in the 20th Entry on 27 August 1929, when he was still only 15, and spent the next three years training to become an aero engine fitter II (E). Among his contemporaries within the 20th Entry was young 'Sammy' Allard (though Allard was an apprentice metal rigger), later to achieve fame as a pre-eminent fighter ace in the Battles of France and Britain. George Berry, a fighter pilot with 1 Squadron who was to be awarded an immediate DFM during the Battle of France, was also part of that auspicious group. Berry also achieved media celebrity status for later shooting down the Heinkel 111 that sank the troop ship HMT *Lancastria*[4], a ship that was attempting to lift British troops and nationals from the French port of St Nazaire, two weeks after Dunkirk.

Passing out from Halton in the summer of 1932, Gray's first posting was to 40 Squadron in Upper Heyford, helping to service the squadron's Fairey Gordon light bombers, getting to grips with the aircraft's Armstrong Siddeley Panther engines. It was while at Upper Heyford, and after the squadron had moved to Abingdon, that Gray volunteered to become an air gunner. In those days, the role was very much a 'part-time' one, with the seat filled by an experienced mechanic who might wear many different hats. It added more variety and excitement to Thomas's ground duties, as well as carrying a little extra pay which was always welcome.

Proud of his 'winged bullet' badge of a qualified air gunner (the air gunner brevet would follow later), he was even more delighted with his promotion to leading aircraftman (LAC) in 1933, and a posting across to 15 Squadron to work on its Hawker Hinds. Gray returned to Halton in 1936 for further training to become a fitter I. Postings followed to 58 Squadron and 12 Squadron, enabling him to work on a variety of different aircraft and engines, and earning him further promotion to corporal. It was while with 12 Squadron at Andover that he first became familiar with the Fairey Battle, a single-engined light bomber powered by a Rolls-Royce Merlin that promised to be at the vanguard of any future war. As it was, when war came, the Battle was already obsolete, its obsolescence matched only by the outdated views of the commanders in the field.

As an air gunner, Gray already had the taste for flying. Now he decided to go a step further, and applied for and was granted leave to take a course at No. 1 Observers' School to train as an observer. Observers in 1939 were expected to undertake a variety of different roles and were the original multi-taskers. It was as an observer, and with the new rank of sergeant, that Gray proceeded with the squadron to France as part of the RAF's Advanced Air Striking Force (AASF), poised to counter any German offensive but in the event, doing very little as the initial action was superseded by the Phoney War. The war, when it did finally arrive, was anything but Phoney, and did not start well for any of the Battle squadrons.

As German troops and armour began pouring into the Netherlands and Belgium, Hitler proclaimed that 'the hour has come for the decisive battle for the future of the German nation'. The RAF too was immediately in the action, 12 Squadron losing four of its aircraft in its first attack on 10 May[5].

Another squadron operating Blenheims lost five of their number on the same day, including a Blenheim IV in which Victor Spurr (15th Entry) was the observer. Spurr and the rest of the crew were killed. Spurr, the son of a serviceman, had arrived at Halton from Middlesbrough Junior Technical School on limited competition.

On that first day of the German Blitzkrieg, no fewer than 24 Battles were lost, either shot down or damaged on the ground beyond repair. The next day a further nine were lost, though mercifully 12 Squadron was spared. The respite did not last long.

It was the morning of 12 May at Amifontaine. A Sunday. On the daily routine orders, Thomas was detailed as the squadron orderly sergeant, a responsibility he would not fulfil[6]. The squadron had been on readiness since 04.00 hours. Three hours later, orders for an attack were telephoned through from headquarters. Two sections of 12 Squadron were to attack two vital bridges crossing the Albert Canal at Veldwezelt and Vroenhoven, to hold up the German advance.

Wing Commander Albert Thackray, the commanding officer, gathered his pilots together, and called for volunteers. Every hand was raised. Nobody wanted to miss out. It was decided on the toss of a coin[7]. Two flights of three were selected: three aircraft from A Flight, led by Flying Officer Norman Thomas, and three from B Flight, led by Flying Officer Donald 'Judy' Garland. A Flight would take on the concrete bridge at Vroenhoven; B Flight the metal bridge at Veldwezelt. Thomas Gray (see opposite) would fly as observer in Garland's aircraft; aside from the odd 'Nickel' – dropping propaganda leaflets rather than bombs – it was to be his first, and as it turned out his only, operation.

The operation went wrong from the start as one of their number suffered radio problems while taxiing out, and in switching to another aircraft, found that that too had trouble with its hydraulics. Six had become five. The remaining aircraft took off in their formations, following a circuit agreed each morning to avoid a number of unexploded bombs from previous enemy raids. All were away by 08.22 hours.

The flight time to the target was almost exactly one hour. Ahead of them, ten Hurricanes from 1 Squadron, led by Squadron Leader 'Bull' Halahan, were to offer fighter cover, three detailed to provide close support. Almost immediately, however, the Hurricane pilots had their hands full, just as the sky seemed to erupt with exploding anti-aircraft fire. The unequal struggle was only just beginning. Messerschmitt Bf 109s broke through the fighter defence with ease and latched on to the slow flying Battles, hacking them down almost at will. Norman Thomas was one of the first to go, all three of the crew miraculously making it out of their burning and bullet-ridden Battle. Pilot Officer Tom Davey was also shot down, his Canadian gunner, LAC Gordon Patterson, having fought a heroic battle with the fighters and claiming at least one of those Bf 109s destroyed. Davey ordered his crew to bail out and then successfully crash-landed to spend the rest of the war as a POW.

'Judy' Garland opted to bring his flight in at very low level but the enemy defenders were not deceived. The Germans had brought up something in the region of 300 light guns of various calibres including highly mobile 20-mm flak guns capable of spewing out thousands of rounds per minute. Garland's flight comprised Pilot Officer Ian McIntosh and Sergeant Fred Marland. McIntosh was hit on his approach to the target, the cannon shells finding his petrol tanks and setting the Battle ablaze. He too managed to crash land and was captured. Fred Marland wasn't so lucky. Shortly after releasing his bombs his aircraft was seen to rear up like a wounded stallion before winging over and smashing into the ground. There were no survivors.

There were no survivors either from the crew of 'Judy' Garland. Approaching the bridge at almost treetop level he kept the aircraft steady just long enough to see his bombs fall away before being fatally hit and diving into the ground, close to where his bombs had just exploded.

The praise and recognition for the heroism shown that day was fast in coming, perhaps, in some way, to mollify the disaster that had unfolded. Air Chief Marshal Sir Cyril Newhall GCB, CMG, CBE, AM, chief of the Air Staff, sent a signal that read:

> 'I send my warmest congratulations on the brilliant attack voluntarily carried out by the pilots and crews of your squadron yesterday. As the first commanding officer, I am proud to see the gallant and courageous spirit which exists and which I know will continue to bring further honour and credit to the squadron.'

Flying Officer Tom Davey was awarded the DFC; his gunner the DFM – the first Canadian to receive a DFM in the Second World War.

The bodies of Don Garland, Thomas Gray and their gunner, LAC Lawrence Reynolds were recovered by local civilians and buried in secret. Later their bodies would be recovered and buried in a Commonwealth War Grave. On 11 June, almost one month to the day of the raid, the *London Gazette* published details of a Victoria Cross awarded to both Garland and Gray.

> 'Flying Officer Garland was the pilot and Sergeant Gray was the observer of the leading aircraft of a formation of five aircraft that attacked a bridge over the Albert Canal which had not been destroyed and was allowing the enemy to advance into Belgium. All the aircrews of the squadron concerned

volunteered for the operation, and, after five crews had been selected by drawing lots, the attack was delivered at low altitude against this vital target. Orders were issued that this bridge was to be destroyed at all costs.

'As had been expected, exceptionally intense machine-gun and anti-aircraft fire were encountered. Moreover, the bridge area was heavily protected by enemy fighters. In spite of this, the formation successfully delivered a dive-bombing attack from the lowest practicable altitude. British fighters in the vicinity reported that the target was obscured by the bombs bursting on it and near it. Only one of the five aircraft concerned returned from this mission. The pilot of this aircraft reports that besides being subjected to extremely heavy anti-aircraft fire, through which they dived to attack the objective, our aircraft were also attacked by a large number of enemy fighters after they had released their bombs on the target. Much of the success of this vital operation must be attributed to the formation leader, Flying Officer Garland, and to the coolness and resource of Sergeant Gray, who in most difficult conditions navigated Flying Officer Garland's aircraft in such a manner that the whole formation was able successfully to attack the target in spite of subsequent heavy losses. Flying Officer Garland and Sergeant Gray unfortunately failed to return from the mission.'

Strangely, there was no posthumous award for Reynolds; there is no sound explanation as to why beyond the vagaries of classism that existed at the time. The controversy raged well after the war and his case was vigorously fought by the Air Gunners' Association to no avail. One of the new accommodation blocks at Halton is named in Gray's honour.

In the horror of those dreadful six days in May, a good many Halton Boys lost their lives. The day before Gray's fatal flight, two of his contemporaries in the 20th Entry were shot down and killed. Sergeant Charles Dockrill and Sergeant Percy Dormer were pilot and observer respectively in a 218 Squadron Battle that failed to return from an attack on Saint Vith. Dockrill, who had passed out as a fitter AE and finished 28th in the order of merit, had come to Halton on limited competition from Isleworth County School. Dormer was a metal rigger (airframe fitter) who'd spent three years at the Electric & Wireless School at Cranwell. He'd been a schoolboy at Newport Grammar School on the Isle of Wight. All four 218 Squadron aircraft that set out that day failed to make it home.

Sergeant Arthur Johnson and Sergeant Christopher Shelton Jones were also both contemporaries from the 20th Entry, as well as being fellow members of 12 Squadron. Johnson, a pilot, was shot down and killed on 14 May, attempting to disrupt the German advance in Sedan. Shelton Jones, an observer, who had passed out of Halton as a fitter armourer, was killed on the same day and on the same raid.

Other Battle crew from the 20th Entry lost on 14 May included George Barker and Herbert Trescothic. George Barker was an NCO pilot with 150 Squadron and had as his observer another apprentice from the 18th Entry, James Williams. They were killed while operating from their base at Écury-sur-Coole, one of four 150 Squadron aircraft lost that day. Trescothic, who had passed out of Halton as a fitter AE, was an observer in 142 Squadron, flying in the crew of 23-year-old Australian Flight Lieutenant Kenneth Rogers. They had the misfortune of being shot down by one of their own side, a French fighter pilot mistaking them for the enemy.

The other essential component of the RAF's AASF was the Bristol Blenheim. Although much faster and more modern than the Fairey Battle, it was nonetheless vulnerable to fighters and flak, and their losses were considerable. The 12th of May was a disastrous day for many squadrons, not least 15 Squadron who lost seven aircraft and crews over Maastricht. Among the 14 men killed was Sergeant Edwin Roberts, observer to Pilot Officer Claude Frankish, a New Zealander. Roberts had been a contemporary of Thomas Gray, as had Sergeant Leonard Merritt, another observer, shot down whilst also attacking Maastricht in a Blenheim of 107 Squadron.

The 27-year-old left a widow, Gwendoline, and an inscription on his grave that could read as an epitaph for all of the Halton Boys killed in the war. It reads simply: 'Their name liveth for evermore.'

4 THE FLYING OLYMPIAN

After the humiliation of the British Expeditionary Force (BEF) in France, slightly assuaged by the miracle of Dunkirk, only the RAF – and Fighter Command specifically – stood between Britain and what seemed like inevitable defeat. The fighter boys had acquitted themselves well against the Luftwaffe in covering the army's withdrawal, and many lessons had been quickly learned in how to fight a modern war in the air. With hundreds of Heinkels, Dorniers, Junkers and Messerschmitts now only 30 or so miles across the channel, it would take all of the RAF's guile, skill and luck to prevent the Germans from gaining the air superiority needed to mount a successful invasion and force a British surrender.

One of the squadron commanders ranged against them was a Halton Boy who already knew what it meant to compete against the best in the world and come out on top. Don Finlay was not only a born fighter pilot, but also a world-class athlete, a talent that was first identified while a schoolboy at Taunton's in Southampton.

Born on 27 May 1909 in Christchurch, Donald Osborne Finlay grew up in a three up, three down in Macnaghten Road in Bitterne Park, Southampton. His father, James, a former naval man and newsagent, died in 1921, leaving Don's mother, Keziah, to bring up her family of eight alone. The front room of their property had been converted into a store, and Mrs Finlay divided her time between the general store and looking after Don's four brothers and three sisters.

Young Donald loved jumping and sprinting from the start, winning his school's long jump championship. He also loved aircraft, and at 16 he left Taunton's to become an apprentice, formally enlisting on 29 September 1925 as part of the 12th Entry. He passed out in August 1928 as an aero engine fitter II (E), 71 in the order of merit.

It was at Halton that he tried hurdling for the first time, and was born to it, with a style – according to the great Harold Abrahams (of *Chariots of Fire* fame) – that had precious little wrong with it: "That does not mean that he has not spent hours, days, weeks and months in attention to the smallest detail. No man can hurdle over 120 yards in 15 seconds without careful preparation."

Such was his natural quality, Finlay equalled the RAF record in his first race (16 seconds) and in 1928 won the first of no fewer than 11 consecutive Service Championships. The following year he clocked 15.8 seconds, and made his first appearance in the Amateur Athletics Association (AAA) Championships at Stamford Bridge, listed as 'D.O.Finlay. RAF (Tangmere)'. He finished third to David Burghley, the Olympic gold-medal winning hurdler and Lord who won with a time of 15.4 seconds.

Although it was as a long jumper that Finlay gained his first international vest, representing England against France, it was in the hurdling that he would find glory. He won a place in the English team for the Empire Games, and at the AAA Championships in 1931 finished second to Lord Burghley in a time of 14.8 seconds, the first time Finlay had broken the 15-second barrier. It was by no means the last time he would achieve such a feat.

More success followed in Los Angeles in 1932, and his first Olympic Games. Having qualified for the final of the 110-metre hurdles, he just missed out on a medal, but in a subsequent movie replay he was elevated from fourth to third by the judges. It was one of the first times that an action replay had been used to settle the outcome of a race, and US athlete Jack Keller graciously surrendered his bronze.

Finlay lost only one of his competitive races in 1933, 1934 and 1935, and steadily improved his times, recording a record 14.3 seconds downhill and with the wind behind him. The record was not allowed to stand.

Selected for the British Olympic team for the Berlin Games in 1936, Finlay was frustrated by what he saw as the poor preparation by the AAA for such an important occasion:

> "Nearly all other countries have government support; modern, up-to-date coaches; many first-class tracks, and excellent administration. We, in England, have one official coach, no support or money, and a dearth of first-class tracks. It is something of a joke that our summer athletics are held in a greyhound stadium and our winter athletics in a swimming pool. Our AAA are about 30 years behind in everything concerning athletics."

Rather than flying to the Games, the British team was obliged to take the long route via the Hook of Holland, followed by a long train journey across Germany, and finally arrived far from fresh for what was to come. Finlay remembers:

> "All along the route the Nazi swastika flew side-by-side with the Olympic flag. We reached Berlin late on Thursday evening, where we were given a splendid welcome by our hosts and by the British contingent in Berlin. Lord Burghley replied to the official welcome with his usual oratorical brilliance."

For Finlay, the most tiring part of the Games was the opening ceremony, standing and marching for the better part of four hours. They were kept waiting by the Fuhrer of Germany, Adolf Hitler, of whom Finlay observed ominously: "I was much impressed by the spontaneous welcome he received everywhere. Hitler is genuinely popular with the masses in Germany."

More than 100,000 people packed the arena, with the loudest cheers reserved for those teams that offered the Nazi salute. The British team did not.

The Games did not get off to a good start; only in the 50,000 m walk did Britain have something to cheer. In his own personal battle, Finlay made it through the heats and the semi-final to face the great Forrest Towns. He recalls:

> "At last came the hurdles final. I drew next place to Towns. A perfect start, all our pent-up energy let loose for a quarter of a minute; a hectic dive for the worsted – and Towns was Olympic champion in 14.2 seconds. The judges could not separate Pollard and myself, and for the second Olympic final a film had to be shown to place me. Thank heaven for the camera; for the second time it showed me in front."

While Finlay was making great strides in his athletics career, he was also progressing through the ranks of the service. The disappointing passing out results from Halton had long-since been forgotten; in Finlay's words: "I pulled up my socks and started to work hard." This was rewarded with an opportunity to train as a pilot, and before heading for Berlin, Finlay was discharged from the RAF on appointment to a commission. Graduating from Cranwell (where he was unsurprisingly captain of athletics) he completed his flying training, one of many Halton Boys who successfully made the transition from apprentice to pilot.

Finlay was at 17 Squadron, Kenley, from 13 May 1935, during which time he not only ran but also played football and rugby for the RAF. He joined 54 Squadron at Hornchurch in March 1936, and the following year was posted to the RAF School of Aeronautical Engineering at Henlow to complete a specialist engineering course.

With the storm clouds gathering he was keen not to be left languishing as an engineering officer, and on 11 August 1940 was posted to 7 Operational Training Unit (OTU) for a refresher course and to learn how to fly the Spitfire. By now a squadron leader, he was given his first operational command as OC 54 Squadron, Hornchurch, on 26 August, taking over from the highly popular James 'Prof' Leathart. All did not go quite according to plan.

Fully aware of his lack of operational flying, Finlay opted to attempt his first sortie as number two to one of the senior flight commanders, the experienced New Zealander, Al Deere. Deere warned him to stay close; falling behind would leave him vulnerable to German fighters. "If you get separated, make inland a bit," Deere warned him. "It's less dangerous there."

The squadron intercepted a large formation of German bombers and fighters stacked from 15,000 ft up to 32,000 ft, at which height a dozen or so Messerschmitt Bf 109s were lurking, ready to pounce. Pounce they did, although almost as soon as it started, the battle was over, by which time Deere could not find his number two.

A rather shaken Don Finlay returned to Hornchurch having been harried by one of the top-cover 109s: "I believe you wanted to get me shot down," Finlay joked later to Deere, "so that you could get the squadron!"

Don Finlay as CO.

The respite was short-lived. The very next day, Finlay was shot down near Canterbury. Nobody saw the combat but one of the squadron's aces, Colin Grey, reported that he had seen a parachute coming down and what he took to be the CO standing in a field and waving, apparently unharmed. This was not quite the case; Finlay had, in fact, been wounded, and spent several weeks in hospital. Upon recovery, Finlay wrote to his old friend, Harold Abrahams: "I am back again and itching to level the score."

Finlay did not return to 54 Squadron. By the time he recovered, the squadron had been pulled out of the line. He was posted instead as OC 41 Squadron in September, opening his account on the 23rd by destroying a Bf 109E over the channel. On 1 October, he was in combat once again as a formation of enemy aircraft headed for London:

> "An Me 109 [sic] attacked from below. It dived steeply with smoke pouring out. I still dived after it. During the dive I momentarily broke off the attack as Green 2 almost collided with me. I continued the attack firing bursts in the dive until the Me 109 dived into cloud at 4,000 ft with black smoke pouring out. No trace could be found under cloud of enemy."

He claimed the aircraft as 'damaged' and noted in his combat report that only four of his eight machine guns were working.

October proved to be a busy month. On the late morning of the 7th, while leading A Flight, he spotted what he took to be a Dornier 215 (it was actually a Dornier 17) about ten miles south-west of Maidstone heading east. He detailed Green Section to attack, but when that failed to materialise, he opted to attack himself:

> "I attacked from astern then broke away to port and attacked from astern. The port engine was smoking badly and I caught up astern just off Dover and fired another burst. Another Mitor aircraft slid over me and I broke off. The 215 was last seen heading for France, smoking badly."

Two days later, leading B Flight in the late afternoon, Finlay almost came to grief for a second time. Flying Spitfire X4558, he engaged around seven Bf 109s:

> "Enemy aircraft were situated approaching from west to east slightly below to starboard. I had already ordered line astern and immediately attacked a 109 by turning sharply on its tail. I closed to about 180 yards astern and fired a short burst. Immediately I noticed smoke and sparks from the bottom of the cockpit. I broke off to evade attack, during which I blacked out and lost the target. For a further 20 minutes I patrolled Ashford district to try to find stragglers. On return to Hornchurch I found my aircraft had been damaged and made a crash-landing. No. 222 Squadron reported that they had seen 109s attack me from above as I attacked and that they engaged these aircraft."

Although Finlay claimed one of the 109s as 'damaged', his own Spitfire required repairs of its own, being classed Category 2. The squadron had been engaged by fighters from JG54, and Finlay's assailant was a well-known fighter pilot who would survive the war, Oberleutnant Hans-Ekkehard Bob.

Finlay took part in two more combats before the month was out, claiming a Bf 109 damaged and sharing in the destruction of a second. Large formations of German fighters were by now no means unusual, but their lack of range and limited flying time meant they often headed for home, rather than engage in an unnecessary dogfight.

November 23 proved to be something of a red-letter day for Squadron Leader Finlay. Twelve aircraft from 41 Squadron were leading a formation of Spitfires from 64 Squadron to patrol the Biggin Hill line when they were vectored onto a large raid heading over Maidstone towards the coast. Half a dozen or more 109s from JG51 were spotted in poor visibility, and Finlay gave orders for individual attacks. Flying a Spitfire IIa (P7666), his subsequent report tells the story:

> 'While leading 41 Squadron in Blue Section, in bad visibility, five 109s

passed across the front of the squadron going east. I immediately called for individual attacks and turned sharply in pursuit. The e/a disappeared in the haze but I caught them again and put a long burst into one. Glycol streamed out and he dived very steeply away. I chased after him and the glycol appeared to stop. Another burst caused bits to fall off the cockpit and further glycol poured out. I could not finish off e/a due to windscreen being iced up. Two more short bursts were made before e/a crashed near Ivychurch, New Romney. Pilot got out and after a short time lit what appeared to be a smoke flare near his aircraft.'

Finlay had fired off almost 1,500 rounds in the combat, closing to a range of only 100 yards. The combined firepower of his eight Browning .303 machine guns at that range and concentration had been devastatingly effective, forcing the unfortunate enemy pilot to crash land. Obergefreiter Günther Loppach, the pilot of the 109, was quickly taken prisoner.

Finlay claimed one more 109 destroyed, on 27 November, his final claim with the squadron. It was by no means his last action. On the evening of 3 March 1941, and with 41 Squadron now based in Catterick, Finlay was scrambled to intercept an enemy intruder. On his return, and in attempting to land in poor visibility and a nasty crosswind, he overshot the runway (the landing lights had inadvertently been switched off) and crashed through the airfield boundary hedge, crossed the A1 near Bainesse Farm, and struck a sand-bagged emplacement with two men inside. Finlay was slightly injured, and the two men seriously so. The Spitfire (X4774) was almost a write-off, but later deemed worthy of repair.

In August 1941, and following another mishap when he suffered an engine failure in June, Finlay was promoted wing commander and posted to 11 Group as engineering officer. Although technically not operational, he still took the opportunity to fly whenever he could, and on 3 March 1942 bagged another Bf 109 eight miles off Cap Gris-Nez while 'keeping his hand in' with 485 Squadron.

On a visit to 602 Squadron at Kenley a few days later, he joined the station commander, Group Captain Victor Beamish, on a 'circus' to northern France, flying as his number two. Escorting six Boston light bombers for an attack on Mazingarbe, they were crossing the coast on the return leg when intercepted by a force of Focke-Wulf 190s. It was the group captain's first experience of the German type as Beamish later recalled:

"I was just behind the bombers and one section of Fw 190s came down in a fairly shallow dive having come through the top cover. I dived to catch the number one but found myself in a steep dive behind his number two. I got a long burst no deflection and this Fw 190 turned over and dropped away, smoking black and white very badly. I did not follow him down but knew he was hit well. My number two temporarily lost me in the manoeuvre and dived to get on the Fw 190s but he saw two aircraft crash in the sea just off the French coast."

Finlay's record had not gone unnoticed by his superiors, and in the *London Gazette* of 10 April 1942, the long-overdue award of a Distinguished Flying Cross (DFC) was announced. The citation said it all and more:

> 'From September 1940 to August 1941, Wing Commander Finlay was the commanding officer of 41 Squadron. He participated in many sorties during which he destroyed at least three enemy aircraft in combat. On one sortie, he attacked a German ship, leaving it a mass of flames. During the period, his squadron destroyed 66 enemy aircraft. Since joining his present unit, Wing Commander Finlay has participated in several sorties. On 3 March 1942, he destroyed a Messerschmitt 109 following a courageous head-on attack, thus bringing his victories to four. This officer has always shown great keenness and he has set a splendid example to all.'

His 'head-on attack' had been while flying a Spitfire VB, but it was when flying a Spitfire IX that he at last got to grips with an Fw 190 on equal terms. Flying a 'Ramrod' operation in the early evening of July 30, Finlay was flying as Red 3 with 64 Squadron when he saw the Red Section leader (Squadron Leader Smith) dive to attack a formation of Focke-Wulf fighters. Finlay followed two of the German aircraft as they fled towards Dunkirk, throwing their aircraft into a series of manoeuvres to evade Finlay's aim. Despite getting to within 300 yards, Finlay could not close the gap any further, but fired several speculative bursts from dead astern:

> "After allowing more for bullet drop at least one hit was secured on the left-hand side of the fuselage or wing root, a small piece coming off. The Fw 190 dived steeply and a moment later the other one further attacked a Spitfire which was simultaneously attacked from almost head on by three Fw 190s. In the ensuing melee, I lost contact, climbed to 9,500 ft, and crossed the coast west of Dunkirk."

He claimed the fighter as 'damaged'. It was the last claim he would make in the war, but it was by no means his final contribution to victory.

In the early summer of 1942, he was posted to RAF Rednal in Shropshire as station commander. Rednal had only recently become home to 61 OTU, helping embryo fighter pilots on their last leg before becoming operational. Finlay was responsible for almost 1,500 officers, airmen and women, as well as the large contingent of French, Belgium and other European flyers who had escaped Nazi occupation. Some of the instructors were Polish, which proved essential in overcoming some of the language barriers. Training was intense, and accidents a fact of life. But there was also time for fun.

One morning the station commander emerged from his staff car outside one of the Flight offices. He had one arm in a sling, a walking stick in the other, and his bandaged head was topped by a new but rather battered hat. The flight commander, a former Battle of Britain man, was heard to exclaim: "Good God, Don, what happened to you?" Finlay replied: "The bastards were playing rugby in the mess last night and they used my new hat as a ball." "How did you get hurt then?" the flight commander enquired. Finlay retorted: "I was still wearing the bloody thing!"

After his stint at OC Rednal, Finlay was posted to the Mediterranean theatre, converting to twin engines. He took command of 608 Squadron in December 1943. This involved flying Lockheed Hudsons on anti-submarine, convoy and escort duties to protect Allied shipping and provide cover for the Anzio landings and campaign which took place on the Italian mainland in the first few months of 1944. He received a mention in despatches. Promoted to acting group captain, he was appointed Senior Air Staff Officer (SASO) at 210 Fighter Group and awarded the Air Force Cross (AFC) on 1 September 1944.

In the new year of 1945, he found himself in yet another theatre, as commander of 906 Wing in Burma, flying Spitfire VIIIs out of Sadaung. A contemporary from Halton recalled:

> "Every morning at dawn he could be seen outside of his caravan doing his press-ups and other exercises to keep fit. The story was that if he caught anyone in a misdemeanour, he would have them out there with him. No-one took the risk that I heard about!"

Finlay was still in Burma when the war ended, and in the New Year's Honours list of 1946, received a second mention in despatches.

Throughout the war, Finlay had never ceased to maintain his fitness, and was a familiar sight pounding an airfield perimeter track in his vest and shorts wherever he served. He also, remarkably, turned out on the right wing for the wartime Tottenham Hotspur FC! It is, however, nonetheless extraordinary that for the 1948 Olympics, at the age of 39, he was still good enough to be selected for the Great Britain team as captain and given the honour of taking the oath on behalf of the competing nations. Although he fell in his heat, he still managed to post new British national and English national records the following year at the age of 40. At the White City cinder track on 16 July 1949, Finlay won the 120-yard hurdles race in a time of 14.6 seconds, making those present wonder just what he might have achieved had it not been for the interruption of six years of war.

'DoN'.

Caricature of Don Finlay.

Reverting to the rank of wing commander, Finlay settled into his peacetime role as an officer in the Engineering Branch, and returned to RAF Halton as the station technical officer (STO) as Group Captain Training. He retired in 1959. He was a hard taskmaster, and not afraid to fail those who were not up to the mark. But he was also a very fair-minded man, and a hero to many who knew him. (He even appeared in a cartoon strip of the time.). At his funeral in 1970, an early death accelerated by a serious car accident, Peter Hildreth, a fellow hurdler and Olympian, recounted how Finlay was always ready to help those who were just starting out:

"John Hart was selected to represent Britain against France in 1946 and was keyed up for it. Only days before the match he received a call from the team manager, Jack Crump, asking if he would stand down in favour of Donald Finlay who had been serving abroad but was just home. But Finlay wouldn't hear of it, insisting that Hart should run as selected and showing up on the day to support and encourage him."

Perhaps the last word should go to a contemporary of Finlay's from the 12th Entry (B Squadron, 2 Wing), Vic White. Both were regulars in the squadron football team and won everything there was to win:

"It was a joy to watch him strolling past opponents or hurdling them if they came in too low! Despite his supreme prowess at any sport in which he took part, Don was the most unassuming and likeable character it has been my pleasure to know."

5 THEIR FINEST HOUR

Sammy Butterfield knew he had a fight on his hands. The 27-year-old former metal rigger apprentice from the 20th Entry was no stranger to combat, but even he knew he may have just bitten off more than he could chew.

His flight had been ordered to patrol Dunkirk. It was 28 May. The Belgian army was on the point of surrendering, and the first of the 'little ships' were arriving to help lift the stranded men of the British Expeditionary Force (BEF) off the beaches. While the soldiers would later curse the RAF and doubt their resolve, men like Sammy were fighting for their lives in the grey skies above them.

Sammy was Blue 2 in a B Flight formation of 213 Squadron coming to the end of his patrol when he spotted nine Bf 109s at only 800 ft. They spotted him too and almost immediately a dogfight ensued. A German fighter drifted into his gun sight and he opened fire with his eight Browning .303s, a two-second burst. It missed and he fired again, thumbing the gun button, this time seeing instant results, the enemy fighter bursting into flames. He spotted another Bf 109 on his starboard side and turned in to attack, a one-second burst from astern and at close range being enough to snap off the fighter's tail as though it were a toy.

As he levelled out, a twin-engined Junkers 88 drifted mournfully across his path and Sammy attacked from his quarter, a longer, five-second burst causing the starboard engine to belch thick, oily black smoke before the bomber half-rolled into the sea. Moments later Sammy felt and heard the sickening thud of cannon fire beneath him, and just had time to glimpse a Bf 110 Zerstörer – a heavily armed twin-engined fighter – as it flew past. Sammy immediately broke away and then attacked, firing yet another five-second burst and once again having the satisfaction of seeing the fighter flip onto its back and dive into the cold grey of the Channel.

Battle had now been joined by many dozens of German fighters, perhaps 80 in all, and with no ammunition left for his guns, Sammy pulled the emergency boost to escape. Twisting and turning for all he was worth, he managed to avoid first one and then several attacks until, inevitably, he was hit. Two shells smashed into his cockpit panel, and three more into his underbelly. The engine stopped dead, and flames began to appear at the wing route. Sammy's Hurricane had been mortally wounded. Now to get out.

Dangerously low, Sammy tried desperately to gain height before leaving the stricken aircraft, crouching in his cockpit and pulling for all he was worth on the stick. At 800 ft he left the blazing Hurricane, banging his head on the main plane for his troubles but fortunately still cognisant enough to pull the rip cord once he was sure he was safe from the prowling fighters. The parachute blossomed briefly until he hit the sea, and his Mae West inflated. Sammy's luck held for he was soon after picked up by a passing paddle steamer, *Sundown*, and landed at Margate. His subsequent combat report records four 'kills' in the space of less than 15 minutes.

Perhaps not surprisingly, Sammy was decorated for his efforts, the citation for his immediate Distinguished Flying Medal reading: 'Throughout the engagement, though greatly outnumbered, this airman displayed great courage, outstanding initiative and determination.'

With the end of the Battle of France came the Battle of Britain, by which time the former Watford Grammar School boy was already an 'ace'. On 11 August, operating from Exeter, he failed to return from combat over Portland. Twenty-five British pilots lost their lives this day, the greatest loss of pilots on any day during the Battle of Britain. His body was later washed up on the French coast at Berck-sur-Mer and his Hurricane, P7389, discovered many years later on the seabed two miles from Lulworth.

Two days before Sammy's epic dogfight over Dunkirk, Ian 'Jock' Muirhead, a contemporary from the 20th Entry had also been in combat and forced to take to his 'chute.

Despite his Scottish heritage, Ian had been born in London before his parents moved to Carlisle. It was while at the Nelson School in Wigton that he applied for and was awarded an apprenticeship at Halton where, in 1932, he graduated at the top of the Entry. His prize for being the best fitter (AE) in his year was a beautiful-ly bound copy of the classic *Machinery Handbook*.

Even though Ian was outwardly fit and active, having swum for his Wing, shot rifles and pistols at Bisley, and winning the Barrington Kennett trophy for sporting prowess, he failed to get into Cranwell on account of high blood pressure. He should have been re-tested and his parents were somewhat upset by the result, but Ian was more sanguine about the outcome. He insisted that to be an officer required having a private income, and with his father at sea and his mother with a business to run, it was just not possible. It was only a temporary setback, however, for his wish to become a pilot was quickly realised.

Upon the outbreak of war, Ian was serving with 151 Squadron as an NCO pilot but with a commission in April 1940 came a posting to 605 Squadron in Wick. On 10 April, in the late afternoon, Ian almost opened his score when Green

Section intercepted a Heinkel 111K out to sea off the north Scottish coast. He attacked the aircraft twice, forcing the bomber to jettison its load, but only being able to claim the aircraft as damaged, despite firing off over 1,100 rounds.

The squadron moved south to Hawkinge in the second half of May, allowing Ian to open his account properly on the 22nd when intercepting a pair of Heinkel 111s near Arras. He claimed one as damaged and a second as confirmed destroyed, having watched the aircraft dive vertically into the ground from 2,000 ft and explode. He claimed three more German aircraft on the 25th: a Henschel Hs 126 reconnaissance aircraft and two Junkers 87 'Stuka' dive bombers – all destroyed.

On 26 May, Ian was flying Green 3 in the early afternoon when his section spotted a number of Bf 110s over Dunkirk and turned to engage. Ian managed a squirt at one, silencing the rear gunner after a long burst. He lost the aircraft momentarily as he flew through smoke from the burning oil tanks below, and as he emerged, he noted it had dived to sea level, heading for Ostend. Before Ian could give chase, his cockpit began filling with glycol and steam. Unaware that he had been hit, but with the aircraft clearly damaged, he headed for a friendly airfield but never made it. With conditions in the cockpit now impossible, he was obliged to take to his 'chute. Unbuckling his harness, he rolled the machine onto its back and dropped out, watching, fascinated, as his aircraft flew on to crash 1,000 ft below.

As he drifted down, he was alarmed to see tiny holes appearing in the canopy above him, and quickly realised that he was being fired upon from the ground. The firing continued even after he landed until he was finally able to convince the Belgians who were shooting at him that they were in fact on the same side. Fate in the shape and shoulder flashes of a Royal Army Medical Corps officer finally saved the day. Ian was able to borrow a car to get to Stene aerodrome to make contact with the Belgian air force authorities. Ian was directed to Ostend and allocated to the SS *Aboukir* for passage to England, teaming up with a number of fellow officers and men from RAF Fighter and Bomber Commands.

The SS *Aboukir*'s departure was delayed, and while they waited ashore in the basement of a French Marine Mission, they were subjected to a raid by a single enemy bomber which dropped a stick of five bombs that burst alarmingly close and scattered smaller incendiary devices that set fire to a railway line and siding. The RAF men decided to leave the 'sanctuary' of the town for the comparative safety of the countryside, returning as the sun rose on a new day. As they waited, they were subjected to regular and heavy air raids but had the satisfaction of seeing some of their Hurricanes fighting back, a sight that gave great succour to the men on the ground. The attacks from all manner of German aircraft – Heinkel 111s, Junkers 88s, Junkers 87s – went on all day, and were indiscriminate in their targeting, Ian witnessing several attacks on defenceless refugees on the surrounding roads.

That evening, as dusk fell, they cast off, and braced themselves for the inevitable attacks from the air and from the sea. Ian teamed up with a 151 Squadron pilot, Flight Lieutenant Ives, in manning a Lewis gun on the wheelhouse deck and put up a spirited defence against the airborne assault. They could do nothing, however, against the torpedoes, and a violent explosion signalled that the steam ship had been hit and was sinking fast. Ian clung to a makeshift raft as the vessel almost literally disappeared beneath his feet. He was joined by three fellow survivors, and between them they watched as their nemesis – an E-boat – proceeded to machine-gun anyone they could see struggling in the water. Ian cautioned the men to stay still and hide, if possible, under their small piece of wreckage. He figured if they were still alive by daylight, they had a good chance of being rescued. And so it proved. They were eventually picked up by the destroyer, HMS *Grenade*, and transferred to HMS *Greyhound* where Ian received treatment to his legs, which he could not move.

Out of a complement of around 230 on board the SS *Aboukir*, Ian could count only around 30 survivors. Among the dead was the redoubtable Flight Lieutenant Ives. He noted in his report: 'I trust his behaviour will be brought to the attention of the authorities.'

Ian's injuries put him *hors de combat* for some weeks, and it was not until July that he re-joined his squadron. In the meantime, he was awarded the DFC, the squadron's first decoration of the war. Returning to operations at the height of the Battle of Britain, Ian added to his score on 15 August and 24 September, and was given command of B Flight. He was shot down once again on 7 October, but again bailed out and survived. He was shot down a third time eight days later, on 15 October, in combat with Bf 109s over Maidstone. Sadly, it was not to prove third time lucky. Ian is buried at Hulme Cultram in Cumberland.

Flight Lieutenant Ian Muirhead DFC was immortalised in one of the now famous pencil portraits of Battle of Britain fighter pilots drawn by the artist and former Royal Flying Corps observer Cuthbert Orde. Orde drew at least 160 such portraits during and after the battle, and perhaps almost twice that number. Several were of former Brats.

They included: 'Sammy' Allard (20th Entry), a metal rigger who won the DFC, DFM & Bar with 85 Squadron and was credited with more than 20 kills in France and over Britain before being killed in a flying accident in 1941; Frank Carey (16th Entry), who also graduated from Halton as a metal rigger only to return for further training as a fitter II (Airframes). As a pilot, Carey fought the Luftwaffe in the Battle of France and the Battle of Britain, and then fought the Japanese in Burma, claiming more than 20 victories and winning three DFCs and a DFM. He survived the war; and Clifford Whitehead (24th Entry) who flew with 56 Squadron in France, was shot down during the Battle of Britain and awarded the DFM in August 1940. He lost his life as a flying instructor two years later.

While in France, the speed of the German advance obliged the British fighter squadrons to abandon their temporary bases, often at very short notice. When 56 Squadron evacuated Vitry for Norrent-Fontes on the evening of 18 May, Whitehead was sent back to destroy the remaining aircraft and stores. With him was another former Brat and fellow NCO Taffy Higginson, an exceptional fighter pilot whose exploits are worthy of wider recognition among the Halton alumni.

The son of a policeman from Swansea, Frederick 'Taffy' Higginson arrived at Halton in January 1929 from Gowerton County Intermediate School as part of the 19th Entry. After three years he passed out as a metal rigger and was posted to 7 Squadron at Worthy Down as a fitter and occasional air gunner to work on the Vickers Virginia. He would occasionally rub shoulders with Aircraftman Shaw, more familiar to the world as Lawrence of Arabia.

Determined to fly, Taffy's wish finally came true in 1935 when he began flying training at Brough (4 E&RFTS) and Sealand (5 FTS), gaining his wings and being posted to 19 Squadron at Duxford in the summer of the following year, joining C Flight. Very soon after his arrival, C Flight was hived off to form the nucleus of 66 Squadron, equipped with the Gloster Gauntlet, and Taffy went with them. He swapped his Gauntlet for the more advanced Gladiator IIs with 56 Squadron in 1937, the squadron soon after re-equipping with the Hurricane 1.

It was with the Hurricane that 56 Squadron went to war, operating flights both from North Weald and various bases in northern France. With B Flight in Vitry-en-Artois in May, Taffy first engaged with the enemy successfully, claiming a Dornier 17 and Heinkel 111 destroyed on the 17th, and a Bf 110 the following day. Taffy and fellow Brat Clifford Whitehead returned to Vitry from their new base at Norrent-Fontes to destroy what had been left behind in something of a rush, for the Germans were just a few miles up the road.

With his return to the UK, Taffy flew fighter patrols over Dunkirk, claiming a Bf 109 on 29 May, but did not score again until 15 July on the eve of the Battle of Britain. Two weeks later he was awarded the DFM, the citation stating:

> 'This airman pilot has led a section during all operations undertaken by his squadron and has personally destroyed at least five enemy aircraft. He has shown the greatest determination in the face of the enemy and his cool and courageous leadership has been an example to his squadron.'

Taffy fought long and hard throughout August and on the 16th successfully attacked a Dornier 17 but was himself obliged to force land after his aircraft caught fire. He made claims on the 25th, 26th and 31st, and continued his successful run into September. His leadership skills were recognised with a commission and the appointment to be temporary commander B Flight. By the end of the battle, his score had risen to at least 12, with several others damaged or probably destroyed.

With the start of a new year came a change in Fighter Command's tactics, taking the fight to the Germans with offensive sweeps over the Channel. They were also called upon to escort light bombers and it was on one such 'circus' that Taffy's luck finally ran out. On operations to Lille, his Hurricane was hit and the control column snapped off at the base. With no means of flying the aircraft he bailed out, but on landing was immediately captured by a German officer and sergeant in a motorcycle combination. While the two men were momentarily distracted by a low-flying Messerschmitt, Taffy seized his chance, turned the motorcycle over and ran for all he was worth.

There then began a series of adventures over the next 14 months that saw him hidden in a brothel, consorting with a traitor, and spirited away within the famous Pat O'Leary escape line. Making his way into Vichy France (the unoccupied zone) he was captured on the Spanish border and imprisoned for six months for being in possession of false papers. Due for release, his sentence was extended in reprisal for a raid on the Renault factory at Billancourt, and he was moved to a new prison in Monte Carlo where he changed his identity. Far from abandoned by his protectors in the O'Leary organisation, a hacksaw was smuggled into his cell (thanks to a Polish priest) and on the night of 6 August, Taffy and four other inmates made good their escape, reaching a safe house in the principality where they were treated to tea by a Scottish spinster. Disguised as a priest, he made for Marseille and the beach resort of Canet Plage, where he was picked up from a dinghy by a Polish trawler employed as a Q ship[1]. From there he was transferred to the HMS *Minna* and landed at Gibraltar.

Taffy's war was far from over. He returned to operations with 56 Squadron flying the Hawker Typhoon (see photo opposite) and was awarded the DFC. He saw out the war with 83 Group's communication squadron, and later pursued diverse careers in civil aviation, engineering and farming. He died on 12 February 2003, five days short of his 90th birthday.

Taffy's escape and evasion was almost a carbon copy of the experiences of another notable Battle of Britain Brat, Roy 'Wilky' Wilkinson. Wilkinson (21st Entry), who was also, coincidentally, a policeman's son, gained the remarkable distinction of temporarily commanding a fighter squadron during the Battle of France while still an NCO and went on to shoot down nine enemy aircraft before being shot down himself.

Wilky had learned to fly in 1937, joining 3 Squadron equipped with Gloster Gladiators. He fought throughout the campaign in France and when his squadron commander was shot down, the acting CO passed over two flight lieutenants to make him a flight commander. Soon after that he became acting CO, thus jumping straight from sergeant pilot to flight lieutenant, missing out two commissioned ranks altogether.

On his return from France, he helped with the formation of 71 Squadron, the first of the RAF Eagle squadrons. However, it was with 174 Squadron, a Hurricane

Apprentices working on a Typhoon.

fighter-bomber unit, that he was shot down, his aircraft receiving a direct hit in the engine from a 40-mm Bofors shell. Despite being dangerously low he managed to bail out, his 'chute opening just in time for him to hit some trees which left him dangling a few feet off the ground.

Evading capture and given food in a local farmhouse, he headed for Paris, stopping for a shave in a local barber shop in which he convinced two German officers he was mad by shouting at them in Arabic – a language he had picked up during an earlier posting after Halton. Like Taffy, he also took refuge in a brothel, where the madam refused to take payment for any comforts. He then took a train to Chagny and headed south into Vichy. In a series of lucky breaks and fortunate meetings, he was eventually given false papers and made his way to Marseille where he met Pat O'Leary, the legendary escape line chief. He crossed the Pyrenees into Spain and on reaching Gibraltar, hitched a lift in a Sunderland flying boat to Plymouth.

After the war, Wilky helped to establish Stansted as a private airport, and ran Elstree Flying Club before setting up a garage on the Isle of Sheppey.

Harry Clack was not one of the celebrated fighter boys. He was not a bemedaled 'ace'. His name is not celebrated in any histories of the Battle of Britain. But perhaps it should be. For he was one of the many hundreds of RAF ground crew who went about quietly, diligently, and skilfully serving their country, keeping the aircraft flying, or doing whatever jobs the RAF asked of them, few of them glamorous. Like the task Harry Clack was given on 25 October 1940, to recover what was left of a German Dornier 215 twin-engined light bomber, shot down on a reconnaissance sortie the previous day.

A former pupil at John Ruskin Central School in Croydon, Harry had joined the RAF as an apprentice, part of the 39th Entry. His chosen trade was engine fitter. His accelerated training finished on 5 October, after which he was posted to Cambridge on salvage and repair duties with 54 Maintenance Unit. When the call came through to recover the crashed bomber, Harry was excited. It was his first 'real' job.

The aircraft had crashed not far from the Crown Inn pub in Eaton Socon, Cambridgeshire. All four crew had abandoned their aircraft, but only one had survived. The bomber was near a power line, and Harry and one other were in charge of the crane needed to lift the wreckage. As the crane was manoeuvred into position, disaster struck. The top of its jib hit the overhead line; there was a loud 'bang', a flash and a smell of burning. Both men were electrocuted.

What is remarkable about Harry's story is not how he died, though that is tragic enough, but rather his age. Still only 16, he was one of the youngest members of the British armed forces to be killed in the war while on active service.

Fred Hain, a fitter IIE of the 38th Entry had been posted to 56 Squadron at North Weald on passing out at the height of the battle. Ground crews tended not to use the hangars for fear of being bombed. Most maintenance was carried out in the open in bays dispersed around the airfield perimeter.

On one occasion he was completing a cylinder block, radiator and propeller check when an air raid siren wailed and he was obliged to take cover on the engineer officer's instructions. On leaving the shelter, he was confronted by a scene of utter devastation, buildings ablaze, transport destroyed, and the upsetting sight of the body parts of 18-year-old airmen who had failed to obey their orders to take refuge in time.

Inspecting 'his' aircraft he found that a piece of shrapnel had gone into a propeller blade and through the radiator, which he quickly replaced. He was ground running the aircraft when there was another alert; a sergeant pilot came running out to the aircraft, Fred leaped out and the pilot climbed on board, strapped in, slammed the throttle lever forward and took off to join the battle with his comrades.

The aircraft never returned.

In total, some 116 Halton apprentices flew in the Battle of Britain, but many hundreds more served as ground crew as fitters, riggers, and armourers. Some of these pilots went on to become notable aces.

Jim Hallowes, for example, was a metal rigger (19th Entry) who was selected for pilot training in 1935. He claimed his first successes above the beaches of Dunkirk, and on one occasion while attacking a Bf 109 his Hurricane was hit in the engine which stopped. While undoing his straps and preparing to bail out, the enemy aircraft overshot and flew in front of him. Hallowes dropped back into the cockpit and opened fire. The German pilot bailed out and Hallowes quickly followed suit. They landed in adjacent fields. Hallowes was awarded the DFM, and a Bar a few months later. Later in the war he added the ribbon of the DFC, having been commissioned, and retired in 1956 as a wing commander. His final official victory tally was not less than 21 enemy aircraft and there were probably more.

Edward Thorn claimed fame with his gunner, Fred Barker, as the most successful Boulton Paul Defiant partnership of the war. Edward arrived at Halton in September 1928 and passed out as part of the 18th Entry three years later. Selected for pilot training he joined 264 Squadron in the late autumn of 1939. The pair accounted for three Bf 109s on 28 May, two Junkers 87s and a Bf 110 on 29 May, and a Heinkel 111 two days later, all confirmed. Not surprisingly, both men were awarded the DFM. Edward and Fred flew throughout the Battle of Britain, adding to their score, and nearly coming to grief on 26 August when attacked by a Bf 109. With their aircraft hit, Edward prepared for an emergency landing but as he did so, the 109 attacked again and Fred shot it down. With their own aircraft now ablaze, the two men were lucky to escape with their lives. A Bar to their respective DFMs followed immediately after. Edward was to add a DFC and Bar before the war ended but did not live long thereafter. On 12 February 1946 he was killed in a flying accident when his Meteor crashed into the ground at high speed after coming out of cloud.

While most of the publicity given to the men who fought and died in the Battle of Britain went to the day fighters, a fierce and dangerous battle was also being fought at night. Defiants, Blenheims and even lone-flying Hurricanes were pressed into service with only limited success. Much of this changed, however, with the introduction of the Bristol Beaufighter which, equipped with the steadily developing airborne radar and the growing confidence and experience of the crews, transformed the night time aerial battle.

Charles Widdows, an apprentice with the 14th Entry, fought throughout the Battle of Britain and beyond as the Officer Commanding 29 Squadron. A pilot of considerable experience, Charles had carried out extensive performance tests on the first production Hurricanes and Spitfires to enter service before the war, having served his own flying apprenticeships on Fairey Gordons in Egypt in 1933. Taking command of 29 Squadron in June 1940, he turned a somewhat lax and demoralised unit into a disciplined, professional fighting force, rebuilding the squadron around a few of the keenest and most able pilots and radar operators who would later go on to become famous aces in their own right.

The first Beaufighters arrived in September 1940, but it was not until March the following year that Charles achieved his first victory, a Junkers 88 shot down with a one-second burst over the Lincolnshire countryside, a few miles east of Horncastle.

The Beaufighter had its fair share of teething problems, not least with its engines, as Charles found one night shortly after take-off. Recognising the danger straight away, he ordered his radar operator to bail out. But as Charles made to leave the aircraft himself, he noted his crewman had been unable to release the rear escape hatch and so was effectively trapped. Charles returned to his controls and skilfully crash-landed in a field – a remarkable achievement in the dark and

Aden pilots have just landed Gordons of 14 Squadron with K2623 in the distance.

with only one engine.

When the squadron moved to West Malling, Charles was promoted station commander but continued to fly[2]. One night in May he attacked a Junkers 88 near Beachy Head but was hit by return fire, putting his radio out of action and obliging him to take violent evasive action. He was also slightly wounded in the leg. Limping back to base he was somewhat surprised to find his regular radar operator, Sergeant Browne Ryall, had bailed out. His body was washed up soon after on a French beach. Charles was awarded the DFC.

Charles' experience was used by Fighter Command as Group Captain Night Operations for 11 and 12 Groups. He was twice awarded a mention in despatches. He retired from the RAF as an air commodore in 1958 and died at the age of 100, a full life fully lived.

Not all were given the chance to prove their fighting abilities or realise their true potential at day or at night. There were men like Philip Cox, for example, who passed out from Halton as a fitter and won a place at Cranwell as a flight cadet. He fought in France with 501 as a flight commander, covering the BEF evacuation from Cherbourg. On 20 July he claimed a Bf 109 destroyed and shared in the destruction of another the same day. A week later, however, he was shot down and posted missing.

His body has never been found.

6 THE RAJAH OF SARAWAK

While the RAF was licking its wounds from its mauling in France, and steadying itself for the Battle of Britain, in the Western Desert men were already fighting a desperate action to stem the advance of the Axis forces. With the belated entry of the Italians into the war on 10 June 1940, the Allies soon had their hands full, desperate to stop the supply and resupply of the Italian army, which already had more than a million men in Libya against a British Army across the border in Egypt that could only muster 36,000 soldiers on a good day. Among those units tasked with hampering the Italian war effort was 211 Squadron, and within their ranks was a former Halton apprentice, Francis Brooks, who went on to distinguish himself in two theatres of war.

Born in Devonport on 7 December 1913, Francis Brooks came from a military family. His father and cousin had both been in the Royal Navy, and he had two uncles in the army. In many ways, therefore, Francis broke with tradition in joining the RAF, having passed his entrance exam and leaving Devonport High School in the autumn of 1929, still a few months shy of his 16th birthday. After three years at Halton he passed out as a metal rigger and was posted to join 57 Squadron, which at the time was based at Upper Heyford.

While the day job called for his skills working on the squadron's Hawker Harts as part of the ground crew, he also trained to become an air gunner, proud of the brass bullet he was entitled to wear on his sleeve. Various other postings followed, notably a spell with 99 Squadron at Mildenhall where he swapped the trim Hart for the mighty Handley Page Heyford, before receiving the first of his overseas postings to 60 Squadron in India, and a chance to work on yet another different airframe, the Bristol Blenheim.

It was in India, and while seconded to the Indian air force, that he undoubtedly acquired the nickname 'Rajah', after James Brooke, the Rajah of Sarawak, a name that was to stick with him throughout his service career. Francis was with 11 Squadron in Singapore on the day that war broke out, and it was not until 16 June 1940 that he was posted to the Western Desert, by which time he had qualified as an observer and been promoted to corporal. He also already had more than 2,000 flying hours in his logbook, a quarter of those at night.

Under the command of Squadron Leader Gordon 'Porpoise' Bax, a pre-war regular, 211 had carried out the first raid of the war in the desert and continued an exhausting series of attacks on Italian airfields (notably El Adem, considered the Regia Aeronautica's finest aerodrome in Libya) and the ports and harbour installations feeding munitions and supplies to the Italian army. Rajah was immediately thrown into the action, flying with a number of different pilots before becoming part of a regular three-man crew comprising himself as observer, Sergeant Thomas 'Jock' McCord as W/Op AG, and 'The Duke' Delaney as the pilot.

With The Duke, Brooks had struck gold. Keen on motor racing, his father had found fame in the Paris-Madrid rally before the war – an event that became notorious and had to be stopped after so many drivers and spectators had been killed. Impossibly good looking, The Duke was perpetually happy and a splendid pilot.

Rajah flew two trips in June, three in July, five in August and 11 in September. Flak and fighters were a constant danger, so too the questionable reliability of their aircraft operating in such a hostile environment. On 15 July, after a bombing raid deep into Libya, Blenheim L1540 with The Duke at the controls, he was obliged to make a forced-landing at Sidi Barrani. Of the eight squadron aircraft taking part that day, not a single Blenheim made it back to base. One landed in enemy territory and the crew were captured, although the pilot later managed to escape.

Derma, Al Gazala and Tobruk all featured as regular targets, the Blenheims typically able to carry a dozen 12-lb and a similar number of 40-lb bombs and smaller incendiaries to create maximum damage, particularly to aircraft dispersed on the ground. Many of these raids were conducted at high level, some upwards of 20,000 ft which took them beyond the range of the light flak but into the guns of the fighters. Occasionally, Rajah could see the results of their bombing; on one raid on 26 September, for example, he noted in his logbook 'four fighter aircraft hit'.

The battle was by no means one-sided. The squadron lost several of its crews in those first few months of the war, including the commanding officer, 'Porpoise' Bax, although he was later reported as a prisoner of war. James Gordon-Finlayson, known either as 'GF' or 'The Bish', took over command in time for the squadron to move to Greece to reinforce the Greek air force and counter the Italian invasion.

Again, the pace of operations was relentless with the ships and jetties around Valona harbour being favourite targets, as well as the nearby airfield. The raids were often conducted at low level. On 6 June, Rajah was flying as observer to the B Flight commander, Flight Lieutenant Doudney, for an attack on Valona. They were formation leaders, and all went well until they reached the target when they were met by intense anti-aircraft fire. This was followed by an attack by six Italian fighters as they left the target area.

Their aircraft made it home with a punctured tyre and a machine-gun bullet in an airscrew, and two other aircraft were damaged but of The Duke there was no news. Subsequently it transpired that he had been seen attempting to land near Argyrokastro on one engine but failed in the attempt. The Duke was killed along with 'Jock' McCord and Sergeant Vynor 'Vic' Pollard, a 22-year-old Yorkshireman who had taken Rajah's place as observer. One other crew also failed to return. Rajah wrote in his logbook simply: 'F/L Delaney and Sgt McCord killed on raid over Valona. My first crew.'

Promoted to sergeant, Rajah began to fly regularly with New Zealander Flying Officer Lindsay Buchanan, one of several Antipodeans on the squadron, attacking targets in Greece and Albania. In February he flew 12 operations, including a raid on an arms and munitions dump at Bousi on the 13th when they were attacked by three Italian G.50s. Their air gunner (Sergeant George Pattison) claimed to have shot one down. Bousi was raided six times in as many days, sometimes twice in a day, and the reception was always intense.

In March, Squadron Leader Arthur Blomfield took command of the squadron, but beyond that little much changed. Rajah flew 16 operations including a joint attack with the Fleet Air Arm on 13 March which he recalled after the war:

> "The Navy Swordfish were given a target of torpedoing ships at anchor in Valona. This operation had to be targeted at night. To keep the defences' attention occupied, a Blenheim would fly over Valona, seconds before the main attack. Being the only sergeant with many hours of night flying, I was detailed for the flight. Approaching the target area, the sky became alight with searchlights and tracers. I released my bombs, on time, just as the low-flying Swordfish came over the water. With my plane getting all the attention, the Swordfish completed a perfect raid."

Another remarkable event was recorded three days later. Rajah was not operating, but another former Halton apprentice, Ronald 'Twinkle' Pearson, certainly was. Twinkle had been a contemporary of Rajah's in the 20th Entry and was one of the squadron's characters. Returning from a reconnaissance sortie, and over the sea, he came across an Italian Cant Z.506 three-engined floatplane and decided to attack. His account of what happened that day was recorded by Tom Wisdom in his well-known contemporary account, *Wings Over Olympus*:

> "We were evenly enough matched – the Blenheim had two guns and the Cant had three, two in the rear turrets and one front. We tackled first the stings in the tail, and with my second burst I got the rear gunner. Just in time, too, for the tracer from the top turret was fairly whizzing past the

cockpit – most unpleasant. Then, the rear guns silenced, I went for the cockpit, and made a series of head-on attacks to drive him away from home. When the 'ammo' in the front gun was exhausted we tried beam attacks to give my rear-gunner a chance. It was jolly good fun. Then we had to come back, regretfully, for the Cant, just above the waves, was still flying, though all his guns were silent. So we landed a little fed up."

He had no need to be disappointed; an observation post on the coast had seen the Italian crash into the sea and sink. Twinkle's celebrations were only slightly muted by a severe ticking off by The Bish for what he took to be a foolhardy stunt[1].

The Germans attacked Greece from Bulgaria in April 1941, and 211 Squadron was forced to evacuate its airfields at Menidi and Paramythia. In the chaos that ensued, Rajah lost his first logbook, destroyed by fire alongside the rest of his kit. It had been the run of two weeks of bad luck, for shortly before abandoning their base his second crew – Lindsay Buchanan and George Pattison – had been killed close to the border of Yugoslavia. Six aircraft had taken off that afternoon to attack German ground units around Florina and not a single Blenheim had returned. All were shot down by German Bf 109s from JG27. Buchanan and Pattison were thought to have survived the initial crash, only to die shortly afterwards in an Albanian hospital.

Rajah's observer's seat had been taken by Squadron Leader Leslie Cryer DFC. Also flying that day had been the area commander, Wing Commander Patrick Coote. 'Paddy' Coote, a former Irish rugby international who had also represented the RAF and Britain in the bobsleigh, was a pilot but had opted to fly as observer to Flying Officer R. V. Herbert. The 31-year-old Coote, who had beaten Douglas Bader for the Sword of Honour at Cranwell, had started out in the 12th Entry at Halton, and was one of the more senior officers killed in the war.

Rajah continued flying with the squadron until the end of May (his last flight was on 11 May with Flying Officer Hugh Clutterbuck as his pilot) when he was posted to 11 Squadron (Blenheims) at Aqir in Palestine.

Under the command of Squadron Leader Alfred Bocking DFC (Bocking had won his award for operations in Palestine in July 1939), the squadron was heavily involved in the occupation of Syria. Flying photo-reconnaissance sorties, initially, with Pilot Officer John Pringle-Wood[2], Rajah soon found himself as the regular observer to the B Flight commander, Flight Lieutenant Rowbotham. A high-level raid on Beirut harbour on 22 June enabled Rajah to score two direct hits with his four 250-pounders on an enemy destroyer, and further successful attacks were mounted on motor transport, fuel dumps, and a fortress. The enemy in this case included the Vichy French, and bombing sorties were interspersed with armed-reconnaissance operations against Vichy shipping. He remained with 11 Squadron until August when he was at last posted back to the UK.

His tour of operations was acknowledged with the award of a well-earned Distinguished Flying Medal which he received, in part, for the joint raid with the Fleet Air Arm on Valona. The award was announced in the *London Gazette* on 22 August 1941, the citation stating: 'This senior NCO has taken part in 62 repeat, 62 raids over Libya and Greece and on all occasions has shown the greatest determination and courage when on duty.'

The emphasis on the number of raids is unusual and remarkable, in the truest sense of the word. It suggests that to undertake such a volume of trips, and survive, was something exceptional. Rajah received his DFM at an investiture ceremony from the King.

Sent on a navigator's course and qualifying as an air navigator second class in April 1942, Rajah was posted to Bishops Court in Ireland, and spent the next two years as an instructor, primarily with an advanced flying unit (AFU) for observers. He was also commissioned. When the Officer Commanding 7 (O) AFU, Wing Commander 'Rex' Boxer, was earmarked for 'ops', he asked Rajah to join him as his navigator.

After a five-day course learning how to use Gee – a radio navigation aid – at 13 OTU at Finmere, Rajah and his new skipper were introduced to the North American Mitchell, a fast and relatively heavily armed light bomber. The Mitchell was a proven war machine, capable of carrying 4,000 lbs of bombs more than 1,600 miles, and with a cruising speed of more than 200 mph. It was popular with pilots and aircrew alike. It was also the bomber in which James Doolittle had executed his famous attack on the Japanese mainland from the carrier USS *Hornet*, soon after Pearl Harbor.

Three weeks of local flying, cross countries, and high- and low-level bombing exercises were followed by a posting to 2 Group Support Unit (2GSU) and thence onward to 180 Squadron, part of the Second Tactical Air Force (2TAF). They arrived on 3 January 1945 two days after Operation Bodenplatte, the Luftwaffe's last-ditch attempt to inflict serious damage to the RAF on the ground.

Under the command of Wing Commander Kenneth Powell, a second-tour man, 180 Squadron was tasked with the bombing of tactical targets – road bridges, railway marshalling yards, troop concentrations, ammo and fuel dumps etc. – to support the Allied advance into Germany. Operations were flown from Melsbroek in Belgium, a former Luftwaffe base under new management and given the Allied identifier B58.

Rajah's first trip with 180 Squadron, and first with Boxer, came on 14 January, an attack on a road bridge at Zaltbommel. Twelve aircraft reached the target but all of them missed and one of their number was obliged to crash land. Eight days later they bombed Wassenberg, again with mixed results. February saw a change in squadron commander, and a change in skipper. Wing Commander Terence Cox (later DSO, DFC) arrived to take charge of the squadron, and Rajah began flying with a New Zealander, Flying Officer Neville Freeman. He flew four trips with Freeman before changing pilots again, being nabbed by one of the flight commanders, Squadron Leader Ernest Sell, as lead navigator.

Throughout February and March, the squadron was heavily engaged in Operation Clarion, the planned destruction of German communication networks, as well as Operations Veritable and Grenade, the former in support of Montgomery's 21st Army Group, and the latter to support the crossing of the Roer River by the US Ninth Army. Interceptions by enemy fighters were comparatively rare; flak was the main danger, and so it proved on the morning of 21 March, when Rajah nearly met his Maker.

The target was the railway marshalling yards at Bocholt. The briefing was very clear: 12 aircraft were detailed with the object of destroying the essential rolling stock the Germans relied upon to rush men and armour to and from the front line. The official report suggests that some bombs were seen to burst on the target, and others over- or under-shot. Flak was heavy and intense, and one aircraft received a direct hit and was seen to explode, scattering debris in a comparatively small area of sky that was densely populated with other aircraft.

At least one of the other Mitchells caught the impact of the blast and was seen to go down with flames and smoke billowing from an engine and a large hole in its fuselage. Only one parachute was observed. A third Mitchell was also hit and the pilot, Pilot Officer Richard Perkins, severely wounded, his right thigh shattered. In a remarkable feat of airmanship, the air gunner, Flight Sergeant James Hall, took over control of the aircraft, and managed to crash land at B90 without further injury to the crew[3].

Three other aircraft were also badly hit: Flight Sergeant Walsh brought his aircraft safely home, with one of his gunners badly wounded; Flight Lieutenant Howard-Jones was similarly hit, and despite extensive damage to the undercarriage and fuel systems, he also managed to make it back to base. The third aircraft to be hit, was flown by Squadron Leader Sell. Rajah recalled this particular raid many years later:

> "Arriving over the target area, my first run had to abort owing to clouds. I attacked again from another angle and again there was no clear target, but my Wing (the attacking aircraft were split into two sections) dropped their loads and turned for home. The bombs fell in a field.
>
> "Being left alone and with the briefing so definite, the flight commander and I decided to go below the clouds. The run was perfect, and the explosion was so huge that the plane felt it. Pulling away we were hit by a barrage of flak. The port engine began losing oil, the starboard engine was

coughing and there was a hole in the front Perspex. The wireless was u/s and the gunner wounded. I gave the pilot an ideal course to fly, to get to a landing strip, in the Netherlands. Having passed the strip before, I had some knowledge of the area. I tended the wounded gunner and read the area to the pilot. Our luck held, and we made it to the landing strip (B78)."

Sell landed at Eindhoven and the wounded gunner, Flying Officer Collard, was immediately taken away in a blood wagon. His leg had almost been shot away. Rajah was furious. He felt the rest of his section had let them down: "The crews that had left us were nearly court-martialled," he said.

Rajah flew his last operation of the war on 24 April, attacking enemy positions near Bremen. Twelve aircraft took off, and all returned safely. It proved to be the squadron's last operation from Melsbroek, and their last under Wing Commander Cox. A few days later, the squadron packed their kit for a move into Germany, flying their last operational sortie on 3 May, by which time Wing Commander J. R. Davenport had arrived to take charge.

By now a flight lieutenant, Rajah left 180 Squadron at the end of May and joined 170 Squadron at RAF Hemswell. In July he learned that both he and Squadron Leader Sell had been awarded the DFC, the citation making specific reference to the raid in March:

'Since being awarded the Distinguished Flying Medal on the 22 August 1941 this leading navigator and bomb aimer has highly distinguished himself during his operational career. He has led squadron formations with determination and accuracy on 51 operations against enemy targets in the Occupied countries and Germany. He has consistently set a high standard of professional skill and has won the confidence and admiration of all whom he had led. On many occasions his aircraft has been flown to its target through heavy and accurate anti-aircraft fire. With complete disregard for personal danger, F/Lt Brooks has at all times pressed home his attacks with high courage and coolness.

'During one flight his aircraft was badly damaged, the aileron control impaired and one engine seriously affected. The air gunner was gravely wounded and in danger of his life. Calmly F/Lt Brooks guided his pilot towards an advanced air strip and thus contributed largely to saving the lives of the wounded air gunner and the rest of the crew. This officer's tenacity, skill and courage have been one of the highest order, and the squadron record has been sustained and enhanced by the fine example which he has set.'

Rajah had enjoyed a long and varied RAF career, during which time he'd flown at

A Vickers Victoria.

least 15 different aircraft types including the Bristol Fighter, the Atlas, Tiger Moth, Hawker Hart, Hawker Audax, Heyford, Wapiti, Victoria, Valencia, Bombay, Blenheim Mk 1, Blenheim Mk IV, Anson and Mitchell. He'd even flown in a Junkers 52 'Tante Ju' of the Hellenic air force. He'd completed well over 100 bombing operations (the recommendation for his DFC by Wing Commander Davenport and dated 15 May gives the number of sorties as 127) and awarded two well-earned medals for gallantry. He retired from the RAF in December 1946 and died in 2001 at the age of 87. He now lies in Mildenhall Cemetery, Suffolk.

7 FOUR-ENGINED PIONEER

Gerry Blacklock failed at his first attempt to get into Halton. Happily, for the RAF and for the young Gerry, he succeeded second time around, and on 13 January 1931 he set off from his home in Grindleton in the Ribble Valley for the long journey into London and then out again to the Buckinghamshire countryside.

A former pupil at Queen Mary's Royal Grammar School in Clitheroe, he remembers a pamphlet about the RAF apprenticeship scheme appearing on a school notice board providing three years' training in one of six trades. But what particularly caught his eye was that airmen would have the opportunity to volunteer for training as pilots. It rekindled a latent memory he'd had of laying in the sun and seeing a tiny dot in the sky – his first aeroplane – and wondering what the ground looked like for the pilot looking down.

On arriving at Halton as part of the 23rd Entry, and being shown into his accommodation, the first thing that struck him was the floor:

> "It was covered in brown linoleum and polished to an almost dazzling brightness. After that I took in the twin rows of beds, lined up facing one another, and beside each bed an open-fronted locker, and on the wall behind, a steel cupboard."

Each of the steel beds had a square brown mattress known as a 'biscuit', on top of which were three folded blankets and two sheets, with a fourth blanket wrapped around them to make a parcel. On top of these was a cylinder stuffed with horse hair. A pillow. This was to be his accommodation, and his level of luxury, for the duration of his stay.

Having passed his medical, and been subjected to the obligatory short back and sides from a less than sympathetic barber, Gerry was attested, given his service number, and provided his preferred choice of trade. His first choice was as a fitter (E), and his second, metal rigger. As was so often the way in the RAF, he received his second choice, and settled into the weekly routine, punctuated only by a bout

Lessons did not stop for haircuts from Sweeny Todd.

of severe tonsillitis that necessitated a stay in IDH – the infectious diseases hospital.

Training was divided between workshop and school, Gerry learning all manner of skills such as splicing ropes and steel cables, brazing, welding, hull and float repairs, fabric repairs, metallurgy and rigging. Most of the RAF aircraft of the time were canvass-covered biplanes, and it was in one such aeroplane – an Avro 504N – that Gerry got to enjoy his first air experience flight.

After three years at Halton, Gerry took his final exams, hoping for an average of 80 per cent in educational subjects, bench work, and the oral exam that would see him pass out as a leading aircraftman (LAC). Unfortunately, he failed to make the grade in the oral and so departed as an AC1. A few of his contemporaries went on to be awarded a cadetship at Cranwell – Ted Bunting, A. A. Kelk, and L. 'Tommy' Atkins. Bunting was invalided out, Kelk killed in a motorcycle accident and only Tommy finished the course.

Posted to Wittering, on the Great North Road south of Stamford, along with six other Brats, Gerry was pleased to learn that the station was home to the Central Flying School (CFS). Although he would have preferred to have been posted to an operational squadron, anything was better than being sent to the Aircraft Depot at Henlow. Many of the other aircraft tradesmen were also ex-apprentices, although apart from Jack Wildman (22nd Entry) and Cecil Chapman (20th Entry), few of the faces were familiar.

Gerry had plenty of aircraft to work on since the CFS had a miscellany of types including Armstrong Whitworth Atlases, Siskins, Bristol Bulldogs and Hawker

Harts. There were also Tutors and Avros. Gerry moved with the CFS when it transferred, en bloc, to Upavon, and was busily minding his own business one day when told he was 'on the boat' which is RAF language for being posted overseas. Issued with tropical kit and given the necessary jabs, Gerry assumed they were being sent out to Abyssinia, where Mussolini was making trouble. As it was, they set sail in the SS *Cameronia* for Egypt via Malta, where they stopped over to refuel. Their final destination was the RAF Depot at Aboukir. They were not alone:

> "By the time we had sorted ourselves out it was dark. Silence reigned until morning, when there was a little excitement as someone who was starting to put his boots on found that a scorpion had got there before him. This resulted in the rest of us taking great care to shake our boots first."

Part of 'J Detail' as the group became known, Gerry and his colleagues worked each night, every night, un-crating aircraft from huge packing cases and assembling the contents into a recognisable aeroplane, labouring as fast as they could. In 1935, the RAF was still responsible for servicing the Fleet Air Arm aircraft, and Gerry later found himself posted to the FAA pool at Amriyah.

> "I was allocated to the Fairey gang since they were occupied, to a large extent, with work on FAA machines. But not a Fairey came our way. We encountered odd things like Blackburn Baffins and Sharks, quite an interesting variety in fact. Our shop was shared with the Vickers gang. Most of whom were engaged on a major inspection of a Vickers Victoria – the then current troop carrier – which, with its great bulbous nose, looked enormous in the shop. When it came to attaching the main planes, everyone in the shop was called on to help."

The 'emergency' ended almost as soon as it began, and Gerry arrived home to be posted to 5 Flying Training School at Sealand. One incident of note was when a mighty Heyford crashed into the Pennines in bad weather, and Gerry and a group of fellow airmen were instructed to salvage what they could: "The broken Heyford was rather a forlorn sight among the patchy snow. There was nothing of the airframe worth salvaging, so it was a case of reducing the metal to manageable proportions for loading, and burning the rest."

About this time, one of Gerry's contemporaries from Halton, Ken Cleghorn, departed to commence pilot training. A short while later, and Gerry was himself put forward as a possible candidate for flying training but failed the medical because of his eyes. He passed at the second attempt (something of a habit) and eventually, after yet another mishap with the MO, departed for 8EFTS at Woodley near Reading. Gerry was not the only apprentice at Woodley. There were four other Brats

An engine overhaul on a Vickers Victoria IV (J8929) of 70 Squadron in the field in Delhi. This is similar to what Gerry would have had to do in the FAA pool.

looking to fledge: Colin Wathey of the 22nd; Bert Baxter of the 23rd; and George Atkinson and Henry Ford of the 24th.

Unusually, Gerry learned to fly on a Miles Hawk. The reason was simple: 5EFTS was run by Philips and Powis Aircraft Ltd, who manufactured the Miles, thus the school was partly equipped with Miles aircraft. He went solo in eight hours and progressed to 3FTS at South Cerney. At the time, South Cerney was only half built and a depressing sight, being almost a sea of mud. Flying training did not start until late December, but it only took Gerry a further six hours to solo in a Hawker Hart, and he was excited by the surge produced by opening the Hart's throttle.

Those destined for fighters flew the Hawker Fury, while Gerry stayed in Harts and Audaxes, with a view to joining Bomber Command. Having gained his 'wings', he and several others were given a short course in air navigation and qualified as an air navigator second class. Gerry then stayed at Manston for further instruction in astro navigation. Shortly after, Colin Wathey was posted to 148 Squadron flying Vickers Wellesleys but was killed within days in a flying accident. Gerry received his posting to 99 Squadron at Mildenhall and was allocated to B Flight. His flight commander was a diminutive New Zealander, Squadron Leader McKee, and called variously 'Square', 'Butch' and 'Mr Cube'.

Despite some initial concerns about flying an aircraft several times bigger than anything he had been used to before, Gerry quickly adapted to the Heyford, and found it a rather satisfying aeroplane to fly. It was not long, however, before the squadron converted to the Vickers Wellington, and Gerry moved to A Flight.

With hostilities now imminent, the pace of exercises increased, and on 3 September they listened to the declaration of war on the wireless from the officers' mess. For the first few weeks of the war, 99 Squadron, now based at Newmarket, nibbled at the edges of conflict, primarily engaged in searches for the German Fleet. Frustrations ended, however, on the morning of 14 December. Twelve aircraft were bombed up with 500-lb semi armour piercing (SAP) bombs to hunt German ships in the North Sea that had supposedly been sighted by a Royal Navy submarine. Orders were given to reconnoitre an area in the southern part of the Heligoland Bight and the north of the Friesian Islands. Gerry flew as second pilot in the crew of another former apprentice, Flight Sergeant Reg Williams[1]. One of their gunners was also ex-Halton – Corporal M. G. Brown, a fitter II.

Setting out at 11.43 hours, the weather at first benign began to deteriorate. At 14.25 hours, and after a few adventures along the way, the formation spotted at least two German warships steaming south. Wing Commander Griffiths[2], the squadron CO, turned to get a better look, and almost at once a number of smaller ships came into view and started firing. The two larger warships also opened up with their pom-poms, forcing the formation to turn away.

As the island of Wangerooge came into sight, so too did a formation of Bf 109s, quickly followed by a number of Bf 110s. A running battle ensued over the next 20 minutes, during which two aircraft collided, three were shot down, and a sixth crashed on its return, killing three of the crew. The Germans did not have it all their own way, however, with two gunners claiming victories.

The raid had been a disaster, despite the AOC's suggestion otherwise when he addressed the survivors after it. Five out of the six bombers that did make it home did so with damage from flak or fighters. Not surprisingly, there was a DFC for Wing Commander Griffiths. There was also a DFM for one of Griffiths' air gunners, Corporal Alexander Bickerstaff, a metal rigger by trade from the 19th Entry. Another immediate DFM went to the air gunner in Squadron Leader R. G. E. Catt's crew, Corporal Cedric Pettit. He had qualified as a fitter AE in the 18th Entry.

Among the dead were a number of ex-apprentices. Flight Sergeant James Healey (18th Entry) had been captain of Wellington N2886, shot down in the sea with total loss of life; Flight Sergeant William Downey (15th Entry) was another Brat, skipper in Wellington N2911, lost when it was struck by the aircraft of Pilot Officer Norman Lewis. Within Downey's crew were two other Brats, Thomas Jones (20th Entry) and Frederick Goodwin (22nd). Within Pilot Officer Lewis' crew was LAC Charles Watson of the 30th Entry.

Sergeant Richard Brace, in Wellington N2986, was also killed that day, shot down by anti-aircraft fire. He had passed out from the 20th Entry as a metal rigger. His second pilot was another Brat and fitter I, Sergeant Charles Caldwell, of the 22nd Entry. He too failed to return.

Gerry did not dwell on the losses, and the aircrew casualties were soon made good by new individuals and crews. Among those joining 99 Squadron was Flight Lieutenant Percy Pickard, the captain of 'F-Freddie' in the film, *Target for Tonight*[3].

After flying a number of further reconnaissance sorties and nickel raids as second pilot to a variety of different pilots, Gerry was at last made captain of his own aircraft, and given his own crew. Among the many operations they flew over the next few weeks was one to Stavanger:

> "The weather had been clear all the way, and although it was 21.30 hours it was not yet dark and the aerodrome was clearly seen. We were each carrying six 250-lb bombs, three of which had a 12-hour delay. I chose to drop them in two sticks of three but two failed to release. Two of those that did fall were seen to burst at the northern end of the aerodrome. We managed to shake the other two off on the way home where we landed after nearly eight hours. I was surprised that on such a beautiful clear evening we had not been intercepted by fighters. There was, however, a certain amount of flak, and although some of it was close, none of us suffered any damage, except possibly Jack Brent who crashed in the Wash on the way home."

With the invasion of the Low Countries on 10 May, many felt that the war had begun in earnest, and 99 Squadron attacked tactical targets in the Netherlands, Belgium and France almost continuously for the next three weeks. Gerry suffered his fair share of flak damage and engine failures, but always made it home. After the evacuation of the BEF from Dunkirk, targets switched to the Ruhr, and Gerry's flying was interrupted only by a medical examination prior to being appointed to a commission, even though he didn't really know if he wanted one. On 17 June, Gerry and his crew decided to have a little fun of their own on a return trip to Essen. While over the Netherlands they spotted a flare path, and although they did not have any bombs, Gerry dived into attack with all guns blazing. The intelligence officer thought the event worthy of telling the station commander, Group Captain Fogerty.

On 1 July, Gerry had a message to report to the orderly room. He had completed 29 operations (at this time there was no recognised number of operations to count as a tour) and fully expected to do several more. Instead, he was ordered to report to Boscombe Down, home of the Aircraft and Armament Experimental Establishment (A&AEE), for 'bomber performance testing'. The bomber he would be testing, was the Short Stirling. Gerry remembers seeing the aircraft for the first time:

> "It was not a good-looking machine, indeed compared to the shapely, if somewhat rotund, Wimpy, it was rather ugly and badly proportioned. The fuselage was too slim for its inordinate length, and the great, complicated-looking undercarriage was so tall that the cockpit was 20-something

feet above the ground. However, this was much the same as the Heyford and that had not proved difficult to land."

Gerry did not get to fly the new aircraft immediately. On 8 July, along with another Halton apprentice, Reg Cox (20th Entry), the two former Brats were allowed one hour's dual instruction before being deemed fit for solo, and since there was nobody qualified to make any further checks, they were both automatically captains designate.

It was while Gerry and Reg were sitting on the grass one morning, hoping for a serviceable Stirling to fly, that the flight sergeant in charge of the technical team asked whether they had seen the paper. He then pointed to the announcement that Gerry had been awarded the DFM.

> "That came as a complete surprise as I hadn't considered that I had done anything special and didn't know that there had been any other decorations for 99 Squadron, apart from those following the 14 December effort. Naturally Reg quizzed me on what I had done, to which I replied that like the stamps we used to get at Sunday school, it must have been for good attendance."

The most notable event from his time in what later became known as the Stirling Development Flight was a visit from 'Boom' Trenchard, Father of the Royal Air Force and also of the Halton Apprenticeship Scheme. He informed them that in the next few days they were to become the nucleus of 7 Squadron even though, as Gerry said later, anything less like a squadron than the few aircrew and ground crew mustered around the great old man it would have been difficult to imagine:

> "I don't suppose he had any idea of the number of his 'Brats' in that small party; the sergeant fitters would certainly all be ex-Halton, as were Reg, Arthur Treble (second pilot and ex-99 Squadron), and Bunny Austin, an ex-Cranwell wireless operator/mechanic; so there could only have been four or five who were not in the 'union'. So on 3 August, I gathered my kit and my crews into the only serviceable Stirling (N3640), and off we went to our new home at Leeming."

The new squadron was officially formed on 1 August, and a large gathering of ground crew was assembled for Gerry's arrival in Stirling N3640 two days later. The next morning, the CO, Wing Commander Paul Harris, informed Gerry that from then on, he was the captain of N3640 – thus becoming the first captain of a four-engined bomber in Bomber Command.

Two more aircraft arrived soon afterwards and the job began of converting pilots to the unfamiliar type. A mishap occurred in October when the twin tail-wheel assembly broke apart on landing at Benson, and the resident ground crews were in no rush to lend a hand. A lifting cradle had to be sought from Boscombe for the aircraft to be repaired.

After only three months at Leeming, the squadron moved to its new home of Oakington and new pilots were assimilated into the unit. Among them were the two flight commanders, Squadron Leader John Griffiths-Jones DFC (ex-149 Squadron) and Squadron Leader Pat Lynch-Blosse[4]. New pilots also included another Brat who had already distinguished himself, Flight Sergeant Dennis Witt DFM, of the 23rd Entry.

The squadron began operating on 10 February 1941. Three aircraft took part in an attack on an oil storage facility in Rotterdam. The three senior captains – Griffiths-Jones, Lynch-Blosse and Flight Lieutenant 'Sask' Smith – assumed the privilege. Gerry flew as second pilot to Smith, and Reg Cox with Griffiths-Jones. The trip was uneventful.

It was a full two weeks before Gerry flew his next operation, during which time he began picking the brains of the teams from Short Brothers and Bristol – the airframe and engine manufacturers – about various technical aspects of the Stirling and how to eke out its best performance. Loading was a particular challenge; how the positioning of bombs and fuel impacted the centre of gravity, and how that in turn affected the aircraft's longitudinal stability. Range was also an issue, and how best to fly the aeroplane and handle the engines to achieve optimum range. His search for information earned him a reputation for technical knowledge that he thought ill-deserved.

Gerry flew from Newmarket on the night of 9 April (Oakington was too boggy), his first trip to 'The Big City'. Gerry was in charge of Stirling N6005, an aircraft prone to undercarriage problems. That night it also suffered from engine problems, the port inner overheating, obliging Gerry to throttle back. Reaching the Dutch/German border at Lingen, in a full moon and no cloud, the Stirling was picked out by a searchlight, forcing Gerry to take evasive action. More searchlights began probing in the dark, and then came a cry from Flying Officer Sid Stock (the squadron gunnery leader) in the rear turret as a night-fighter swooped in to attack:

> "The fuselage was immediately filled with the clatter of machine-gun fire and the acrid stink of cordite, interrupted by a dull thump. Within seconds the attack ceased and the searchlights were doused. Stock said that the fighter was a Bf 110 and he was sure he had hit it."

While Stock was indeed confident that he had seen off the enemy fighter, they too had been hit. Subsequent examination of the Stirling on its return showed machine-gun bullet holes in the tail unit fin and tail plane, rear turret, port side fuselage, port main plane and one petrol tank. The 'dull thump' they had heard was an exploding incendiary in the number one fuel tank that was fortunately empty save for a few petrol fumes. It had been a lucky escape.

A daylight raid to Emden, Gerry's first in a Stirling, on 10 June also nearly proved their undoing. Halfway across the North Sea they were intercepted by two Bf 109s. 'Jock' Graham, who was now Gerry's permanent rear gunner, promptly shot one down and along with the front gunner, 'Ash' Ashton, frightened the other one off[5].

In the next two weeks, the crew went to Huls, Düsseldorf, Brest, and Kiel (twice). On 28 June, they were briefed for a sneak daylight attack on Bremen in the company of Squadron Leader Richard Speare and Flight Lieutenant John Collins:

> "We were well on the way back when Jock reported another Stirling about two miles behind us and on a track to the south of ours, being attacked by fighters.
>
> "I turned back to give him some support but before we could reach him, we were ourselves attacked by nine yellow-nosed Bf 109s[6]. This time we were flying the CO's aircraft (N3663) which had a mid-upper turret and Taffy Price (the flight engineer) had taken up position there as soon as fighters were mentioned, so we had six rearward-firing guns. Jock's directions proved that a good bomber, properly guided, could be a match for a fighter, or even nine fighters, for we were not even scratched during the attack, while Jock notched up another Messerschmitt and he and Taffy claimed two more 'probables' between them."

The other Stirling was 'Q' Queenie, with Flight Lieutenant Collins at the controls. Gerry tried to raise him on R/T and then with the Aldis lamp but without success. Gerry took up station beside 'Queenie' as protection from further attack, noticing that her starboard outer had failed:

> "I don't remember that is was feathered, but his speed fell off to such an extent that it was difficult to maintain formation. It was not long before he hit the sea. When the spray cleared, we could see that the fuselage was broken in two just behind the wing and the rear half had disappeared, and within a few seconds the front half too slid below the surface. After circling for about ten minutes, with all eyes on the water, we saw nothing and set course sadly for home."

The drama, however, was not quite over. As they approached the Suffolk coast they were attacked by fighters again, but this time they were 'friendly' Hurricanes from a Polish squadron. Happily, they broke off the attack before any damage was done.

For his effort to save Collins, Gerry was awarded the DFC, though always felt that the plaudits should have gone to his gunners.

Gerry's four-engined tour continued with further attacks, primarily aimed at the enemy's capital ships. They hunted the *Scharnhorst* at La Pallice with armour-piercing bombs, three captains being detailed and all three former Halton boys: Reg Cox, Dennis Witt, and Gerry Blacklock – or 'Freeman, Hardy and Willis' as Reg called them when asking control for permission to take off. Once again while over the target they were set upon by fighters, and once again they were beaten off by intelligent teamwork and skilful flying. Gerry took the Stirling down to sea level to escape the danger and landed at St Eval, exhausted, after a long and arduous flight home.

Gerry's final flight took place on 28 August, a relatively quiet trip to Duisburg. It was another city to add to a list of targets that included Karlsruhe, Magdeburg and Cologne. Dennis Witt finished his tour the same night, and Gerry fancied they must have been among the first in Bomber Command to have completed two tours.

Immediately after finishing his tour, Gerry's opinion was sought in formally establishing a training syllabus for flight engineers, who until then had been schooled on a squadron-by-squadron basis. For the remainder of the war, Gerry fulfilled a number of technical training appointments, and with the war's end, undertook a variety of overseas roles, including a survey of Ascension Island. As a group captain he commanded the station at Hullavington before taking early retirement in 1961. He died in 2011 at the age of 96.

Gerry was unusual and fortunate in receiving his DFC and DFM from the hands of the monarch at two separate ceremonies. But what gave him equal pleasure and pride was the assessment of the wing commander of his abilities as a bomber pilot at the end of his 7 Squadron tour. It was a word that summarises the life and achievement of this former Halton apprentice. Exceptional.

8 FIGHTING BACK

In a small corner of the Trenchard Museum, dedicated to the memory of his beloved Brats, is a small glass cabinet containing a duplicate set of medals awarded to an early 'bomber boy' whose flame flickered briefly before it was extinguished too quickly for those who he left behind. Alan Coad, somewhat inevitably nicknamed 'Morse', had been with the 26th Entry and volunteered for flying duties before the war. He flew Handley Page Hampdens with 50 Squadron from March 1940 onwards from Lindholme to all manner of targets across enemy territory, completing his first tour and being awarded the DFM for showing 'the utmost determination and courage in pressing home his attacks'. Notification of his award came in the *London Gazette* of 12 December 1940, but by then he was already dead, killed in a training accident while 'resting' from operations.

Many of those early bomber boys' names have long since disappeared into obscurity, if they were ever really known at all. A contemporary of Morse Coad's in the 26th was Jamie Pitcairn-Hill, the son of a clergyman who was one of the truly outstanding young airmen of Bomber Command in those early days. Within a year of the war starting, he had been awarded both the DSO and DFC, and was a squadron leader flight commander within 83 Squadron. He won his DSO for an attack on the Münster viaduct on the Dortmund-Ems canal in the same action that led to the award of a Victoria Cross to 'Babe' Learoyd of 49 Squadron. His luck finally ran out on 18 September when he led an attack on Le Havre. His Hampden was struck a mortal blow and crashed into the Seine estuary, killing all on board. He was still only 24[1].

Coincidentally, the Officer Commanding 49 Squadron to which Babe Learoyd belonged was another Halton apprentice, 'Wally' Sheen. He'd been at Halton in 1923 as part of the 7th Entry and was very much a man who led from the front. From 49 Squadron he took command of 61 Squadron and was awarded the DSO. He later went on to command 13 Base and was appointed deputy director of (Bomber) Operations. He retired in the rank of air vice-marshal.

Wally was by no means the only former Brat who went on to command a main force bomber squadron. There were many. One who perhaps deserves to be better known is Robert Carter.

When the Germans occupied Northern France, they also occupied the ports on the west coast that gave them open access to the Atlantic. It meant their surface ships and submarines could range freely and cause havoc to Allied shipping. The ports of Brest and La Pallice (La Rochelle) became targets of immense interest to Bomber Command, called upon by their service colleagues to hunt down and destroy the Nazi menace in its own backyard.

On 24 July, Bomber Command planned a series of attacks on enemy shipping, targeting in particular the battle cruisers *Scharnhorst* and *Gneisenau* that intelligence reports suggested were lurking in the area. A comparatively large force of 79 Wellingtons and Hampdens were detailed for a daylight raid, without fighter escort. Among the squadrons taking part was 150 Squadron at Snaith. Its commanding officer was a former Halton apprentice, Wing Commander Robert Carter.

Born into a naval family and educated at Portsmouth Grammar School, Robert Carter had a complicated early life being brought up by his aunt and uncle after his parents left for Uganda. Fascinated by aircraft, he took his entrance exams for Halton and arrived as part of the 16th Entry to train as a fitter (AE). He excelled both in academics and sport, being described as a good keen worker and slightly above average in the workshops. In terms of sport, he was a strong swimmer and a tidy rugby player who also won no fewer than five Barrington Kennett medals, something of a record. He was a contemporary of the great Don Finlay on the athletics track though, he conceded, "the blighter always beat me".

Awarded a cadetship to Cranwell, Robert served on the North-West Frontier (where he picked up some colloquial Urdu) with 27 Squadron and 11 Squadron before returning home in 1936 to join the School of Aeronautical Engineering. An interesting assignment followed as the officer commanding a pilotless aircraft flight (engaged in anti-aircraft co-operation) – at one stage showing off to German military visitors – before a spell in research and development at the Ministry of Aircraft Production.

With war came an operational posting as a flight commander to 150 Squadron (which at the time was flying the single-engined Fairey Battle), becoming squadron commander in June 1941. The following month, and with the squadron now equipped with Wellingtons, he led his men to Brest where they came under sustained and heavy attack from enemy fighters and found the harbour bristling with guns. One of the enemy battle cruisers (contemporary reports suggest the *Gneisenau*) was hit and the dock areas extensively damaged but it came at a heavy cost. Ten Wellingtons and two Hampdens were lost; 12 per cent of the attacking force. Robert was awarded the DSO. A brief segment of the citation provides an example of the leadership he showed that day:

'...the section was then attacked by two single-engined enemy fighters. The first attacks were feeble and inconclusive. A more determined attack, which caused damage to number three aircraft, was countered by skilful manoeuvre of the formation by Wing Commander Carter, and this resulted in the rear and front gunners engaging both enemy aircraft in turn. The leading enemy aircraft was hit and was last seen turning away in a stalled condition with the airscrew idling. Tracer from all guns was seen to enter the underside of the second aircraft which dived vertically and was later seen by the second pilot of the leading aircraft to crash into the sea.'

In September 1942, Robert took command of 103 Squadron during the difficult period of conversion from Wellingtons to Halifaxes. The conversion was short-lived for soon after the squadron swapped its Halifaxes for Lancasters, and it was in the Lancaster that Robert was again leading his men on bomber operations against industrial targets in the Ruhr. The 'Battle of the Ruhr', as that period of operations came to be known, was the most difficult of his flying career. With his promotion to group captain in April 1943 he was awarded the DFC, being described as 'an ideal leader' who has 'consistently shown great devotion to duty'.

As the station commander of RAF Waltham, the home of two Lancaster squadrons, he continued to fly whenever he was able, often with a new crew to instil confidence. It was a dangerous habit, for many a novice crew failed to return from their first or second trips. Experience counted. He was twice mentioned in despatches.

Robert enjoyed a full post-war career, including a spell with the Royal New Zealand Air Force and Senior Air Staff Officer at Transport Command.

He retired as Air Commodore Robert Carter CB, DSO, DFC and died in 2012 at the age of 102.

On 15 January 1944, almost 500 four-engined 'heavies' set out for their first major attack on the city of Brunswick. Brunswick was much smaller than Bomber Command's usual targets, especially during the period known as 'The Battle of Berlin', and it was not a success. Very little damage was achieved, with many of the bombs falling harmlessly in the surrounding countryside. The mood in Bomber Command headquarters after the raid was not improved by the losses inflicted by night-fighters, who engaged the stream from the moment it crossed the German frontier. Thirty-eight Lancasters were shot down, including many experienced crews and captains of aircraft. One of the most experienced was the Officer Commanding 166 Squadron, Wing Commander Colin Scragg.

Colin Scragg had arrived at Halton from King Edward VI School in Southampton as part of the 10th Entry. On passing out he was one of the lucky few to qualify for training as an NCO pilot, gaining his wings in 1931 and joining No. 1 (Fighter) Squadron to fly Siskins and Hawker Fury biplanes. An accomplished pilot, he was soon selected to take part in the famous Hendon air displays as a member of the RAF aerobatic team, thrilling crowds with his inverted flying. Very occasionally he pushed his luck too far, including one incident in November 1931 when he crashed a Siskin of 1 Squadron at Upwaltham, his aircraft cutting a swathe almost 100 metres long through the wood and finally ending on its back after felling a large tree. Colin emerged scratched and bruised, but otherwise in one piece.

Identified as ideal instructor material, and having been commissioned, Colin completed an instructor's course and was posted to Canada as chief flying instructor at Medicine Hat, Alberta. He was noted as a strict disciplinarian but also for his fair and even treatment of those who came under him, regardless of nationality or experience. Medicine Hat was an effective training unit, and Colin played a key role in building and then maintaining the unit's impressive wartime record. He was recognised by the award of an Air Force Cross.

Colin returned home in 1943, and in December of that year was appointed Officer Commanding 166 Squadron at Kirmington, assuming command from Wing Commander Reginald Twamley DFC on the 15th. Twamley had been wounded in the leg during a sortie to Leipzig[2]. Colin's tenure was to last only four weeks until he was shot down by a night-fighter, his aircraft crashing in the target area. He was the only survivor from his crew and would later reflect on how he managed to make it out as the Lancaster fell blazing to the ground, when the others did not. He spent the remainder of the war as a POW.

This is certainly not the end to Colin Scragg's story, however. After the war, he played a key role in the Berlin Airlift, devising an air traffic control system that helped to better manage the flow of aircraft in a highly congested and restricted airspace for which he was awarded a Bar to his AFC. Later still, as director of Operational Requirements at the Air Ministry from 1955 to 1958, Colin was closely involved in the decision to develop the TSR-2 strike and reconnaissance aircraft to replace the Canberra which had entered service as the RAF's first jet bomber in 1951. He continued his support for the project as deputy controller of aircraft at the Ministry of Aviation in the early 1960s, and never quite recovered from the decision by James Callaghan to cancel the programme in his first budget speech.

Colin retired at his own request as Air Vice-Marshal Sir Colin Scragg KBE, CBE, CB, MBE, AFC & Bar.

Many of the main force squadron commanders of 1943/44 had earned their spurs earlier in the war, completing tours in aircraft such as the Armstrong Whitworth Whitley and Handley Page Hampdens that were already past their sell-by date in terms of operational performance. Granted the German defences – the night-fighters, flak and searchlight concentrations that went to make up the infamous Kammhuber Line (named after the general who devised them) – were not yet in full sway, but the dangers were nonetheless real. Certainly they seemed so to Ian Swales, a young sergeant pilot from Yorkshire on his first tour of operations with 38 Squadron.

Educated at Scarborough College, Ian had enlisted as an apprentice with the 23rd Entry in January 1931 and finished 26th in the order of merit[3]. He passed out as a fitter (AE). Trained as a pilot before the war, he flew some of the RAF's earliest bomber sorties over the winter of 1939/1940, usually as a second pilot on reconnaissance and wide-ranging sweeps across the North Sea. On one occasion, after more than six hours above the freezing waters, his Wellington suffered severe icing on its mainplanes and tailplane that could have been fatal. He was fortunate to make it home.

With the shift from the 'Phoney' to the 'Real' war in May 1940, the Wellingtons of 38 Squadron were deployed on different targets, attacking roads and bridges to disrupt the enemy advance, and destroying ammunition and petrol dumps behind their lines. They also ventured into Germany, when the weather allowed. Again, Ian flew as second pilot, often to the B Flight commander, Squadron Leader Horace Hawkins.

Throughout those spring and early summer months, Ian was in good company. Among his contemporaries were Flying Officer Ian Cross, brother of Kenneth Cross (a famous fighter leader in the desert who went on to achieve air chief marshal rank) and later shot in the Great Escape, and Flying Officer Vivian Rosewarne, the anonymous author of *An Airman's Letter to his Mother* published after his death. There were also a good many Halton Boys, including Sergeant Alfred Skelton (21st Entry), an observer who had served on flying boats in Seletar before the war and who was awarded the DFM for his tour at 38, and Alan Cousens (22nd Entry), another observer, who would also go on to be recognised for his gallantry.

Ian became a captain of aircraft in July and by the end of the summer had completed his tour and been awarded the DFM, the award being announced in the *London Gazette* the week after his commission. He returned to operations after a 'rest' the following year, joining 15 Squadron at Wyton in time for the squadron's conversion from the twin-engined Wellington ICs to the four-engined Short Stirling. He flew regularly throughout the early winter months, before being chosen as one of the lead pilots responsible for testing an early form of blind-bombing device known as 'Trinity'. The device was trialled during a series of attacks on enemy warships at Brest in December and January.

On the first, Ian's aircraft was hit several times by flak. He said afterwards: "Every gun seemed to be concentrated on my own aircraft." On a similar raid the following day, he found himself coned by a searchlight for a full three minutes as he dived and weaved to escape its deadly intentions. Not surprisingly he came back with an aircraft pockmarked by shrapnel wounds and damage to its two mainplanes. On 16 December he flew his most dangerous mission yet, as 20 or more searchlights chased him around the skies and flak peppered his starboard wing. He was keeping his ground crews busy.

It was for these experimental raids, often involving comparatively small numbers of aircraft, that Ian received a DFC. In the draft citation (that did not make it into print), Ian is credited with 242 operational hours of flying:

> 'This officer has carried out 28 sorties on Wellington and 18 on Stirling aircraft, involving attacks against the majority of important and highly defended targets in Germany and in occupied territory. Flying Officer Swales took part in five "Trinity" raids against enemy warships at Brest and played a good part in the success of these attacks in their experimental stages. On 7 November 1941, he participated in a raid on Berlin and, despite intense opposition, he coolly carried out a successful bombing attack. This officer has always shown courage and determination in the face of the enemy.'

Ian stayed with 15 Squadron until the end of his second tour in April 1942, when he was posted to assume command of the conversion flight, helping pilots and crews transition from two engines to four. He returned to operations a third time as commanding officer of 622 Squadron, which itself had been formed from a nucleus of 15 Squadron aircraft and crews and was part of main force equipped with Lancaster Is and IIIs. Ian was posted in at the beginning of February 1944 and began operating almost immediately, steering his squadron through the last days of the Battle of Berlin and the watershed of the Nuremberg raid at the end of March.

'Blondie' Swales, as he was known, proved a popular and highly successful main force squadron commander, driving his men to the peak of operational efficiency. When his tenure came to an end, he was given the farewell party to end all farewell parties, such was the esteem with which he was held by air and ground crew alike. He was also officially recognised with the DSO, the citation stating that he was an inspiring leader who had 'rendered much valuable service'.

Happily, Ian continued to serve in the post-war RAF, retiring in 1963 as Group Captain I.C.K. Swales DSO, DFC, DFM.

Ian Swales was not the only former apprentice involved with the development of blind bombing and other aerial devices with which to confound and frustrate the enemy defences. Charles Victor Willis, always known as 'Vic', had excelled at Halton, finishing third in the order of merit in the 28th Entry and top in his educational studies. As befitting his achievements, he was offered a cadetship at Cranwell where again he pleased his masters by being awarded the King's Medal, the J. A. Chance Memorial Prize, and his colours for hockey and soccer.

As a pilot he initially flew London and Sunderland flying boats with 201 Squadron, and upon the outbreak of war flew patrols over the North Sea hunting for surface raiders. In July 1940 he joined the recently formed Blind Approach and Training (BAT) Development Unit at Boscombe Down and was one of the first group of pilots to investigate the invisible beams that guided German bombers to their targets during the early Blitz. The data Vic and his colleagues collated, often in difficult and dangerous circumstances, formed the principle for the development of blind-landing techniques based on the German Lorenz beam. This in turn became the basis of Oboe[4], the ground-controlled blind-bombing system that brought devastating levels of accuracy to Allied bombing attacks. The development unit morphed into 109 Squadron, and Vic became a flight commander.

In October 1941, Vic was flying in the Middle East, as a pilot in a specially equipped Wellington designed to provide electronic countermeasures to support an Allied advance in Libya. Operating from advanced landing grounds (ALGs) out 'in the Blue', he was especially tasked with jamming communications on the 28 and 34 megacycle bands used by enemy armoured columns. On one such operation, in company with one other Wellington, his aircraft was attacked by Italian fighters, one of which was despatched by Vic's gunners. The other two, however, inflicted serious damage on Vic's Wellington, and accounted for the other. Vic's rear-gun turret was put out of action, as well as the gunner and other members of his crew. Vic managed to escape into cloud and limp home where his aircraft was struck off as being damaged beyond repair.

It was not the only time he had to fend off a fighter attack. A few days later, while deep over enemy territory, he was stalked by a Luftwaffe fighter who saw an easy target. The German did not reckon on the skills and tenacity of the Wellington pilot or his gunners, who managed to do sufficient damage to the German that he broke off the attack.

On his return to the UK, and after another spell with 109, Vic was given command of 192 Squadron, a new unit created to conduct exploratory flights over hostile territory to find and jam the enemy's radar. Initially Wellingtons, Mosquitos and Halifaxes were used with missions over Germany, France and the Low Countries. Flights were also made over the Bay of Biscay to check for radar being deployed against Coastal Command's anti-submarine patrols.

After 18 months in command, and on continuous operations, Vic was awarded the DSO and promoted to group captain. The citation reads:

> 'Since being awarded the Distinguished Flying Cross, this officer has completed a large number of sorties, many of them demanding skill of a high degree. His appreciation of the responsibilities entrusted to him, his ingenuity and his determination to complete his allotted task have contributed in a large measure to the success of the operations in which he has taken part. He is a fine leader, whose example of courage and devotion to duty has been worthy of the greatest praise.'

He relinquished command to take over as station commander at RAF Foulsham, where his squadron and other 'spook'-type units were based. After the war he continued to work in the secret world of signals. He retired as an air commodore OBE, DSO, DFC.

To give some idea of the unpreparedness of the RAF to fight a 'modern' war in 1939, one Bomber Command observer in 58 Squadron, Pilot Officer John Mitchell[5], flew his first operation over enemy territory with less than ten hours night-time flying experience in his logbook.

A contemporary of John Mitchell's at 58 Squadron in those early days of fighting back was Leslie Crooks of the 15th Entry. Originally from Bishop Auckland, Leslie passed out from Halton in 1930 as a fitter (AE) and volunteered for flying duties. As a sergeant pilot he served on the North-West Frontier and Iraq between 1935 and 1937, and by the start of the war had been commissioned and posted to 58 Squadron at Linton-on-Ouse.

On the night of 20/21 July 1940 he almost came to grief when his aircraft was badly damaged by flak over Düsseldorf. The fuselage was holed and the port mainplane hit. Happily, he made it home, but only after a nervous few hours coaxing the stricken bomber over the North Sea. On the night of 10/11 August on the way back from Frankfurt he was obliged to force land at Hemswell through lack of fuel and a failure of the battery systems. The undercarriage collapsed on touching down and the aircraft came to grief across the flarepath.

At the end of November, targets switched temporarily from Germany to Italy; of the five 58 Squadron detailed to raid Turin on the night of 26 November, only one – with Leslie at the controls – made it to the target and bombed, the rest failing to gain enough height to cross the Alps. Leslie was again obliged to land away from base when running short of fuel, crashing at Horsham St Faith.

Leslie completed his first tour in February 1941 and was awarded the DFC. He did not return to operations until 1943 when he joined 426 (Thunderbird) Squadron at Dishforth. The 'Thunderbirds' were a Canadian squadron formed at the tail end of 1942, equipped with Wellingtons. It was not declared operational until 11 January, 1943 and flew its first operations three days later under the command of its CO, Wing Commander Sedley Blanchard. When Blanchard was shot down on the night of 14/15 February, Leslie Crooks was appointed in his place.

On the night of 26/27 April, Leslie took off in the early hours with nine other aircraft from 426 Squadron to attack Duisburg. They were part of a much larger force of more than 550 bombers detailed to attack Europe's largest inland port.

Twenty miles short of Duisburg, over Wesel, a night-fighter (probably a Bf 110) attacked from below and raked the Wellington with gun fire. The first the rear gunner was aware of things was when he saw deadly beads of tracer arcing towards his turret. Damage was sustained to the Wellington's intercom, hydraulic and electrical systems. One aileron and half the port tail plane were shot away and the sighting gear in the rear turret was badly damaged. The rear turret was to all intents and purposes u/s.

Leslie took evading action, putting the aircraft into a dive to port to attempt to avoid further damage and to shake off the attacker. The rear gunner (Sergeant How) returned fire with a short burst of 50 rounds from all four guns as the enemy disappeared but did not observe any strikes. The damage was extensive. The Wellington had lost all the fabric from the port tailplane and three feet of trailing edge from the port mainplane was also gone from near the fuselage. Damage was also sustained to the port aileron and centre bomb door.

Soon after being attacked, Leslie was alarmed to see the Wellington's port engine beginning to overheat. He still continued with the bomb run but then found the bombs could not be released. He abandoned the attack. An attempt to pour any available liquid into the emergency hydraulic system failed – coffee from Thermos flasks and oil from the rear turret were attempted without success. The wireless operator tried for over an hour to fix the system without any joy, and in the end had to admit defeat. The undercarriage could not be lowered, and the bomb doors remained steadfastly shut.

Regaining the Yorkshire coast, Leslie apprised Dishforth Flying Control of their predicament and gave his crew the order to bail out. When certain they were all clear, he similarly took to his 'chute but landed heavily, injuring his spine in the process and having to be hospitalised. One other member of the crew also broke his foot. The aircraft crashed harmlessly near Stonegrove. Not long after this incident, Leslie was awarded the DSO:

> 'This officer's courage and skill were admirably demonstrated during a recent attack on Duisburg. When approaching the target his aircraft was raked by cannon fire from an enemy fighter. Wing Commander Crooks skilfully evaded the attacker but his aircraft had sustained much damage. Although one aileron and half the port tail plane had been shot away, while the hydraulic and electrical systems were rendered inoperative, Wing Commander Crooks flew the bomber back to this country. Unfortunately, it was impossible to make a safe landing, but when the crew were forced to abandon aircraft, all descended safely. In the face of heavy odds, Wing Commander Crooks set an example worthy of high praise.'

Leslie continued to lead 426 throughout the summer months, completing a further half-dozen operations and overseeing the successful conversion of his crews from their Wellington Xs to the Hercules-powered Lancaster IIs. On the night of 17/18 August 1941, the squadron was briefed for its part in the attack on the secret research establishment at Peenemünde. It was to Leslie's ninth operation of his second tour. It was also to be his last.

Leslie's Lancaster came down three kilometres south of Greifswald. It was observed to be on fire and attempting a forced-landing. The aircraft was seen to bounce two or three times and then burst into flames. Leslie's body, and those of four of his crew, were recovered from the wreckage. There was only one survivor, Sergeant K. W. Reading. The seventh man, the navigator, bailed out but his parachute failed to fully deploy.

The squadron's ORB paid tribute to their CO. It says simply: 'In the period he led the squadron he earned the respect and admiration of all.'

The attack on Peenemünde is significant since it was the first to be formally led by a master bomber, a single skipper tasked with orchestrating an entire raid. The master bomber in this case was former Brat, Wing Commander John Searby of the 19th Entry.

Searby was accepted for pilot training only two years after passing out as a fitter (AE), and was commissioned on the outbreak of war. He was one of the earliest to complete a specialist navigator (Spec 'N') course, and spent time in Ferry Command on the North Atlantic run before finally joining 106 Squadron as a flight commander. One of his fellow pilots and squadron OC was Guy Gibson. John was later given command of 106 and then 83 Squadron, a Pathfinder squadron, with whom he was serving when appointed to lead the Peenemünde raid. He was awarded an immediate DSO and promoted to group captain. He retired as an air commodore.

John Searby is one of a number of former Brats who commanded the elite Pathfinder Force squadrons in the latter stages of the war. Some, like Wing Commander Reg Cox (20th Entry) of 7 Squadron, and Wing Commander Joe Northrop (19th Entry) of 692 Squadron are perhaps well known; others, like Wing Commander Charles Dunnicliffe (17th Entry), the founding OC of 582 Squadron at Little Staughton, and Wing Commander Alan Cousens (22nd Entry) of 635 Squadron perhaps not so. Cousens, who had flown as a sergeant observer in 38 Squadron, was unusual in that he was a navigator, demonstrating that not all squadron COs were pilots. Arthur Lowe, the main force OC of 77 Squadron in 1942/43, was more unusual still; he was an air gunner.

The vast rump of Bomber Command boys from Halton were, not surprisingly, flight engineers. With their practical skills and ability to fix virtually anything with a piece of chewing gum (as the doyen of flight engineers and ex-Brat Ted Stocker DSO DFC once said), they were vital members of the crew.

Of the 19 flight engineers who took part in the Dambusters raid, for example, five were former Brats: Ronald Marsden (32nd Entry), flight engineer to Warner Ottley; David Horsfall (33rd Entry), flight engineer to 'Dinghy' Young, the A Flight Commander; Guy Pegler (37th Entry), fight engineer in Lewis Burpee's crew; and Alastair Taylor (39th Entry), flight engineer to Vernon Byers were all killed. Ivan

Whittaker, the more experienced of the five, survived, and came through the war.

Ivan, a Geordie by birth, arrived at Halton as part of the 38th Entry in January 1938. After passing out, he spent the first 18 months of his service life using his trained skills at various RAF bases, including Ouston and Catterick, before commencing his aircrew training in January 1942 as a flight engineer. After spells at Air Gunnery School and OTU, he was posted to 50 Squadron in May 1942 and crewed up with Flight Lieutenant Mickey Martin, an Australian recognised as being one of the finest low-level pilots of his time.

Ivan Whittaker.

Ivan completed a tour of operations with 50 Squadron and was commissioned before accepting an invitation from his skipper to join him for a special operation with a new squadron forming at Scampton. Weeks of training culminated in the now famous raid, Ivan's aircraft flying in the first formation ordered to attack the Möhne Dam. On the bombing run their Lancaster was hit several times but not fatally so, and they had the satisfaction of seeing their bomb explode on target. It did not deliver the mortal blow, however. That honour went to the bomb aimer in David Maltby's aircraft, Flying Officer John Fort who, coincidentally, was a Brat from the 19th Entry and who was flying only his second trip[6].

After the Dams raid, the surviving crews were not immediately pressed into action, but held in reserve for further 'special' operations. After one such operation in September 1943, Ivan was awarded the DFC in recognition of a sustained period of bravery and his particular skills as a flight engineer:

> 'During a long and strenuous tour, Flying Officer Whittaker has taken part in many missions of a daring and hazardous character including the attack on the German Dams. In September 1943, he flew as a flight engineer in an aircraft detailed for a low-level night operation. His sortie was completed in the face of adverse weather and heavy opposition from enemy defences. This officer's skilful manipulation of the throttles while the aircraft was flying in low-level formation contributed largely to the outstanding performance of the crew. He has always displayed high devotion to duty and courage.'

On 12 February 1944, Micky Martin, with Ivan sitting alongside, set out to attack the Anthéor Viaduct in Southern France, a vital artery for the supply of troops, armour and materiel to the Italian Front. The Lancasters were carrying 12,000-lb bombs. The raid proved something of a disaster. On the run-up to the target, Martin's aircraft was heavily engaged by flak and searchlights. Round after round from a 20-mm cannon on the bridge slammed into his Lancaster doing terrible damage, knocking out two engines, scything through the bomb aimer, Bob Hay, and seriously wounding the flight engineer in both legs.

Thanks to the skills of the pilot, and Ivan's careful handling of the two remaining engines, they made it to Sardinia to pull off an emergency landing on a tiny airfield only recently in American hands. Ivan was awarded an immediate Bar to his DFC, the citation stating that despite being wounded in both legs…

> '…Flight Lieutenant Whittaker coolly made a detailed examination of the aircraft and gave his captain a full report of the damage sustained. He displayed great fortitude and devotion to duty and his efforts were of much assistance to his captain who flew the damaged bomber to an airfield where a safe landing was effected.'

After the war, and having recovered from his wounds, Ivan continued flying as a flight engineer on VIP duties with 511 Squadron flying dignitaries such as Prime Minister Clement Attlee and the heads of state of many Commonwealth and foreign countries. He eventually attained the rank of group captain and retired from the RAF in 1974. He died in 1979 and is buried in Halton Village Churchyard.

No bomber squadron could function without the commitment, skills and dedication of the ground crews, and this was as true in 617 as it was of any squadron. That they are not always given the credit they deserve is because their war is considered less 'exciting' but one Halton Brat, Henry Watson, may have wished for a little less adventure during his career as an armament officer.

Henry 'Doc' Watson, from the mining community of Fishburn in County Durham, had no wish to follow his brother down the pit, wanting instead to become a pilot. Sadly his eyesight let him down, and so he trained at Halton as a fitter armourer with the 21st Entry and on passing out, joined 26 Squadron at Catterick.

After overseas postings to Iraq (with 55 Squadron) and Malta, he returned to the UK as a sergeant with 106 Squadron and was sent to the Air Armament School at Manby for further training, becoming a qualified senior armament instructor. Promoted again, on the outbreak of war he was posted to 83 Squadron at Scampton and received a mention in despatches in September 1941 for his contribution to the squadron's operational efficiency. While there is no published citation for the award, it may also have had something to do with a hair-raising incident described after the event by the pilot (Pilot Officer Ian Robertson) concerned:

> "I remember a very, very, brave armourer, Warrant Officer Doc Watson. I had just started to taxi out with a large load of 40-lb anti-personnel bombs for an intruder operation which was one of the first against the searchlight

belt. Suddenly, one of the bombs fell from one of the wing carriers. I shouted to Doc to get rid of it, and as he was somewhat slow, I urged him on in no uncertain terms. As Doc ran off carrying the bomb, I suddenly realised that it became live as soon as it had dropped from the carrier; luckily neither Doc nor the bomb came to any harm."

Doc was again awarded a mention in despatches in March 1942, by which time 83 Squadron had replaced its Hampdens for the ill-fated Manchester, and a few months later was awarded the MBE. This time, the citation left no doubt as to what it was for:

'This warrant officer has been in charge of the armament section since February 1941. It has been due to his untiring efforts that operations have never been delayed despite short notice of bombing up or last-minute changes of bomb load. During recent weeks when the squadron has been re-equipping from Hampdens to Manchesters, in spite of bad weather conditions and grave shortage of equipment he has always managed to have the aircraft ready in time for take-off. He has at all times set an outstanding example of keenness and efficiency. On a recent occasion when an aircraft crashed on the aerodrome, he was immediately on the spot and rendered great assistance to the station armament officer by rendering the bombs safe without regard to his personal safety.'

Recommended for a commission, Doc was assigned to Squadron X (which was to become 617 Squadron) and spent 12 weeks at Marston, assisting the inventor of the bouncing bomb, Barnes Wallis, in how the device could be accommodated within the belly of the 'special' Lancasters. He was also present at the trials of the bombs at Reculver and trained the 617 armament crews into how to best handle the four-ton bombs and load them into their cradles[7].

After the Dams raid, Doc heard that the RAF was looking for volunteers to serve in the Far East, and after receiving a mention in despatches for a third time, set off for RAF Salbani in India where he became armament officer for 184 Wing. The wing comprised 355 and 356 Squadrons operating the Consolidated Liberator on long-range, deep-penetration sorties. By the war's end, and the Japanese surrender, he was a flight lieutenant.

In civilian life he returned to the shop floor within an engineering business but was swiftly promoted. He also created a new training organisation to provide apprentices to local industry, always acknowledging the start he had been given by Halton. He died in February 1995.

The Halton Roll of Honour lists more than 2,000 Brats as killed in action during

the Second World War, of which more than 400 were flight engineers. Ivan Whittaker is believed to be the only flight engineer to win the DFC and Bar, in the same
way that Ted Stocker, who flew an incredible 108 bomber operations, all in four-en-
gines, was the only RAF flight engineer to win the DSO DFC 'double'.

The second highest award to the Victoria Cross is the Conspicuous Gallantry
Medal (CGM) and, like the VC, only one has ever been awarded to a Halton Boy.
It went to pilot Harold Vertican of the 23rd Entry.

Harold 'Mickey' Vertican was a Yorkshireman, educated at Ilkley Grammar.
Successfully navigating his way through Halton, he was accepted for pilot training
in 1938 and upon gaining his wings was posted to 70 Squadron in Iraq. He flew
a tour of operations with 148 Squadron, a Wellington-equipped squadron in the
Middle East, often flying from ALGs that had been set up to deal with the constant
ebb and flow of the desert war, and place them nearer to their targets in Benghazi
(referred to as 'the mail run' for the frequency of their attacks) and Crete, dropping
supplies to partisans and troops holding out in the mountains.

Converting from two engines to four, he flew Halifaxes with 462 (RAAF) Squadron, being awarded the DFC after 40 operations for his part in an attack on Leros.
Having successfully bombed the target, one of his engines faltered and then died.
This in itself was not too serious – a Halifax was designed to fly on three engines,
or even two, but range was a problem and so too landing. The dangers were compounded by thick fog over base, requiring Mickey to find an alternative landing
ground. Steadily losing height, Mickey ordered the crew to throw out everything
that wasn't nailed down, including guns and ammunition so that they were now
defenceless. After a flight of more than 700 miles, Mickey managed to get the
bomber down in one piece without any further damage. The citation for his DFC
made specific mention of his 'superb airmanship in very trying circumstances'.

On the night of 6/7 May 1943, Mickey was detailed to attack enemy troop
concentrations and motorised transport on the roads leading to Tunis. Two-and-a-
half hours into the flight, the starboard engine failed, a now familiar occurrence,
and Mickey decided to abandon the operation and return to base. Jettisoning his
bombs over the sea, all went well until the port engine gave up the ghost. With
only two good engines, Mickey went through the now familiar exercise of littering
the desert with everything but the kitchen sink (although he did throw out the
Elsan toilet!).

With significantly reduced power, and battling strong winds, the Halifax struggled to maintain height and direction, and was easily blown off course and over
the sea. When the third of the four engines failed, and with the aircraft now down
to less than 1,000 ft, Mickey had no option other than to ditch, a difficult enough
exercise at the best of times.

All things considered, given the rough seas and unreliability of the aircraft,
Mickey pulled off something of a miraculous landing 70 miles off the coast of

Tripoli, and succeeded in getting his crew safely into the dinghy. They were alive but in a parlous state, with little food beyond a few barley sugars and Horlicks tablets, only two bottles of water, and no way of signalling for help. After three days drifting at sea it rained, improving their water supply but drenching the men who were already soaked through and freezing. They had the extremes of the baking heat during the day, and the perilous cold at night.

After 11 days at sea, and exhausted with sea sickness, they drifted close enough to the coastline for two of Mickey's crew to jump into the water and drag the dinghy through the surf and onto a beach near Homs. Local Arabs, encouraged by the promise of gold sovereigns and other such riches, brought water from a nearby village and took a message to the nearest military base – a friendly one. They were eventually picked up by a Sudanese patrol and taken to Homs and safety. In July, news of Mickey's award appeared in the *London Gazette*. There were also medals for the navigator, Flying Officer John Tempest, and the two NCOs who had swum ashore, Clifton Curnow and James Gordon.

Subsequently commissioned, Mickey returned home to become a test pilot and embark on a new career in air traffic control.

9 FROM CRADLE TO GRAVE

Halton has many famous old boys, an impressive number of whom have achieved air rank. But there are few better examples among the ex-Brats who have risen from apprentice to senior command than 'Pat' Connolly, and fewer still who have later come back as commandant of the very same air force establishment that gave him the opportunity to sprout wings and fly in the first place.

Pat Connolly's story is perhaps all the more remarkable given that he came to Halton as an orphan, and against his remaining family's wishes. Counting Dublin as his home town, Pat came from a military family; his father was in the Indian Army. Indeed, it was in India, as a child, that Pat first became interested in aviation:

> "I remember being fascinated and excited watching the fly-overs by old aircraft, including Bristol fighters of First World War vintage. Once I was in the RAF, as an apprentice, I realised it was possible to get into the flying game through that door, and I decided to do that at the earliest opportunity."[1]

Pat arrived at Halton in 1931, as part of the 24th Entry, and immediately threw himself into service life. It was to be the making of him: "The training I received at Halton was of tremendous value to me in my future service career. It gave me an ideal combination of service training, technical training, and just straight-forward character building."

Passing out as a leading aircraftman (LAC) in 1934, Pat was immediately post-ed to India, an assignment he had requested:

> "In those days an aircraft crew consisted of a pilot, a fitter and a rigger, with one of the latter two acting as air gunner. I quickly became a part-time gunner. I remember how proud I was when I was first able to pin on the air gunner's badge – a brass-winged bullet which we wore on our sleeves, and for which we received the princely sum of one shilling and sixpence per day extra."

Flying as part of the crew of an ageing Westland Wapiti biplane on the North-West Frontier had its appeal, but Connolly had his eye on the bigger prize: to fly the aircraft himself. Thoughts quickly turned to becoming a sergeant pilot, and he applied for pilot training. Happily, he was one of only a handful to be selected:

> "Competition in those days of the pre-expansion RAF was fierce, and very few of the comparatively large numbers who applied were selected. I considered myself very fortunate when, within two years of leaving Halton, I was sent back to England to enter pilot training."

Pat learned to fly at the Bristol Flying Club School in Yatesbury, mastering the ubiquitous DH98 Tiger Moth until he could take off, land and perform a series of other basic flying exercises solo to his instructor's satisfaction. From the Tiger Moth he progressed to advanced training on Hawker Harts and Avro Ansons (the latter being twin-engined) at Ternhill in Shropshire, immediately appreciating the increased power and performance that both aircraft had over the de Havilland. Pat was awarded his wings in 1938, just as Germany began agitating for war, but despite a brief posting to an operational squadron, Connolly was soon back in the training regime, this time as an instructor.

Reporting to the Central Flying School, which at the time was at Upavon in Wiltshire, Connolly qualified as an instructor in 1938, thanks in no small part to the qualities of his teacher, George Clift (who later went on to fly Boeing 707s with BOAC). He was posted to Hullavington:

> "We had all passed out as C Class instructors but, to cut a long story short, I was re-categorised B well within six months and, in 1940, was commissioned and attained the highest instructor's category of A1 CFS."

Pat was commissioned on 15 October 1940 for the duration of hostilities, which by then were already over 12 months old. He also had the pleasure of receiving the Air Force Medal (AFM) in the King's New Year's Honours of 1941. His exalted status, however, was to be his undoing in terms of his desire to see action: "It did cause me frustration because the acute shortage of instructors made any attempt to get an operational job virtually impossible."

Connolly remained an instructor for almost three years before being 'rescued' and posted to Pathfinder Force (PFF). From the middle of 1942 onwards, Pathfinders were in the vanguard of every Bomber Command attack, identifying and marking targets for the main force to hit. As such, Pathfinder squadrons could have their pick of experienced pilots and crews, and Pat had clearly impressed. Joining 35 Squadron at Graveley as a flight lieutenant, he moved to Downham Market in March 1944 when B Flight of 35 Squadron helped to form the nucleus of 635

Squadron to meet the increasing demands of Bomber Command in the run-up to the opening of a second front.

All Pathfinder crews, regardless of their previous experience, initially flew in a 'supporter' role, the first to bomb and add further incentive to main force to do their bidding. Only later did they progress through the Pathfinder hierarchy in a range of different roles described by a language unique to PFF: illuminators; backers-up; blind markers; visual markers. The best became primary blind or visual markers (depending on whether the target could be seen 'blind' – i.e. by using a dedicated ground-scanning radar called H2S – or 'visually', in better weather conditions where the target could be illuminated). The very best became master bombers, who along with their deputies were tasked with orchestrating the entire attack.

Pat's first op with 635 was a comparatively 'simple' trip to Rouen, to bomb the railway marshalling yards. Transport and infrastructure were common targets at the time as the Allies prepared for the invasion of northern France. The Germans relied heavily on the railway network to move men and materiel; knock out the railways, it was argued, and you reduce the German army's capacity to fight.

Pat had only been with the squadron a few weeks when they suffered the blow of losing their popular commanding officer, Wing Commander Alan Cousens. Cousens, who was highly experienced and equally highly decorated with the DSO and DFC 'double', had been with Pat at Halton, though two years his senior. He was the most senior officer to be lost on operations from the 22nd Entry, and it was a tremendous blow to a new squadron just getting into its stride.

On 3 June, prior to an attack on a coastal battery near Calais, another tragedy hit the squadron when one of their number clipped a hangar and crashed on take-off with a full pay-load on board. The power of the explosion could be felt and heard several miles away. Pat later wrote:

> "We knew something had happened soon after take-off. There was a great flash of light which seemed to have come from the direction of the base. Sadly, we learned later that a Lancaster had crashed and we felt sorry for the poor buggers. They didn't deserve that. No crew does."

In a main force squadron, a typical first tour of operations was 30 trips. Aircrew could then be called back for a second tour of 20 trips. In Pathfinder Force, however, they signed up for a 'double' tour of 50 operations straight off, such was the demand. By the end of July, Pat had flown more than 20 operations, including three as deputy master bomber, once to the new squadron CO, Wing Commander Walter Brooks, once to Squadron Leader Rodney Roache, and on the third occasion, on July 30, to Squadron Leader Ian Bazalgette.

Targets had changed once again, with a key focus on the flying bomb sites and storage depots, as well as specific attacks to support Allied ground troops as they looked to extend the Normandy beachhead. Attacks had also shifted from night-time to daylight – a particular challenge for an ostensibly night-time bombing force. The raid on 30 July was Pat's 31st, and it was particularly successful. Working closely with Bazalgette as the master bomber, Pat – who was now a squadron leader – flew as low as 2,000 ft to confirm the accuracy of the Oboe markers. These were then successfully 'backed up' to enable the main force aircraft to do their work. Theirs was one of only two successful raids that day, the four other attacks being thwarted by heavy cloud.

Pat's own first op as master bomber on 1 August proved a most unsatisfactory affair. He was forced to abandon the mission because of low cloud and jettison his bombs over the sea. He retained, however, his markers, as were the orders of the day. He was not on the Battle Order for the attack on the V1 site at Trossy St Maximin, the raid for which Ian Bazalgette was awarded a posthumous Victoria Cross. Another Halton apprentice, Squadron Leader Dennis Witt (23rd Entry), was in the air that day, one of his crew describing the flak as being so thick that it was "like flying through a brick wall in places. Very accurate. Very loud."

The squadron and Bomber Command returned to more 'traditional' targets in the autumn, Pat flying as primary visual marker for an attack on Bremen on the night of 18/19 August that the city's own records later described as 'the most destructive raid of the war', with the whole of the centre and the north-western parts of Bremen, including the port area, being devastated. Pat's own post-raid summary simply states: "Bombed well on the TIs and observed some really large fires and several large explosions in the aiming point area."

On 12 September, Pat flew as a blind sky marker for an attack on Frankfurt (the last major raid against Frankfurt of the war), and while Pat was happy with his night's work, he also commented on the weight of the German defences, seeing several aircraft hit on the route home and commenting on the warm welcome by flak and searchlights on the run up to the target. He also had the pleasure of additional company for the trip, taking Wing Commander Hugh 'Speed' Le Good with him as an observer[2].

The pace of operations as autumn merged into winter saw no signs of letting up. Pat was by now a flight commander and the strain was beginning to tell. Wing Commander 'Tubby' Baker had replaced 'old man' Brooks as the CO, and the calls on the squadron's time were relentless. German night-fighters, flak and searchlights were not the only enemy; the weather could also be a deadly foe, and on the night of 30 November Pat had to fly dangerously low in order to counter the effects of icing on the wings and rudder which were making the aircraft difficult to fly. He also notes 'the crew seemed very tired today'.

Awarded the Distinguished Flying Cross (DFC) in early December, Pat flew his 50th trip with the squadron on the night of Thursday, 28 December, an attack on the railway yards at Mönchengladbach that was again hampered by cloud and of limited success. The new year of 1945 saw Pat promoted wing commander, and on the night of 13 February he was blind marker for the now infamous and devastatingly destructive raid on Dresden. Pat retained his TIs as the H2S 'set' was playing up, and bombed on the master bomber's instructions. (Pathfinder aircraft, it should be noted, carried bombs, even if they were a marker crew.) He remembers the centre of the city being well alight, and such was the intensity of the fires that they could actually feel the heat in their aircraft, even at 16,000 ft. He also remembers the intensity of the German defences, his aircraft – not for the first time – receiving several hits from heavy flak.

Dresden proved to be Pat's swansong, for he was soon afterwards taken off operations and posted to PFF HQ. It is worthy of note that by the end of his tour, all of Pat's crew had been decorated and commissioned. Pat himself was awarded a Bar to his DFC, the citation reading:

> 'Since the award of the Distinguished Flying Cross, Wing Commander Connolly has completed many further sorties against such vital targets as Stuttgart, Essen and Munich. He has pressed home his attacks with the utmost determination and vigour and has always completed his tasks, however arduous, with outstanding cheerfulness and confidence. As flight commander, Wing Commander Connolly has displayed fine leadership and he has always maintained a high standard of courage and devotion to duty.'

His squadron commander and friend, Tubby Baker (later DSO & Bar, DFC & Bar) had similarly no doubt of Pat's talents as a captain of aircraft, flight commander and friend:

> "Pat was a first-class bomber pilot and always gave great attention to details on operations. He was always the one to come up with great ideas in the 635 Squadron planning room. He made me laugh and without doubt he made an excellent flight commander and master bomber. We shared some good moments on and off duty."[3]

With the war finished in Europe, Pat was to become part of 'Tiger Force' to defeat the Japanese in the Far East, and was in fact on his way to Okinawa as a member of the advance headquarters of an element of British Bomber Command when the enemy surrendered and the world war finally came to an end. He thus found himself as part of the RAF contingent accepting the surrender of Hong Kong from the Japanese.

Various assignments followed in Hong Kong, Ceylon (now Sri Lanka), and at Bomber Command Headquarters. He attended the RAF Staff College, the Joint

Services Staff College, and the Imperial Defence College, learning how to run a peacetime operation. He also enjoyed a tour as wing commander (flying) at Binbrook (taking over from another 'Brat', Hamish Mahaddie) which at the time had the only operational jet bomber unit in the world, composed of four squadrons of Canberras.

It was during this period that he was captain of a Canberra that set a new official world record of nine hours and 55 minutes for the flight from London to Nairobi – a record that stood for some time largely, in Pat's words, "because nobody bothered to try to better it officially". In the co-pilot's seat for the trip was none other than the then C-in-C

Pat Connolly (right) during his record-breaking flight.

Bomber Command, Air Marshal Sir Hugh Lloyd, with Squadron Leader Danny Clare DFC as navigator. A more 'veteran' crew it is difficult to imagine with four DFCs, an MC, AFM, and a couple of 'K's' between them. Pat was awarded the Air Force Cross in the New Year's Honours of 1953.

A particular highlight in his career came soon after his promotion to group captain when he took command of RAF Waddington, home to the first of the Vulcan V-bomber squadrons. His most enjoyable tour was his time spent as Group Captain Air Staff (Plans) and chairman of the Joint Planning Staff with the Far East Air Force, flying all around the world from the US to New Zealand.

On his return he was posted as commandant of the RAF's Central Flying School which he considered "the plum of all of the RAF's flying jobs". One amusing incident occurred during the 50th anniversary celebrations of the school and an inspection by HM the Queen Mother. With the formalities completed, Her Majesty was being treated to lunch in the officers' mess and was confronted by a dining table sparkling with newly polished silver. As the Queen Mother went to use the condiments, the lid of the salt cellar fell off, covering her plate with a small mountain of white crystals. Quick as a flash, Pat whipped the plate from under her nose and substituted his own, thus avoiding a potential social disaster. It was a story Her Royal Highness apparently liked to recount in later life.

Pat held the post from 1961 to 1963, during which time he demonstrated an early production model of the Folland Gnat T1, just after its selection as the RAF's

Waddington ex-apprentices.

new advanced training aircraft, at the Paris Salon of 1961 (now the Paris Air Show). His final posting involved a return to his alma mater as commandant in 1967. In an interview in the early 1960s, while CFS commandant at Little Rissington, he said that to the older generation, flying must seem rather complex:

> "But the young are sufficiently technically minded to keep abreast of advances in technology. To them, complexity is commonplace. Their eyes are in space, which is where they ought to be, and I hope that before very long the RAF will be in space too. Flying is still lots of fun, and as far as I can see it, it is going to remain fun for many years."

Air Commodore H. P. 'Pat' Connolly CB, DFC & Bar AFC AFM, aide-de-camp to HM the Queen died in office on 11 December 1968. The *Halton Magazine* recorded his passing:

> 'No one who met and worked with Hugh Patrick Connolly will ever forget his sincere love and concern for Halton. Commencing his service at the

school in 1931, Air Commodore Connolly was delighted to return as its commandant. Affectionate and cherished memories of his own apprenticeship days enabled him to bring inspiration and enthusiasm to the present generation of young men about to enter the RAF. We are sad that Air Commodore Connolly's life was cut so dramatically short at a time when Halton needed his warm-hearted and generous leadership.'

Pat was succeeded by Air Commodore Robert (Bob) Weighill DFC, a veteran of two tours with 2 Squadron (and post-war CO) and a former captain of the England rugby football team.

Before he died, Pat was able to reflect on his own time at Halton: "I am extremely proud of being an ex-apprentice and, looking back, I think this was of immense importance at a very formative age."

10 THE FLYING GOLDFISH

John Clements had one principal aim in joining the RAF: to become a sergeant pilot. It was an objective, in his own words, that he singularly failed to achieve. A rather different career beckoned, a career that saw him fly convoy patrols in a Sunderland flying boat, survive a ditching in the Bristol Channel and, by the beginning of 1945, complete some 300 flight tests of ten different types of airborne radar equipment in 18 different aircraft. It also saw him attain air rank, retiring as an air commodore after 39 years of service.

It was John's fascination with the First World War fighter pilots and the novels of W. E. Johns that drove his desire to become a pilot. Still three months short of his 16th birthday, John arrived at RAF Halton but failed the medical due to an alleged defective eye and was therefore immediately deemed unfit for any future pilot training. Along with a classmate at Cotham Grammar School in Bristol, Norman Courtman-Stock, the pair opted to become wireless operator mechanics – a role that still held out the possibility of regularly flying. A few days later they arrived at Electrical & Wireless training school at RAF Cranwell to begin their training as part of the 36th Entry.

John performed well at schools, was appointed a leading aircraftman, and even managed to swing a further medical examination that found nothing wrong with his previously troublesome eye. A cadetship looked a distinct possibility but fate, in the shape of the outbreak of the Second World War, put paid to such thoughts for the foreseeable future.

On the day war was declared, John was in hospital with chickenpox, and had to watch helplessly as his classmates left for postings to operational stations. A few days later, they were all back, the Air Ministry having decided to recall the entry and shorten its course by six months. As such, they passed out in January 1940 in the newly designated trade of wireless electrical mechanic (WEM). By then, John had been trained on the ground and in the air:

"We had been instructed in the maintenance and operation of air and ground wireless transmitters and receivers, in workshop practices including the use of lathes, in aircraft and car wiring, and petrol-electric sets.

"In our last week we had been taught the servicing and operation of the Type X machine, an electrically operated cypher machine just coming into service and very similar to the German Enigma machine; we were forbidden from taking notes."

John's first posting, along with Norman and fellow Brats Jan Axford, Tom Olliver, Doug Phillips, Walt Warren and Jack Hicks, was to 32 Maintenance Unit (32MU) at St Athan, South Wales – a major airframe and engine repair base. The MU was also responsible for the installation of the newly developed aircraft-to-surface vessel (ASV) and aircraft interception (AI) equipment being fitted to Hudson and Blenheim aircraft respectively, and John's job was to test the equipment both on the ground and in the air.

The MU had been trained in its task by an airborne group from the Air Ministry Research Establishment, whose number included the eminent scientist, Dr Bernard Lovell. John remembers Lovell as something of an eccentric: "When I first caught sight of Dr Lovell he was wearing a teddy bear coat and had a soldering iron in his hand, modifying a 1936 television set!"

Whereas previously the highest frequency John had worked with was 20 MHz, it was now 200 MHz. Pulse widths, pulse recurrence frequencies, and saw tooth waveforms were all new concepts. Aerials with which he had been familiar as lengths of wire trailing ten yards or more from the back of an aircraft were now solid tubes of only a foot. Earphones had been replaced by the green flickering pulses on a cathode ray tube.

"Our 'on the job' instruction proceeded in a scenario where there were no technical publications, no servicing manuals, and no special-to-type test equipment. All we had was an Avometer, a 0-100v AC voltmeter, and a WEM's toolkit. To check that a transmitter was working one put a screwdriver near the lecher lines and hoped for a spark!"

It was not until 17 March that John received his first instruction on the flight testing of the ASV Mk 1 in Hudson N7335 and two more instructional flights took place in April. On 10 April, with just over two hours' experience of ASV flight testing, John was sent out on his first solo. He was just 18. The five other WEMs also succeeded in passing their probation: "We were the forerunners of the breed that about 15 years later were formally recognised and known as air electronic operators."

As well as ASV and AI, John was also responsible for installing and testing IFF – Identification Friend or Foe. The aircraft received a signal from a ground-radar station and returned it in an amplified-coded form to allow the ground station to identify it as friendly. John and Jan Axford installed an aerial on the roof of a C-type hangar for a modified IFF Mk 1 set; the modification allowed the set to respond to the transmission from ASV-equipped aircraft, thus acting as a homing beacon, giving range and bearing. Credit for this idea went to another apprentice, Squadron Leader Sidney Lugg (2nd Entry, Flowerdown), who was then on the staff at Coastal Command HQ. He arranged for a similar beacon, known as Mother, to be installed in the control tower at Leuchars. There it was of great benefit to Hudson crews returning from patrols in the North Sea in bad weather and undoubtedly saved many lives.

Lugg retired as a group captain having rendered splendid service to the 2TAF on the use/misuse of radar for which he was recognised by both the UK and the US governments. He was not the only former apprentice, however, whose innovation saved lives. Keith Street is perhaps one who has never been given the full credit he deserves for his development of the first airborne VHF.

Keith was in the first landplane to arrive at the Seletar Air Base in December 1930. While in Singapore, he became dissatisfied with the airborne RT equipment, then operating in the 3-7 Mhz range. A keen amateur radio enthusiast, he began building a simple airborne VHF (30 Mhz) set and after some successful, unofficial local trials persuaded his flight commander to authorise a formal range test along the Malayan coast. At 10,000 ft near Malacca and at a range of about 100 miles from the base station, the signal was loud and clear. Keith persuaded the pilot to fly even higher in order to get a measure of the maximum possible range. At 16,000 ft, the engine stopped as abruptly as the trial, and the pilot was obliged to force

The prototype Blackburn Iris flying boat, one of only five built.

land on the beach. Although none too popular with his flight commander, Keith had proved that VHF worked and worked well. It was ten years later that VHF RT sets became standard fit in RAF aircraft and were an indispensable aid in achieving victory in the Battle of Britain.

On 13 April, John was sent with a small party to Pembroke Docks to fit ASV sets to the Short Sunderland flying boats of 210 and 228 Squadrons. The pace was relentless: "We settled into a routine: first day cable preparation; second day aircraft wiring; third day ground and air testing."

Convoy patrols – many of eight hours or more – proved the value of the ASV, and for wont of a change, John also fitted and tested an ASV set in a Stranraer taking his one and only flight in a biplane flying boat. He flight-tested his final Sunderland at Pembroke Docks before again putting away his toolkit to join a fitting party heading for Mount Batten to fit those aircraft of 10 Squadron RAAF. A few weeks later he was on the move again, returning to 32 MU where he pursued his ambition to fly. Having passed his LAC trade test board, a necessary pre-requisite, he was somewhat taken aback when told that the Air Ministry had decreed that wireless trades were not to be sent on pilot training: "Flight Sergeant Lawrence, a grizzled 14-18 veteran, said 'hard luck' and proceeded to tear up my application in front of me, consigning the shreds to the wastepaper basket by his table."

By now the ASV Mk 2 (also called the Long-Range ASV or LRASV) had been produced and was being fitted, initially, to Armstrong Whitworth Whitleys. In the first few weeks of 1941, John was part of a fitting party sent to Greenock to work on Catalinas, then being delivered as part of the 'Lend-Lease' agreement with the US, although his first task was to upgrade a Shorts 'G' Class flying boat being modified for operational use:

> "While working on X8273 I met Eric Madger (34th Entry) who was with the Marine Aircraft Experimental Establishment. Eric had achieved some fame the previous summer when the Lerwick in which he was the wireless operator force-landed off the coast of Ireland through engine trouble. Eric sent the SOS which resulted in the crew being rescued and for which he was awarded a mention in despatches."

Back at 32 MU, the AI Mk 4 programme in Beaufighters was now underway and not without its perils. Two incidents in quick succession led to a lucky escape for Jan Axford and his pilot in a crash-landing, and the deaths of two other technicians (including Walt Warren) when their night-fighter blew up in mid-air. John spent almost 12 months in Greenock and therefore missed most of the excitement, but was kept more than busy with his Catalinas, and flight testing the LRASV Liberators at Prestwick.

In the early part of 1942, a programme commenced to fit ASV Mk 2 sets to a small number of Blackburn Bothas. The Botha was a failed torpedo bomber that was woefully underpowered and did little to endear itself to the pilots who flew them. Relegated to training roles, they were to be fitted with ASV for radar-training purposes. On 7 April, John joined LAC Colbert, a member of the first group of Canadian radio mechanics, on a flight test with Flying Officer Sheppard at the controls and Pilot Officer Gatrell as the test flight engineer. John remembers the flight in detail:

"As the aircraft climbed towards the Bristol Channel, I went through the switching on procedure. Gradually the equipment warmed up and land mass echoes appeared on the tube; then the time base started to jitter badly. This was often the sign that the main power supply voltage was too low. Gatrell was by my side, lifted my helmet away from my ear and shouted: 'We're losing power, going in the drink, follow me down the back!' I remember seeing Gatrell release the rear hatch presenting a view of the blue of the rapidly approaching Bristol Channel. The thought went through my head, conditioned no doubt by my recent experience on flying boats, that the Botha, particularly as it was a high-wing monoplane, would ditch horizontally and reasonably elegantly. How wrong I was. I remember only blackness, a feeling of rotating, and then nothing."

John opened his eyes to see nothing other than large, cotton-wool clouds against a blue background and felt it must be heaven. Then a face loomed over him and life returned to his body with a vengeance. His whole body was racked in pain; Colbert gently lifted his head and an amazing sight hit his eyes:

"Both engines had been torn out by the force of hitting the water and the bottom of the fuselage was ripped wide open for about half its length. I was laying on the inside of the top of the Perspex cockpit with the waters of the Bristol Channel lapping over me. I must have travelled a distance of about 30 feet from my position in the rear of the fuselage when we hit the water; another few feet and I would have been bobbing about in the Channel."

With Colbert at his side, John attempted to move but could not put any weight on his right foot. He did, however, manage to crawl until he reached the starboard wheel and draped himself over it. Gatrell had done much the same on the port side. Sheppard was in the water, 50 yards away, swimming towards the shore. The effect of shock and the cold of the water caused John's knees to knock violently together. Happily, they were soon rescued by a boat from a small coastal ship, although the rescue attempt seemed to take an age while the boat's crew determined the best way of getting the injured men on board.

An ambulance and some medical orderlies were waiting for them when they eventually came ashore and they were taken to the sick bay at Fairwood Common, a nearby night-fighter station. John was diagnosed with a broken right ankle and broken ribs; Gatrell had a chipped left knee bone and Colbert was untouched. Of Sheppard there was no news. Sadly, they would later learn that the gallant pilot had drowned.

On recovering, John was soon back to the routine of flight testing and at the end of May completed the installation of the first AI Mk 5 in a de Havilland Mosquito. The Mk 5 differed from the Mk 4 in that the operator's indicator had two displays. A strange incident occurred while flight testing a Mosquito in early June; the A scope time base broke up into a lattice work of sine waves of varying amplitudes. On the ground, however, the set performed perfectly. A few weeks later, a flight test in a different Mosquito yielded a similar result. The problem was handed to the Royal Aircraft Establishment (RAE) at Farnborough to resolve and the reason was soon explained: the Germans were jamming their sets.

On 22 August, tragedy struck when John's good friend Jack Hicks was killed in a flying accident. He had been detailed to flight-test the AI Mk 4 in a Beaufighter and give instruction to Pilot Officer Tony Ward who had recently arrived. The Beaufighter took off and began to climb at an alarming angle until it stalled and crashed about 100 yards from the sergeants' mess. It was a full 24 hours before the bodies of the dead men could be recovered from the wreckage. Rumour had it that the control wires to the elevator trim tabs had been crossed.

Early marks of AI suffered in that their range was limited by the altitude of the aircraft. This was not a problem with the Mk 8, and John's training on the new radar at Malvern coincided with his interview for a commission. In the event, 32 MU did not get the task of fitting Beaufighters with the new Mk 8 but was instead tasked with fitting the Mk 2 version of the H2S ground-scanning radar to aircraft of Bomber Command.

John took his first flight-test with the new equipment on 10 June 1943 in a Halifax and spent the next few weeks conducting further tests in Halifax and Lancasters. He also continued to fit AI equipment and had a scare on one flight in late July when the set caught fire and started to fill the fuselage with acrid black smoke:

> "We were commencing our approach to the target aircraft when I could smell burning. I looked down to my left-hand side and saw small tongues of flame and smoke coming from the modulator's cooling louvres. I immediately switched off the set, turned my seat around, got out of my harness and made my way as fast as I could down the fuselage to where the fire extinguisher should have been stowed. It wasn't there.
>
> "I told the pilot to get down at a rate of knots which he did. Fortunately, we were not far from the airfield as the smoke was making it very diffi-

cult to breathe. As we came to a halt at the end of the runway, the fire tender was there to greet us."

Throughout his time flight-testing at 32 MU and on his various temporary postings, John got to fly with a number of pilots of varying abilities and eccentricities, including one who insisted on wearing a red and white knitted bobble hat and another who had resigned a short-service commission only to re-enlist as a sergeant. Among the more notable pilots were Karel Kuttelwascher, a well-known Czechoslovakian fighter ace and ground-strafing expert who was 'resting' at 32 MU, and Geoffrey Page, the Battle of Britain fighter pilot and arguably the most famous of Archibald McIndoe's 'Guinea Pigs'. With Page, John was testing a new set of American design that had both an ASV and AI capability and was being fitted to the Fleet Air Arm's Fairey Firefly.

In-between flight tests, John tried again, in his words, to become more actively engaged in the war. WOM/AGs were being sought for Coastal Command; John applied but heard no more. Another attempt at pilot training also ended with yet another failed medical, this time on account of sinusitis. When John challenged the findings, he was told that as a 22-year-old flight sergeant he was 'too old' for pilot training:

> "In more recent years I recalled the remark with wry amusement when I read that a squadron leader of 51 was flying Jaguars in the Gulf War and the first WRAF officer to be selected for pilot training was 29."

In all, John carried out 19 test flights in Fireflies with six different pilots and at the end of January 1945 was told to report to No. 8 Radio School at Cranwell on a pre-commissioning radar course. It had been more than two years since he had originally sat for his commissioning interview and five years since he had arrived at St Athan. In that time, he had flown some 300 flight tests testing ten different types of radar and navigation equipment in 18 different aircraft. For some reason best known only to the RAF, he never received a flying brevet, even though the Air Ministry had introduced a radio operator's brevet (AMO A17/41) that required candidates to attend a three-week radio operator's course and complete five hours of flying instruction to qualify. A further attempt, ten years later, to qualify for the air electronics officer (AEO) brevet was similarly declined. The rather brutal dismissal of his application reads:

> 'Whilst Squadron Leader Clements may possess technical qualifications which enable him to carry out the function in some measure of an AEO, he cannot be said to fulfil the requirements of QR815 (2) which states that the flying badge is not deemed to have been fully earned until the holder

has been posted to, and has actually undertaken productive flying duties in a qualified capacity on, an operational or non-operational unit.'

John's post-war career was a busy mix of training and instruction, initially in India and then back in the UK, working on Rebecca and Gee, and flying four sorties to Gatow as aircrew during the Berlin Airlift, including one as the stand-in navigator when the regular nav was sick. Whilst at Wünsdorf, John witnessed a remarkable incident when a Tudor II of Don Bennett's new airline was attempting a ground-controlled approach (GCA) landing. Although it made a normal touchdown, its tail refused to come down:

> "As the tail came down towards the tarmac the astrodome opened, and a small figure appeared. I was told later it was the wireless operator who had been sacked as the aircraft was taxiing to the hardstanding. There the station commander and AVM Bennett walked to the rear of the aircraft where the red elevator locks were clearly visible. The aircraft had been landed using only the elevator trimmers; a remarkable feat of airmanship. No marks can be awarded for pre-flight checks."[1]

John never stopped trying to become a pilot, taking lessons with the university air squadron at Southampton while studying on a post-graduate course. From Southampton John went to the Radar Research Establishment (RRE), Malvern where he carried out the development flight trials of Blue Study, a radar-bombing system in the Canberra. He joined the RRE flying club and gained his Private Pilot's Licence in a Tiger Moth. By the end of his tour at RRE he had clocked up over 800 hours operating 22 different type of radio equipment in 29 different aircraft ranging from biplanes to jets. At every turn, however, his dubious medical record returned to put the spanner in the metaphorical works to gain any formal recognition of his flying abilities. It was, however, the only frustration in an otherwise rewarding RAF career that saw John rise to the rank of air commodore and retire in a top signals appointment as air officer signals, RAF Support Command. His immediate boss in his last job was another ex-apprentice, John Bowring, who went on to become an air vice-marshal. Bowring later found fame for his work in the US, as part of the design team for the first manned space capsule.

Of those others who had travelled with John to St Athan from Cranwell in those early days of 1940 as newly qualified WEMs, Doug Phillips managed to qualify as a pilot just as the war came to an end, and enjoyed a successful peace with Aer Lingus and SkyWays before being killed in a flying accident in Libya in 1959. Norman Courtman-Stock similarly gained his wings and was commissioned but flew principally as a flight engineer because of a surplus of qualified pilots. He retired from the RAF in 1964 and became a teacher. Tom Olliver left 32 MU for

Sealand and stayed in the RAF after the war. In 1961 he was appointed the first CO of 38 Tactical Signals Unit and awarded the MBE in the 1966 New Year's Honours list.

Perhaps the most remarkable of post-war careers fell to Jan Axford. He trained as a navigator in Canada, was commissioned, and flew operations with 192 Squadron. He left the RAF to join the colonial police, serving throughout the Malayan Emergency and was badly injured when a small patrol he was leading was ambushed by a 30-strong band of communist rebels. Jan was hit 11 times and left for dead but survived to take his revenge. A few months later, having recovered from his wounds, he received intelligence that the rebel group would be in a particular place, at a particular time, and laid on a welcoming committee. The rebel gang was all but wiped out. Shortly afterwards, Jan converted to Islam and became a citizen of Malaysia, taking the given name Ibrahim. His last appointment was as chief police officer (superintendent) of Muar, a district in the state of Johore.

Of other contemporaries, Peter Henson, a particular friend, qualified as an instructor at CFS, only to lose his life in 1956 as an exchange pilot in the US when his F-84F Thunderstreak crashed into the Gulf of Mexico. Though he was seen to have bailed out, the body of Squadron Leader Henson was never found.

As for John, on retiring from the RAF he joined Marconi Defence Systems where he initiated the proposal for the Brimstone missile, still used by the RAF today. At the time of writing he is living happily in outer London, on the edge of Hertfordshire, and reflects that in his career he carried out the duties of five different aircrew categories but doesn't have a single brevet to show for his efforts. Nor does he own the coveted pilot's wings.

11 POLES APART

When Vyacheslav Mikhailovich Molotov, Stalin's minister of foreign affairs, signed the Nazi-Soviet non-aggression pact with Germany's foreign minister Joachim von Ribbentrop in August 1939, it effectively gave Adolf Hitler the 'green light' for his invasion of Poland. It also sealed the fate of tens of thousands of Poles, wrenched from their homes, herded into cattle trucks and forced eastwards, to the harsh hinterlands of Siberia. Many never made their unknown destinations; illness, malnutrition and the harsh conditions took their toll, especially among the sick and the old. Only the lucky survived with the pathetically few personal possessions they managed to take with them.

Forced to live in freezing, overcrowded wooden barracks, the men were immediately put to work in the surrounding forests, sawing and stacking wood while the children – some as young as ten – were forced to clear around them. Food was in desperately short supply, and dependant on the Poles meeting 'targets' for the work they were given. Many died from hunger and exhaustion. Medical care was non-existent. Typhus added to their misery. In one camp alone, 600 people died out of the 1,700 or so who had originally arrived.

Those initially chosen for deportation included the families of teachers, doctors, judges, soldiers and policemen. Selection could be arbitrary; all were simply identified as 'dangerous elements' that needed to be removed. Among them was the family of 12-year-old Eugene Borysiuk.

"My father was a former policeman, so perhaps he was on a list of public sector workers or government employees. Whatever the facts, we were chosen for a special holiday.

"We were quite poor, and my father had returned to working the land. Despite this we were deported along with hundreds of others from our village – Hajnówka – and the region of Polesia on the eastern border of Poland. The last time I saw my father was just before we departed. He was summoned into some sort of administrative building to sign various documents. He was still in there when we were loaded into trucks and driven away. I never saw him again."

Eugene, his mother and his elder brother languished in the region of Novosibirsk, by the Ob River, until June 1941, and Hitler's invasion of Russia. In a stroke, the non-aggression pact was torn into a thousand pieces, and Britain found herself with a new, unlikely ally. It also meant that Russia was now an ally of Poland, and large numbers of the Polish military who had been imprisoned by the Soviets were now released. Among them was General Anders, who set about re-establishing the Polish Army in exile.

This was by no means a simple task, but Anders set to his duty with tremendous vigour, even succeeding in moving large numbers of men across Russia into Persia and then Iraq. Eugene's brother, who was nine years older than his sibling, was among the first to volunteer, leaving Eugene alone to care for his mother. Families were also now allowed to travel, though the Russians were largely obstructive and showed little enthusiasm or sympathy for their former enemy's plight. Eugene recalls the journey to the south-eastern border of Russia:

"The journey to Tashkent in Uzbekistan took many weeks and was undertaken in terrible conditions. We were once again herded onto cattle trucks and had very little food or water and certainly no money. No supplies were provided to us either. It was hell, and many on our train died from hunger or the cold."

In Tashkent, Eugene was immediately put to work on a collective farm, waiting patiently for his onward passage to be approved. Three times he was told it was his turn, only to be disappointed on the day. At last he travelled to Krasnovodsk on the eastern shore of the Caspian Sea, where he was put on a boat with hundreds of fellow refugees and disembarked at Pahlavi in Iran. Quarantined for six weeks and issued with clean clothes, Eugene was no longer a prisoner of the Soviet Union. Arrangements were made for an onward journey to Palestine, a trip that again took several weeks but in considerably better and more humane conditions. They travelled by road across the mountains of northern Iran to Tehran, and then across the border into Iraq where they arrived in the middle of September. It was not until November that they finally reached Palestine.

While Eugene had been travelling, the Polish military had been busy. Various military training schools had been established throughout the region and even further afield, and in the spring of 1943, a Polish air force mission arrived to select and recruit candidates for training by the RAF at No. 1 School of Technical Training at RAF Halton. Eugene was among the 264 boys who were eventually chosen:

"My mother had died in Tehran and with my brother in the army and my father missing I was essentially on my own. Anders had originally created a cadet force which I joined, in Palestine, and when they called for volunteers to go to Britain and train as RAF apprentices, I put my name forward and was accepted. It seemed like a good option at the time; the romance of a uniform, and the chance to be properly fed and looked after well."

After yet another long and arduous journey, this time via Suez, Eugene arrived in England on 12 August 1943. It was raining. Two days later, having entrained from Liverpool, Eugene and his fellow trainee apprentices – nearly all of them ex-deportees – arrived at Wendover for the short march to Halton. They were each given their first RAF pay of ten shillings and allocated to barrack blocks nine and ten.

The Poles' assimilation into service life was far from easy. While officially between the ages of 15 and 17, many of the boys were unbelievably small and under-developed for their age. Partly this was to do with their hard upbringing, and years of malnourishment; partly, also, it was because some of the boys had lied about their age, or genuinely did not know when they had been born. This led to practical challenges such as uniform size, and some had to wear kit usually reserved for WAAFs as they were so slight.

At first, the Polish boys were eyed with some curiosity by the English apprentices; language was a particular problem, as one contemporary report notes: 'It was weeks or months before talk between the two became possible, and then only with the help of gestures.'

The same report says that life was far from easy for the new arrivals: 'They were strangers in a strange land and learning English for the first time, they had to try and come up to the British standard, fit into the British timetable and syllabus, and conform to King's Regulations. Their new, unknown surroundings held lots of surprises in store for all of them.'

The boys first had to learn the English language before they could hope to train for any one of the number of technical trades open to them. For some, this was their first real schooling of any kind, and their education included lessons in history and geography. English textbooks were translated, and Polish-speaking teaching staff and instructors drafted in to help. Restoring their trust in adults was a considerable task, given their experiences, and it was not until the start of 1944 that work could begin in earnest in turning these young men into qualified airframe fitters, engine fitters, armourers, electricians and instrument makers.

Despite the RAF's best efforts to integrate their new charges, there were obvious differences in culture and discipline. Their drill was nuanced in how they swung their arms across the body rather than fore and aft. Fights were inevitable, though there was plenty of scope for the young boys to exert their energies in sport and physical training, and the Poles quickly impressed with their skills on the football pitch, the boxing ring, and the pool.

Holidays also proved a problem, especially at Christmas since the Poles had no families. Surrogate families, however, were swiftly found thanks to a newspaper appeal by their Honorary Guardian, the actress Virginia Child-Villiers, Lady Jersey[1]. Eugene found himself as a guest of Harry and Gertrude Ward in Tunbridge Wells, a contact he retained for many years after the war.

He recalls only one specific incident where the clash of cultures exploded into something more difficult:

> "We were queuing for food and a minor scuffle broke out. One of the English lads stood up and said something like 'bloody Poles go back to where you belong'. As a unit, we downed tools and left in protest. It became something of an incident and the commandant, Air Commodore Titmas, was obliged to intervene. He had the airman on the carpet and smoothed things over. He was very good to us and this incident was the exception to the rule."[2]

In January 1944, 100 of the apprentices were transferred to the Air Apprentice Wing at Cranwell to study wireless at the No. 1 Radio School, though Eugene remained at Halton to train as an instrument maker. He quickly warmed to the task; he was a keen student and passed his final exams with distinction. He was on parade for the inspection early in their tenure by General Sosnkowski, who had taken over from General Sikorski as the commander-in-chief of the Polish Armed Forces, and given the signal honour of escorting Lord Trenchard, the founding father of the RAF and Halton, on his inspection of the Polish apprentices towards the end of their training.

The first group of Polish apprentices, Eugene among them, passed out in July 1947 alongside the 49th Entry. Of their number, Eugene was one of only seven to attain the rank of leading aircraftman. Sixty-nine passed out as AC1s and the remainder as AC2s.

At the end of his training, Eugene and his compatriots faced something of a dilemma. The war was now over; should they return home? For Eugene, the answer was somewhat easier than most. His home was no longer part of Poland:

> "We had begun to like England but it was still not my home. Some did decide to return, of course, and others decided to go further afield to the United States, Canada and even Argentina. For me, without the chance of going home, and with the offer to sign up as a regular with the RAF for five years, it was the easy option to stay and an easy way out of my dilemma."

Eugene was duly posted to 32 MU at St Athan, no longer an apprentice, but still very much as a junior in learning mode. Further postings followed to RAF Hemswell, from where he was detached to Mildenhall to work on calibrating bombsights, and to Gibraltar where, by his own admission, he didn't take full advantage of the opportunities open to him. He worked mainly on large, wartime aircraft such as the Lancaster and its post-war derivative, the Lincoln. He was at RAF Abingdon when his service came to an end.

Given 'disembarkation leave', Eugene was staying with his adoptive family and considering his future. An advertisement in the local paper caught his eye; Marconi was recruiting for qualified technicians, so Eugene duly applied, was invited for interview, and offered a job. "The interviewer asked me when I could start and I replied 'right now'. The job was based in Chelmsford and they put me up in a hostel. Within 48 hours I was a Marconi employee."

By now married to a fellow Polish refugee, Eugene's wife encouraged him to go to evening college further to build his technical knowledge, studying more advanced electronics engineering with the full support of his employer.

During his career at Marconi, Eugene was able to work on a number of interesting projects, including a large-screen projector for TV that was subsequently used in flight simulation. The project was not without its challenges, and trips to the US to iron out various technical problems were not uncommon. Invariably, Eugene found the solution and fast gained a deserved reputation as troubleshooter and 'fixer'. It was for this reason that on another occasion the former airman found himself all at sea:

> "The navy was interested in a technology that we were developing that allowed a wet film to be viewed as an actual picture without the negative having been developed. The Fleet Air Arm perceived a role for it in their aircraft, for the rapid turnaround of photographs after a reconnaissance sortie. They were experimenting with the positive/negative viewer on an aircraft carrier, and the equipment needed fine tuning. Muggins was duly despatched while the carrier – HMS *Centaur* – was at sea."[3]

Eugene spent three weeks on the carrier and was treated like royalty. Buying drinks in the mess, however, proved a challenge:

> "I wanted to buy a round but of course they didn't take cash. You had to sign a chit. I was told to write 'Marconi' which I did, and by the time we returned I had accumulated quite a number of chits that Marconi honoured. A nice letter from the navy saying how helpful I had been no doubt helped!"

Eugene retired from Marconi in 1992, having risen from instrument maker to quality assurance manager for GEC Avionics, part of the Marconi 'family'. He is

The unveiling of the Polish memorial plaque at RAF Halton in 1947.

justifiably proud of his achievements, and the role that Halton played in his formative years.

In total, of the 207 who entered Halton, 169 young Polish apprentices completed their training with the 49th and 50th Entries between August 1943 and February 1948. Of these, 102 joined the RAF as regular airmen, 60 entered civilian life in the UK or emigrated, and only five returned to communist Poland and an uncertain welcome.

The youngest and believed to be the youngest apprentice in Halton's history, was Stefan Petrusewicz. 'Peter', as he was known, gave his date of birth upon arrival as 12 January 1927 but he was actually born three years later and was only 13-and-a-half when he landed in the UK in 1943. He served as ground crew in the RAF until 1953 when he joined English Electric and then later BAC at Filton. He studied for a degree in Maths and Thermodynamics and Structures at the University of Southampton before studying for a PhD in Noise Control. He stayed in academia as a lecturer at the School of Engineering at the University of Bath where his students included Stephen Dalton, now Air Chief Marshal Sir Stephen Dalton.

On 21 June 1947, in the presence of Air Commodore Titmas and other senior dignitaries, a Polish memorial plaque was unveiled in No. 1 Wing, and has since become the focal point for reunions, though their numbers have now dwindled. It reads: 'Polish Avenue – These birch trees were planted by the Polish aircraft apprentices to express their gratitude to the British people for the hospitality, care and training that they received in the RAF at Halton in the years 1943-1947.'

12 THE GREAT ESCAPERS

In St George's Church are a series of stained-glass windows, the brainchild of a former RAF Church of England padre, Richard Lee, commemorating the Halton Boys and their achievements. Among the windows dedicated to specific entries are those for particular groups, winners of the highest awards for gallantry – the Victoria Cross and the George Cross – and those that immortalise Brats from all corners of the former British Empire. There is even one for Lewis, the legendary and much-loved mascot goat.

In one corner is a small, square window of subdued colours that is nonetheless striking for its simple image of a guard tower and a hut, surrounded by a barbed wire fence. On the one hand it might symbolise the struggle of all of those former apprentices who found themselves in the prison camps of Germany in the Second World War, but this one commemorates three men in particular, three apprentices who paid the ultimate price in their desire to make it home, recaptured and murdered in the greatest of Great Escapes.

William 'Jack' Grisman, whose father, a postman, had served in the 9th Norfolk Regiment, arrived at Halton on limited entry from Hereford High School as part of the 23rd Entry, and immediately threw himself into service life as a keen engineer and apprentice. He was similarly a keen sportsman, winning medals for rugby, swimming and athletics, and being awarded the Barrington Kennett trophy.

Finishing 46th in the order of merit as a fitter AE, Jack passed out as an AC1, and was posted to 10 (B) Squadron at Boscombe Down before heading out to Iraq for his first stint overseas, by which time he was an acting corporal

William Grisman.

(though unpaid!). Two years in Iraq, including a seven-month spell at the British embassy in Baghdad as a driver, was followed by the inevitable posting to India, joining 28 (Army Co-operation) Squadron before his request for aircrew training was granted and he returned to the UK at the end of 1938 to join 1 Air Observer School (1 AOS) on the first leg of his journey to fly.

Six months of tuition on the ground and in the air led to the award of his 'flying arsehole' and a posting to 99 (B) Squadron at Mildenhall on the eve of the Second World War. Among his contemporaries were Gerry Blacklock (a fellow Brat), Percy Pickard of *Target for Tonight* fame, and Tom Kirby Green, with whom he would later share a similar tragic fate.

In those early days, Jack was not part of a regular crew, but was rather chosen to fly with a number of different skippers. Early operations included 'nickel' raids, the rationale being that 'a potential weapon in time of war is the dissemination of suitable propaganda in enemy territory', though they had to be careful not to infringe Belgian, Dutch and Luxembourg neutrality. Armed reconnaissance sorties were also required, hunting the German fleet in and around Heligoland with only limited success.

The war started proper for the young observer in April 1940, as the bomber boys sought to support the ill-fated, short-lived expedition to Norway. Jack flew a number of operations as navigator to one of the squadron flight commanders, Squadron Leader Stanley Bertram (later DFC and commanding officer of 142 Squadron), though again their success was often limited. Long and dangerous slogs over the North Sea to bomb the airfield at Stavanger often ended in the despair of failing to find the target, though they did have some success on the night of 26-27 April when the squadron completed a successful attack, only to be shot at by some of their own destroyers!

The German invasion of the Low Countries put a new slant on bomber operations, and 99 Squadron was heavily engaged from the outset. Jack flew with Bertram as well as the squadron commander, Wing Commander Griffiths, to attack road and rail infrastructure to frustrate the German advance, as well as specific troop and armour concentrations where they could be found. In the second half of May and into early June, Jack flew as the regular navigator to Sergeant Valentine Hartright, a second pilot who had now been made captain of his own aircraft. Hartright was a former Halton boy of the 22nd Entry. The new team flew seven operations in 14 days, and on the night of 11-12 June scored a direct hit on an ammunition dump near the Fôret de Saint-Michal that resulted in 'shells bursting in all directions'[1].

A few days later and Jack was chosen by the Wingco for a special operation that saw a small force of Wellingtons audaciously attack Italy from a temporary base at Salon near Toulon in the south of France. Two raids on Genoa achieved little beyond a small propaganda victory and a thumbing of the nose to Il Duce.

Jack's qualities as an airman had been recognised by his commanding officer, and on his return from France he was sent to an officer training unit and commissioned. Over the summer he was also married, and received notification that he had been mentioned in despatches 'for gallant and distinguished services'. The newly appointed Pilot Officer Grisman reported for flying duties at 109 Squadron in December 1940, a comparatively 'secret' squadron for its time that had only just emerged from the shadows of the wireless intelligence development unit. Jack was tasked with various duties to help identify enemy methods of using radio beams and developing radar aids for use by the RAF. As well as the 'regular' RAF crew, the aircraft often carried technicians and scientists from the Telecommunications Research Establishment (TRE) at Malvern, and it was on one such flight, and with one such scientist, that Jack's luck finally ran out.

On the night of 5-6 November 1941, Jack was flying navigator to Pilot Officer Lester Bull on a special duties operation when their aircraft ran into difficulties over Lorient, losing the starboard airscrew. With the pilot unable to maintain any meaningful control of the Wellington, he ordered the crew to bail out. All made it out in one piece, coming down in and around the town of Pontivy. Les was captured immediately but Jack remained on the run for at least 24 hours before hunger and fatigue obliged him to take a gamble. Seeking help at a local farm, he was betrayed, and soon after arrived at Stalag Luft 1 at Barth for the first of his two-and-a-half years of captivity. He began planning to escape almost immediately.

At home, his wife was expecting their first child, a child he would never see.

Edgar 'Hunk' Humphreys arrived at Halton exactly one year after Jack Grisman to become part of the 25th Entry. Born on 5 December 1914, just prior to the first Christmas of the war to end all wars, Edgar was educated at Ackworth School near Pontefract, an independent Quaker school that clearly prepared the young student well for he easily won his place at Halton under open competition to train as a fitter II. (He started as a metal rigger and was remustered.) The fact that his father

Edgar Humphreys.

was a serving officer in the RAF and had been awarded the Air Force Cross in North Russia in 1919, certainly did not act as a barrier to progress.

With his apprenticeship completed, Edgar passed out in 44th place in the order of merit with the rank of AC1 and followed the traditional path of pre-war service life. Always keen to fly[2], his application to train as aircrew was eventually granted and upon the outbreak of war, he was a qualified sergeant pilot. Identified for a commission in the early part of 1940, Edgar joined 107 at Wattisham in the summer of the same year and was immediately thrown into the action.

The squadron, equipped with Blenheim IV twin-engined light bombers, had returned to the UK after a torrid time in France and now it was tasked with defending Britain from the very real threat of invasion[3]. Operations throughout August tended to be focused on attacking enemy airfields in France, Denmark and the Netherlands, and on 4 September Edgar recorded a very successful raid on Abbeville. Flying through concentrated flak, he delivered a low-level attack, the official report confirming several buildings ablaze as he left the target.

As the Germans moved men and materiel to the French channel ports in preparation for Operation Sea Lion, 107 Squadron switched targets: on the night of 8-9 September, Edgar was part of an attacking force tasked with bombing barges and tugs in and around Ostend. They identified the targets by first dropping flares, a very early version of pathfinding, and repeated the technique ten days later in a similar attack on Calais, although one of their number fell victim to flak. Of the four aircraft detailed for the raid, two were flown by ex-Halton apprentices, the second being Sergeant Roy Ralston of the 22nd Entry.

The pace of operations continued throughout September and into October with raids on Boulogne (led by the squadron CO, Wing Commander Duggan) and Le Havre, as well as attacks deeper into Germany such as the marshalling yards at Hamm where Edgar did well to avoid intense flak and a barrage of balloons. As the immediate threat of invasion passed, targets again switched back to enemy aerodromes and on the night of 15-16 November Edgar attacked the airfield at Poix from 800 ft and had the satisfaction of scoring a direct hit on an enemy aircraft as it attempted to take off. A few nights later he had similar success during a raid on Amiens-Glisy, diving through heavy anti-aircraft fire to drop his bombs on the runway. November ended with two raids on German targets, the railway marshalling yards at Dortmund and an armament works in Cologne, but much of December's effort — including a planned attack on the Fokker aircraft factory at Bremen — was hampered by poor weather.

On the night of 19-20 December, seven 107 Squadron aircraft were detailed to attack two enemy airfields — Lannion and Lorlaix — though only one of their number was able to drop its bombs. The rest returned safely to base with the exception of Blenheim T1860, flown by Pilot Officer Edgar Humphreys. Edgar and his two crewmates — Sergeant G. R. Griggs (observer) and Sergeant L. F. Brand (W/op AG) — were captured.

Soon after, Edgar's wife Lilian received formal notification that her husband was safe and a prisoner of war.

Tom Leigh was the youngest of the three men, born on 11 February 1919. His father was British and his mother Australian. They lived in Shanghai but returned to Australia for the birth of their second son, Tom, and his younger sister. Tragically, Tom's mother died young in 1926, and their father moved the family back to the UK. He died six years later and so at the age of 13 Tom was parentless and was brought up by a combination of boarding schools, family friends and a guardian.

Tom's first thought on turning 15 was to join the navy, and he took the entrance exam for the Training Ship (TS) *Mercury*. The ship was moored in the Hamble and was little more than a floating dormitory and classroom that would not have looked out of place in a Dickensian novel. Within months, however, Tom was studying for the entrance exam at Halton which he passed,

Tom Leigh.

joining the 32nd Entry on 20 August 1935. Although he showed early promise, and was promoted leading apprentice (which meant being in charge of a group of 21 junior boys and having a room of his own), his passing out exams were something of a disappointment, finishing in 336th place in the order of merit and giving the lowly rank of AC2. He was posted to 48 Squadron, servicing Ansons at its base in Eastchurch as a fitter II.

With war on the horizon, Tom volunteered for aircrew training and qualified as an air gunner. While his academic abilities may have let him down, his leadership qualities were still very much in evidence and he was identified as officer material. In the meantime, however, he had been posted to 76 Squadron, a heavy bomber squadron based at Linton-on-Ouse which soon after moved to Middleton St George. It was here that the squadron flew its first four-engined operations on the night of 12-13 June, and thereafter became a central part of Bomber Command's plans to destroy Germany's ability to wage war.

Tom's first op with 76 Squadron followed soon after, a successful raid on Kiel. Three days later he took part in another successful attack on the same target, though one of their number was lost, the first Halifax to be reported missing from air operations. On both of these operations, Tom was flying with a very experienced skipper, Austin Byrne. Byrne, an Irishman, already had more than 20 operations under his belt with 10 Squadron before exchanging his twin-engined Whitleys for the four-engined 'Halibag'.

On the night of 5-6 August, the target was Karlsruhe. Ninety-seven aircraft were taking part on what was a busy night for Bomber Command with three separate attacks. Halifax L9516 with Byrne at the controls made good progress and bombed the larger of the two fires they could see below. As they turned away from the target they were 'coned', and the pilot threw the aircraft into a series of gut-churning manoeuvres to escape the deadly beam. Despite his best efforts, the flak soon found them, and the shrapnel of exploding shells began tearing through the fuselage.

Byrne thrust the column forward to maintain some semblance of control, and at the same time ordered the crew to bail out. Each crew member in turn called out as they exited the aircraft, but there was no response from the second wireless operator, Brown. Byrne was also disconcerted to see his parachute pack disappear out of the forward escape hatch, and so was left with little option other than to remain with the aircraft. He later wrote:

> 'I stayed and managed to regain control of the aircraft. Eventually I was shot down from a low height by a fighter and by sheer luck managed to pull off a landing of sorts at the expense of a black eye, a broken cheekbone, and sundry bruises.'[4]

Byrne was indeed fortunate; he was knocked out on landing and spent some weeks in hospital recovering from his injuries and shock. Brown was not so lucky.

Of the rest of the crew, all made it out and were captured. Tom ditched his parachute harness and was on the run for only a few hours before he was spotted and arrested and taken to the barracks at Worms where he was interrogated. He was also reunited with another of the crew, Cyril Flockhart[5]. Soon after the pair were transferred for more formal interrogation at the Dulag Luft at Oberusel, and thence onward to a more permanent camp.

While in captivity, Tom's promotion to pilot officer was published in the *London Gazette*.

The story of the Great Escape has been well told on many occasions. The digging of three tunnels, Tom, Dick and Harry in a bid to achieve a mass breakout from Stalag Luft III, where all three of our Brats eventually ended up, is the stuff of legend.

For the escape from Hut 104 on the night of 24-25 March 1944 a long list of more than 500 names was created. The first 100 were those who had either contributed the most to the escape, and/or were considered to have the best chance of making a 'home run'. Jack Grisman, Edgar Humphreys, and Tom Leigh were all in the first batch.

Jack Grisman had known Squadron Leader Roger Bushell, the mastermind behind the Great Escape, since they had been fellow 'Kriegies' at Barth. As well as throwing himself into his studies, Jack had also committed himself to escaping. He was one of Bushell's most trusted lieutenants, and on the night of the escape was to act as a marshal, one of a dozen or so men who would wait in the forest after breaking free and 'collect' a pre-selected group of ten men who would be led westwards to give them the best start to their escape. Jack's group were some of the 'hard arsers', those who would rather trust to their feet rather than the trains.

Jack had been clear of the camp for no more than 50 minutes when the alarm sounded, and he set off on foot for Gorlitz. Not surprisingly he was not at liberty

Squadron Leader Arthur Cork MC
Apprentice in the 11th Entry

Top: *Graham 'Blondie' Hulse (left), one of the UK's least known but bravest fighter pilots who flew with the USAF in Korea.*

Middle: *The Military Cross won by Arthur Cork of the 11th Entry, defending his party from air attack en route to Greece.*

Bottom: *Canberras on the airfield at Luqa in Malta being prepared for operations against Suez.*

Top: *Close up of the wing of Pete Goodwin's Venom FB4, damaged by a cannon shell in a ground-attack operation in Aden.*

Bottom: *A fabulous air-to-air shot of a Venom F4B of 8 Squadron over Kormaksar, 1957.*

Opposite, top: *An underwing view of the damage done to Pete Goodwin's Venom showing how close he came to disaster.*

Bottom left: *Charles Long of the 56th Entry joined the Kenyan Police and won decorations for bravery both pre- and post-independence.*

Bottom right: *A post-war recruitment poster that captures some of the youth and excitement of an RAF apprenticeship.*

Left: *Taffy Holden of the 47th Entry with the Lightning in which he found himself unwillingly airborne.*

Squadron Leader Akmal Khan
Royal Pakistan Air Force
Apprentice in the 63rd Entry

Middle left: *Mohammad Younis was one of a number of apprentices from Pakistan who made senior rank and was said to have shot down an Indian spy plane in 1959.*

Middle right: *Medals awarded to Muhammad Akmal Khan of the 63rd Entry, who bravely fought off an attack by Indian commandos in the India-Pakistan War in 1965.*

Bottom: *Wally Epton in 1972 fulfilled a childhood dream in becoming a Spitfire pilot with the RAF Historic Aircraft Flight.*

Top: *Halton apprentices are expected to work on all manner of aircraft, including this Westland Whirlwind HAR.10.*

Middle: *What the best dressed station commander was wearing in 1996. Dusty at Lossiemouth, where all his birthdays came at once.*

Bottom left: *Instructing an apprentice on the intricacies of a modern jet's cockpit.*

Bottom right: *Brothers in Arms. Dusty Miller (210th Entry) at Lossiemouth in 1997 with his brother Clive who was also a Brat (in the 219th Entry).*

Top: *Guard of honour. Halton Boys flank the gun carriage carrying the body of Winston Churchill.*

Middle: *Apprentices at work in a neatly posed publicity shot.*

Bottom: *Nearest the camera is F.6 Hunter XE656, now part of the Auto und Technik Museum in Speyer, Germany*

Top: *An instructional airframe which was once a complete Jet Provost T-3, built in 1959.*

Middle: *Complete Jet Provosts were rather more common visitors to the Halton workshops.*

Bottom: *Jaguars and Harriers await the Brats' attention. The Jaguars in the foreground are from 17 Squadron; two Harriers furthest from the camera have 4 Squadron markings.*

Top: *Air Cdre Mike Evans presenting Dame Felicity Peake with a cheque for £1000 on the occasion of the dedication of a stone to commemorate all former RAF apprentices and boy entrants. Former apprentices MRAF Sir Keith Williamson (former CAS) and AM Sir Eric Dunn (former chief engineer RAF) are standing right.*

Bottom left: *The tribute to Halton apprentices, representing the brass cube test undertaken by every brat under training.*

Bottom right: *The memorial stone set in the pavement on the south side of St Clement Danes.*

for long and was soon once again 'in the bag' but facing a more uncertain future. He was taken to a collection point for escaped prisoners with 18 fellow POWs at Gorlitz prison and told that he would never see his wife again.

Along with Jack in that party of officers was Tom Leigh. Tom had been one of the first 50 to make it out and was another determined to keep to the woods and fields, rather than risk the railways and roads. He was on the run for several nights in near freezing conditions (several of his contemporaries suffered from frostbite) before his luck finally gave out.

Hunk Humphreys, 54 out of the tunnel, paired up with the next in line, Flight Lieutenant Paul Royle, an Australian, getting clear of the camp at around 02.30 hours. They headed south-east and made comparatively steady progress, despite the deep snow. As dawn broke, they opted to lie up for the day so as not to be seen, starting off again at dusk after little more than a couple of hours sleep between them.

Against their better judgement, they opted to keep to the road rather than the woods that would have offered them better shelter and protection. While the going was quicker, they were forever diving for cover to avoid contact, but eventually their luck ran out when confronted by a party of elderly Volksturm. Hunk and Paul attempted to bluff their way out but the Germans were having none of it. They were taken to the village of Tiefenfurt and shoved into a tiny cell in the local jail. They were only about 20 km from the camp.

On 30 March, three large sedans arrived at the prison in Gorlitz, and six prisoners were taken away. Among them was Tom Leigh. None of the men were ever seen again. The next day, Humphreys and nine others were taken away by the Gestapo in a covered truck. All were shot, and Hunk's remains cremated at Liegnitz.

On 6 April, at Gorlitz, Tony Bethell, a fellow prisoner, heard a list of names being read out that included Jack Grisman. Jack was never seen again. His body was cremated at Breslau and his remains are now buried at Poznań Old Garrison Cemetery.

All three men were awarded a mention in despatches.

Many years after the war the murderers of the 50 were brought to trial. By then, however, the killers of Humphreys and Leigh, Gestapo agent Lux and Wilhelm Scharpwinkel, were already dead, one in battle and the other in Soviet captivity in 1948. Scharpwinkel, the more senior of the two, was also responsible for the death of Jack Grisman. The man believed to have selected the 50 to be shot, SS Gruppenführer Arthur Nebe, was himself executed, ironically, for his part in the 20 July plot to assassinate Adolf Hitler.

In 2009, Air Vice-Marshal Nick Kurth of the 231st Entry represented the RAF at an international gathering of dignitaries and relatives of those who died in the Great Escape at an unveiling of a replica of Hut 104 from where the escape was mounted.

13 SPECIAL DUTIES

Bob Lewis came from a large service family. When originally applying to join the RAF, he did not have his birth certificate and neither could he get it, since his father was at sea. Eventually part of the 40th Entry (the last of the pre-war entries), Bob qualified as a fitter IIE after a truncated course of only 20 months, and on passing out was posted to a repair and salvage unit, 67 MU in Taunton.

He attempted to remuster for pilot training only to have his ambitions thwarted by his commanding officer who deemed his expertise too valuable to lose. It was therefore not until the summer of 1942, shortly after his 18th birthday, that Bob took advantage of the introduction of new four-engined aircraft and began aircrew training in the new category of flight engineer.

After gunnery school at RAF Walney Island in Barrow-in-Furness (10 AGS), during which he attained an above average rating firing at drogues from the turret of a Defiant, Bob completed his flight engineer's course at St Athan in December 1942. His logbook is signed by the senior training officer at 4 School of Technical Training, and fellow apprentice, Gerry Blacklock.

Very specifically, Bob passed out as a flight engineer on flying boats, and one in particular – the Consolidated Catalina. The Catalina was a very long-range, ocean patrol flying boat which entered service with the RAF in early 1941. It was popular with its crews and also popular with the men of the Atlantic convoys for whom it offered anti-submarine protection. It was the observant crew of a Catalina that spotted and shadowed the *Bismarck*, after contact had initially been lost, and helped ensure her destruction.

Posted to 131 OTU Killadeas in Fermanagh, Northern Ireland, Bob flew training flights with a number of pilots over the succeeding months[1], also qualifying as a first fitter on the designated type and no longer having to be accompanied by an instructor. In May 1943, he teamed up with an Australian pilot who was to become his regular skipper and a firm friend, Flying Officer Bruce Daymond. In the summer, some of the men of 131 OTU formed an operational flight under the command of South African-born Squadron Leader Frank Godber DFC, and flew sorties, escorting various merchant ships (including the RMS *Aquitania*, a former luxury liner) and convoys passing in range.

Posted to 302 Ferry Training Unit (FTU) in November 1943 pending service with a squadron overseas, Bob flew in a Sunderland as a passenger on a long-haul trip to India via Gibraltar, the Gambia, Sierra Leone, Nigeria, French Equatorial Africa, the Belgian Congo, Kenya, Tanganyika, Madagascar, the Seychelles and the Maldives before finally emplaning at Madras. In all the journey took just one day short of a month.

Now part of 240 Squadron, Bob recommenced operations almost immediately, flying anti-submarine patrols over the Indian Ocean. On one occasion they did a sweep of an area where a Japanese sub had been reported. A badly damaged merchant vessel, heavily listing to starboard, was all the proof they needed of the danger that lurked below.

In March 1944, Bob and his skipper joined 628 Squadron (via 357 Squadron to which they had been briefly attached), a unit formed to provide special duties but for much if its life carried out long and arduous Met reconnaissance. On 6 September, however, Bob and his crew were detailed for a special operation – code name Balmoral – to drop three agents (two US army lieutenants and their Malay guide) on Davis Island on the Burmese-Siam border. The agents' mission was to send back movements and strength of Japanese shipping and forces operating between Singapore and Rangoon. They were also to reconnaissance the island's suitability for a future landing.

The nine-man crew included two pilots – Squadron Leader Peter McKeand and Flight Lieutenant Bruce Daymond. A tenth man – a US major general – was also onboard to supervise the operation[2].

For three days prior to the operation, the crew practised taking off with the extra weight. At the briefing, they were told that some opposition was to be expected, and as such they would be escorted by a second Catalina ('R' Robert flown by Flight Lieutenant J. O'Meara) to provide additional firepower as needed. Liberators would also carry out a diversionary raid on the railways at Hnohngpladuk to keep the Japanese looking the other way[3].

The take-off did not go as planned, the pilots finding it impossible to get the flying boats to leave the water in the confined space of a harbour. Even when towed out further to sea, it took Bob's Catalina a run of more than three minutes (and six extremely bad bounces) before she finally began flying rather than floating, and not until her hull had been badly dented in the process. The second flying boat was also damaged.

On the long leg to the drop-off point, they sighted a Japanese submarine and dropped to below 50 ft to avoid detection by enemy radar. They were obliged to take further avoiding action when they emerged through a storm cloud and heavy rain to find clear skies and a small convoy of enemy merchant vessels escorted by two destroyers. Gunners on the destroyers opened fire but without effect.

By 18.00 hours, the Catalinas had made landfall, but encountered a problem. Told that the island was uninhabited they arrived to find that it was anything but. A large Japanese troopship was lying in anchor and several Japanese soldiers were walking on the beach. Bob's aircraft turned in and opened fire, strafing the ship and the men on the shore. Some of the soldiers returned fire, but the Catalina sped away without being hit.

Without any chance of being able to land the agent on Davis, the US general decided to explore Chance Island as an alternative. As far as was discernible, the enemy was nowhere to be seen, and a landing was attempted. They did so in a heavy swell, causing the boat to leak. Bob's contemporary account of the operation needs no embellishment:

> 'Taxiing towards the shore, a machine gun opened up on us from the jungle. The pilot opened up the engines and got out of sight around the north corner of the island. We stopped engines and anchored about 60 yards from the shore. It was quite dark by now as the moon had not risen.'

By 19.00 hours, it began to become light, and the agents prepared to land:

> 'They blew up their dinghy and loaded it. Their work had to stop on two occasions as several large sharks threatened to overturn the dinghy. They pushed off at 19.20 hours and paddled for the shore. It was very bright by now and there was only the sound of the surf on the reef. A ship was reported as approaching but passed very close to us without seeing us as we were lying with the jungle at our back.'

The crew waited anxiously as the agents paddled to the shore. An hour passed without word that they were safe. Then the walkie talkie crackled to confirm all was well: "Hello ashes and cans. Hello ashes and cans. Everything quiet. Over."

With their mission now accomplished, the pilots restarted the engines and turned the boat into wind for take-off. Again, they were not helped by the swell and after several large bounces – and further damage to the hull and the port float – they finally groped their way into the sky. Bob could see fires and explosions some way off the starboard beam, proof that the Liberators had found their target and were having a busy night of it.

They returned to base without further incident after a marathon trip of 25 hours and ten minutes, landing alongside their support Catalina. Bob's boat was considered too badly damaged to repair.

Now with something of an appetite for special duties work, it was not long before the crew was once again called for a secret mission, this time involving an agent known as 'Barn Owl'. Operation Barn Owl I called for a landing at Bentinck Island, 14 miles to the west of Mergui, to collect eight Japanese prisoners who had been captured by four British agents under the command of 'Captain Nicholls' of the Kachin Levies – a Special Force in Burma, created and commanded by the British but comprising mainly Kachin people. One of the Allied party was also wounded.

Operation Barn Owl I was spectacularly unsuccessful. Daymond on this occasion was the lead captain, with Flying Officer C. Brown DFC in the second pilot's seat. Captain Toms of the Burma Frontier Force was acting as supervisor. Bad weather and appalling visibility led the skipper to abandon the operation and head back to base, discretion being the better part of valour.

Two days later, on 4 October, and with the same crew and brief, they tried again, this time with considerably better luck. But it was not without its excitement. No word had been received from the agents since the squadron's first attempt at rescue on the 2nd. A Mosquito had been sent in to attempt visual contact but chased away by Japanese fighters. Bad weather was an ongoing issue, but more concerning was whether the Japanese prisoners were still alive or whether they had over-powered their captors. Hand grenades and sub-machine guns were loaded onto the Catalina; they weren't taking any risks. They would also once again have a support boat, though the second Catalina's pilot had strict orders not to land if the primary boat was caught on the water.

The long flight out was particularly strenuous for the pilot after George, the automatic pilot, packed up almost immediately. They spotted the island shortly after 21.00 hours and approached at 20 ft. Almost every pair of eyes, if not looking for enemy fighters, was staring into the night, hoping to spot a torch, blinking three, five-second flashes to indicate all was well. The rear gunner spotted an aircraft above, and they held their breaths as it passed over, but without them being seen.

Although no signal came, the skipper decided to land, bringing the boat down in yet another heavy swell. He taxied closer to the beach and then cut his engines. Every gun was trained on the shore, ready to open up at the first sign of trouble. Half an hour passed and then a small boat was spotted, and then another. The sound of an aircraft's engines could be heard overhead, and the crew were relieved to see it was their support boat, preparing to land. Three small boats were now heading towards them as Bob later wrote:

> 'At last no-one could stand the suspense of waiting whilst these boats were
> coming in so the skipper shouted, "Halt! Who goes there?" There was no
> answer, so he shouted again: "Halt or we fire!" This time a voice came from
> the leading boat but we could not make out what was being said. It cer-
> tainly didn't sound like English. "Give the password," the skipper said, and

this time very clearly came the cry, "Victory". At last we were relieved to recognise Captain Nicholls in the leading boat. Nick told us that he hadn't expected us, and that his wounded man was ashore. He also informed us that the prisoners had tried to escape and were all shot and killed, and their bodies dumped in the lagoon for the sharks. This was quite a relief to us as we had not liked the idea of carrying the prisoners with us.'

Nick explained that he had not used his torch as there were too many Japanese about and he did not want to give away his position. His wireless was also broken, so they were glad of the spare parts and the two spare men they had brought with them. After some to-ing and fro-ing, the wounded man was recovered to the Catalina, good-byes said, and best wishes given. The only concern was that there was now no sign of their support boat.

Notwithstanding the challenges, accentuated by a shortage of fuel, FP134 managed to make it safely to base. On arrival they discovered their fellow travellers had already landed, but their boat had sunk, having hit some coral on take-off. The wounded agent was taken to hospital where he quickly recovered, and the mission was chalked up as a success.

No. 628 Squadron was disbanded in the first week of October, and Bob transferred to 240 Squadron under the command of Wing Commander Basil Wood, a flying boat specialist and world-class fencing champion. Barn Owl III led to tragedy, and the loss of K240 shot down by Japanese fighters, with Flight Lieutenant Rolf Luck DFC at the controls. Two other secret operations – Biff I on 29 October, and Biff II two nights later – were a success. So too Barn Owl IV, the operation that led to an immediate DSO for Bob's skipper, Bruce Daymond.

In an interview given in 2004, Bob described those days in some detail, and in particular made reference to his flight on the night of 4 November:

> "We operated during the moon periods flying along the Ten Degree Channel between the Andaman and Nicobar Islands, and into Burma, Malay and Siam, picking up and dropping off agents.
>
> "The operations were 'hairy' in that they necessitated flying at night before the moon had risen, not above 100 ft, to keep under radar coverage. We had asked for radio altimeters but these didn't arrive. The 14th Army in Burma is always described as the forgotten army, but actually everyone was forgotten out there. Consequently, when flying on operations we calibrated our altimeters at last light by trimming the aircraft nose-up, then descending slowly; when we touched the water the altimeters were set.
>
> "Some of the flights were of 25-hour duration or more (the aircraft were specially adapted with additional fuel tanks) which required incredible

concentration, especially from the pilot. We had six crews initially but only two at the end. After one operation to pick up a group of men from an island in the Kra Archipelago we arrived with a back-up aircraft to find a Japanese submarine waiting; presumably they thought the pick-up was going to be by an Allied sub. My skipper (Bruce Daymond) decided to land anyway. After a great deal of hassle, we picked up the agents but our back-up aircraft disappeared in the melee."

Bob dramatically underplays events that night. The agents signalled from the shore that they were ready to be picked up. They had seen the submarine earlier in the day but were convinced it had gone. They did not realise it had returned during the night, and they were now in great danger. Daymond asked Bob to man the bow turret to keep a sharp eye out for obstructions as they came into land. It was only at the last moment that Bob spotted the enemy submarine, but Daymond was committed to his approach. He had no intention of leaving the agents to the enemy.

As they zoomed over the sub's conning tower, they expected a searchlight or the crackle of cannon fire but there was nothing. Daymond killed the engines and allowed momentum to take them closer to the shore. Being a Devon lad with sailing experience, Bob dropped a lead line to measure the depth of the water and get them as close to the shore as possible.

The agents on the beach began to row frantically towards the Catalina in a rubber dinghy, urged on in stage whispers by the crew. Keen hands grabbed at the men – one of whom was seriously ill with malaria – and hauled them on board in double quick time. They punctured the dinghies with knives and let them sink. Draymond restarted the aircraft, reassured by the power of the Pratt and Whitney engines, and began churning up the water that was otherwise dead calm. It would help shorten the take-off run. The submarine was by now aware of their presence and sought to block their escape. With more than a dozen men in the aircraft, conditions were cramped, and the additional weight would be an issue.

The Catalina needed about 75 knots at least to become airborne; the pilot opened up, as the navigator called out the speed. Just when it looked like they wouldn't make it Bruce hauled back on the stick and just cleared the sub as it opened fire. Now they were through, but not yet out of danger.

Their journey home would take them close to a Japanese fighter base on the Andaman Islands but again the enemy must have had other things on their minds, or else the decision to head south at 50 ft through an horrendous squall had foxed their controllers. Neither Bob, nor his skipper, can explain how they got away with it. On the water they would have been sitting ducks, and even in the air they did not rate their chances against the nimble Zeros. All of the guns had been removed to save weight and maximise fuel efficiency. They were effectively defenceless.

"At debriefing it was decided that our skipper should be up for a VC but due to the secret nature of the operation, and the fact a citation in the *London Gazette* would be required, he was awarded an immediate DSO. The two surviving skippers collected three DSOs and four DFCs between them."

The operation did not go unnoticed and resulted in a congratulatory note from Air Marshal Guy Garrod (later Air Chief Marshal Sir Guy Garrod GBE, KCB, MC, DFC), deputy commander-in-chief, South East Asia. It stated:

'I have read with interest the report of sortie 7, dated 4 November, by your squadron. I would like to congratulate the Captain, Flight Lieutenant B. G. Daymond and the crew of Catalina F of your squadron for their excellent work on this occasion.'

In the same note, Garrod references four recent operations conducted by the crew totalling 95 hours and 11 minutes of flying time.

Japanese surrender in 1945.

Bob continued flying into the new year, completing his final special duties flight (Operation Influx) on the night of 30 January with Wing Commander Wood and Flight Lieutenant Ridgeway at the controls, both of whom were subsequently decorated. He also found time when not operating for some dual instruction on a Tiger Moth with Group Captain Brougham.

By now commissioned, he returned to the UK tour-expired in April. Prior to his departure, he was rated by Wing Commander Wood as being above average, the CO describing him as 'a very efficient and keen member of aircrew who has shown stamina and initiative in several very long-distance special duties operational flights'.

Joining 230 HCU at Lindholme with the intention of returning to the Far East as part of Tiger Force, the end of the war saw a posting to Portreath (as station adjutant) before eventually retiring in 1948 in the rank of flight lieutenant. In peacetime he helped run a Cornish hotel before going into business as a wholesale baker with one of his five brothers, another Halton apprentice of 1931 vintage. He retired in 1983.

14 MiG KILLER

Many a Halton Brat trained as an apprentice and went on to fly fast jets, but there are few, if any, who not only flew Spitfires in combat but also F-86 Sabres, and fewer still who could claim victories over an Italian Macchi, Croatian Messerschmitt and a Chinese MiG. Graham Hulse managed all of these achievements and more, for he also had a price put on his head by Jewish terrorists during the post-war struggle for Palestine.

Originally from the railway town of Crewe in Cheshire, Graham Hulse was born on 11 April 1920, and from an early age had always been interested in aircraft. As a journeyman student at Newcastle-under-Lyme High School, he successfully navigated the entrance exam for Halton, and arrived at the camp in January 1936

Graham Hulse (third from the left in the back row).

as part of the 33rd Entry – the self-proclaimed 'famous' entry that served under three kings – George V, Edward VIII and George VI. He passed out three years later as a fitter II, finishing 123 in the order of merit.

Determined to fly he was finally granted his wish, qualifying as a sergeant fighter pilot and receiving his first operational posting, to 122 'Bombay' Squadron, in the summer of 1942. The squadron had moved to Hornchurch in March, and was for a time commanded by a Belgian, Squadron Leader Léon Prévot. Prévot was shot down over France on 30 July, and so at the beginning of August, and coinciding with Graham's arrival, a 31-year-old New Zealander was in charge: Squadron Leader John Kilian, a pre-war regular. Kilian had joined the RNZAF in 1937. He later went on to command 504 Squadron and survived the war. Among Graham's contemporaries at 122 was another notable apprentice, Jim Hallowes.

Fighter sweeps were the order of the day, Graham being involved in a number of circus, rhubarb and rodeo operations, either escorting small formations of light bombers or simply flying in pairs, shooting up any targets of opportunity that came into range of his cannon. Standing patrols and scrambles were also a routine part of everyday squadron life.

Graham flew his first patrol on the morning of 3 August, but it was not until the afternoon of 11 October, more than two months later, that he had his first notable contact with the enemy. Six squadron pilots had taken off at 13.20 hours on a rodeo when they spotted a force of some 20 or so Fw 190s over St Omer. Three of Yellow Section (led by Yellow 1 – Flight Lieutenant Charlton 'Wag' Haw DFM) peeled off to attack the fighters which were 4,000 ft below them. Possibly because of the dive, Graham – flying as Yellow 2 – came in too fast and almost came to grief as his subsequent combat report attests:

> 'I opened fire with a one-second mixed burst but was going so quickly that I had to cease fire and push my stick forward, thus going underneath to avoid ramming him. I saw strikes on the port trailing edge and engine cowling. I did a climbing left turn to get back in position but by this time the enemy aircraft had dived away inland.'

Graham claimed the Fw 190 as damaged.

After almost six months with the squadron he was posted away to North Africa, and after six weeks of doing very little was posted from the Reinforcement Pool to 81 Squadron at Bône in Algeria, arriving in February 1943. At the time the squadron was under the command of another New Zealander, the mercurial Colin Gray, prior to his promotion to wing commander.

The Allies had won splendid victories at both the first and second Battles of Alamein, and the once mighty German Afrika Korps was steadily being squeezed into defeat. The Luftwaffe, however, was still very much a force to be reckoned with, and combats were far from one-sided.

Often flying from temporary airfields with matted runways Graham claimed a Bf 109 damaged on 8 March after an early morning scramble, a probable on April 28 during a freelance sweep over Medjez el Bab, and a Macchi MC202 as damaged on 14 June while on a sweep of Comiso. All were claimed while flying a Spitfire IX. On 16 July, flying a clapped-out Spitfire V, he claimed another Bf 109G as a probable – a remarkable feat given the aircraft's comparatively poor performance at height.

By now, and with the Germans defeated in North Africa, the squadron had withdrawn to Malta to cover the Allied landings in Sicily, hence coming into more regular conflict with their Italian counterparts. By now also, Graham had been commissioned and already promoted.

It was as Flying Officer Hulse that Graham began flying with 94 Squadron in the late spring of 1944 (81 Squadron had deployed to the Far East at the end of 1943) based out of Bu Amud in Libya. Much of the early summer was spent supporting Marauder and Baltimore bombers of the South African Air Force (SAAF) on bombing operations to Crete. The squadron moved bases no fewer than three times in as many months, much to the annoyance of the ground crews and administrative personnel and the disruption this caused. In September, the squadron was pulled out of the line, resuming operations in late October from Kalamaki. It did not start well. On their arrival at Kalamaki, two Spitfires collided on the runway and caught fire. One of the pilots escaped, but the second, a South African, burned to death. The month ended badly with the loss of their Australian squadron commander, Squadron Leader Russell Foskett DFC. His aircraft developed engine trouble and Foskett was obliged to take to his parachute. Though he landed in the sea, he could not be saved.

Briefly under the command of Squadron Leader Hugh McLachlan DFC, a Canadian, until the arrival of a permanent replacement, Squadron Leader Jack Slade DFC, the pace of operations accelerated in the last winter months of 1944 as the Germans were expelled from the Greek mainland and operations moved across the border into Yugoslavia. This was a testing time for Graham and the squadron, which as well as its British and Commonwealth officers and NCOs, also had a contingent of Yugoslav pilots, some of whom were wont to make trouble for their supposed Allies. Revolution and rebellion, even at a squadron level, were never far away.

Early operations in November were often flown in the company of Wing Commander Patrick 'Woody' Woodruff DSO DFC, a former bomber pilot, including a successful armed reconnaissance at the start of the month. On 9 November, Graham had a lucky escape. Flying as section leader, he was briefed for a strafing attack on the railway running between Veles and Skopje[1]. He successfully shot up a locomotive and some wagons but was met by a barrage of deadly flak and his Spitfire Vc was hit. Happily, he made it home, no doubt chastened by his experience. Two days later he was part of a two-section attack on a concentration of rail traffic, during which the Spitfires also claimed a Bf 109 as damaged to the north of Priština.

In December, their targets changed again. Rather than harrying the Germans in retreat, the squadron was called upon to support the British Army as it sought to counter a communist uprising in Greece led by the Greek People's Liberation Army (ELAS), the most powerful armed resistance movement. A civil war erupted in Athens between ELAS and those Greeks still loyal to the King.

Graham returned to operations as a flight commander with 213 Squadron. The squadron was commanded by Squadron Leader Peter Vaughan Fowler whose principal claim to fame was as an SOE pilot, flying agents in and out of France at the dead of night in unarmed Lysanders.

For Graham it meant yet another change in aircraft, exchanging the doughty Spitfire Vs and IXs for the Packard Merlin-powered Mustang III, flying as part of the Balkan air force in Biferno. This was a continuation, in many ways, of his recent operations over Greece, tasked with fighter sweeps over Yugoslavia and Albania. Armed-reconnaissance operations were also a preferred role, the sturdy and reliable Mustangs being adapted to carry 1,000-lb bombs.

Despite the war steadily drawing to a close, throughout the spring of 1945, Graham was flying almost every day, attacking marshalling yards, railway locomotives, motorised transport and anything else that came into his gunsight. He also flew escort missions for SAAF Beaufighters operating in the area. On 17 April, in a bombing attack, he scored a direct hit on a bridge but because of the time delay on the bomb, he only succeeded in holing rather than destroying it. On 19 April he flew two sorties in a single day, and for the latter was guided onto his target (a gun emplacement) by a ground controller, the first time such a practice had been executed.

Graham made his final claim of the war on 23 April 1945. Three aircraft (Graham was flying a Mustang IVa) took off in the late morning from Prkos on an armed reconnaissance, though one of their number was obliged to return early. The two remaining Mustangs carried on to attack a concentration of motorised transport and locomotives, with little success, and were then jumped by two Bf 109s with yellow tails and spinners from 2. Lovacko Jato ZNDH. Almost immediately, Graham's wingman, Flying Officer Francis Barrett, called up to say he had been hit in the port wing. As the Messerschmitts broke off the attack, Graham followed them, chasing them down to 2,000 ft and closing in for the kill. He opened fire on one of them at close range, striking the enemy aircraft on the port wing and fuselage. Bits of the aeroplane began to break off and black smoke began billowing from its engine. With his leader now out of ammunition, Barrett – having recovered from his earlier scare – began firing on the enemy himself, but was forced to break away as his own aircraft was hit by flak. Only Graham's Mustang managed to make it back to base. Barrett was posted as missing and was later confirmed as killed in action. Graham was allowed to claim the 109 as damaged.

Incidentally, a very different version of events is told in the book *Aircraft of the Aces – Legends of the Skies* (Tony Holmes, Osprey Publishing, 2004). The two Messerschmitts were being flown by two Croatian pilots, satnik Ljudevit Bencetic (in a 109G-10 Black 22) and his wingman, porucnik Mihajlo Jelak (in a 109G-14 Black 27). They were returning from an uneventful patrol east of Zagreb when they spotted the two Mustangs and positioned themselves to attack. Bencetic opened fire from a range of 260 ft, hitting the Mustang's radiator and wings and setting the aircraft on fire. Barrett attempted to escape, but a second burst from Bencetic's guns at an even closer range tore into the Mustang's fuselage and the aircraft was seen to crash. Jelak, the wingman, claimed to have attacked Graham's aircraft and shot him down, prior to two more Mustangs arriving on the scene and forcing him to crash land near Velika Gorica. Bencetic's victory was his 16th and last of the war credited to a Croatian pilot in the Second World War.

With the war's end, Graham moved with the squadron to Brindisi and then onwards to Ramat David (today one of three principal airbases used by the Israel air force), located south-east of Haifa. He was also awarded the DFC for his sustained period of operations, the announcement appearing in the *London Gazette* on 21 August.

This was a difficult time for the British armed forces and the RAF especially, finding themselves in the middle of a growing conflict between the Arabs and Jews in Palestine. The British had refused entry to more than 100,000 Jewish immigrants, heightening tension in the region and causing the Jewish underground fighters to unite.

A conference between the Jews and the Arabs in September 1946 ended in deadlock, coming as it did after the more extreme Jewish terrorist groups had conducted a series of atrocities, including the bombing of the British Officers' Club in Haifa and the bombing of the King David Hotel, resulting in more than 100 deaths.

It was against this background that Graham and 213 Squadron flew a number of reconnaissance patrols, principally on the lookout for illegal shipping. He was also, from November 1945, temporarily in charge of the squadron, until the arrival of Squadron Leader Nash. It was on one such patrol that he spotted and reported the approach of an illegal refugee ship, the *Enzo Sereni*, attempting to break the Royal Navy blockade[2]. His report led to the ship's capture by a Royal Navy destroyer. He was no doubt dismayed to later hear his name being given out on Jewish radio, amid calls for retribution should he be caught.

Graham was granted a permanent commission and converted from piston engine to jet engine with ease. Peacetime flying, however, still had its dangers, as Graham was to discover on more than one occasion while instructing at the Central Flying School at Little Rissington in the summer of 1950.

The date was 29 June, and Graham was flying a Gloster Meteor T Mk7 (WA668), practising manoeuvres for a forthcoming Farnborough display. With a reputation for daredevil flying, especially inverted, no-one was particularly surprised when they saw the Meteor race across the airfield and pull up, passing through 500 ft at about a 40-degree climb. They were surprised, however, to see both sides of his tailplane fall apart, and the aircraft continue to climb until it fell apart completely, the wings parting company with the fuselage and falling to earth. Somehow Graham managed to release his harness and bale out from what was left of his aeroplane, his parachute opening only moments before hitting the ground.

Gathering his canopy and shroud lines he noticed a car coming towards him and flagged it down. The old lady who stopped asked him if he was the pilot of the aircraft she had just seen break apart in the sky. When he said that he was, she told him he ought to be more careful, and promptly drove off, leaving the crest-fallen fighter pilot by the roadside.

Not long after this incident, Graham was despatched to the US to demonstrate the Boulton Paul Balliol as an advanced military training aircraft. He was also awarded the King's Commendation for Valuable Service in the Air in the New Year's Honours of 1951 and a request that he join the United States Air Force on an exchange posting. The exchange proved to be both a blessing and a curse, for it coincided with the growing hostilities on the Korean Peninsula that ultimately led to a full-scale war between the North and the South, and the intervention of US, Chinese and Russian forces that for a time might well have escalated into a third global conflict.

Graham was attached to the 336th Squadron of the USAF 4th Fighter Interceptor Wing, flying the powerful F-86 Sabre, and given command of C Flight. Converting to the type took eight weeks. Highly manoeuvrable and with a General Electric turbojet engine giving it a top speed of approaching 700 mph, the North American F-86 was considered the only jet aircraft that could take on the Russian Mikoyan-Gurevich MiG-15 'Fagot' on equal terms. Its .5-inch machine guns were no match for the cannon-armed MiGs, but the Sabre pilots had the benefit of experience, a large number of them having flown combat missions in the Second World War.

Houston Tuel, a contemporary of Graham's at Kimpo airbase, a rather desultory spot surrounded by paddy fields, said Graham's pilots idolised him. He was always keen to impart his knowledge to the junior men in his flight. Tall, blond and affable, fellow pilots would listen enthralled by Graham's tales from the war: 'His skill as a storyteller was legendary,' Tuel wrote later[3].

Another contemporary, Jim Thompson, who knew Graham well, similarly remembers him as a worthy addition to the unit:

"Graham was well regarded and was a with-it, skilled pilot with whom and for whom I flew wing. I remember him well, as I do another junior English pilot who would always cry 'Tally Ho' when he saw the enemy."[4]

Graham's skills as a fighter pilot also quickly achieved legendary status as they were thrown into combat against the North Korean forces.

Graham opened his scoring at the end of October 1952 when he shared in the destruction of a MiG-15 near Sinuiju (the fighter had been shot up by the flight leader) and followed this up in the second week of December with a confirmed MiG-15 near Wonsong-Dong. Graham had been escorting a Lockheed RF-80 reconnaissance aircraft at 30,000 ft on a photo-recce operation when the ever-alert Englishman spotted two MiGs some 25,000 ft below. As he recounted to a journalist from *Flight* magazine at the time: "They were just across the Yalu at 5,000 ft," he recalled, "so I dived after them and shot one down."[5]

The camouflaged MiG with its distinctive red stars had at first tried to outclimb him, but Graham had built up considerable speed and momentum in the dive and the MiG was unable to escape him. He gave it three bursts, hitting the wings and the fuselage. Then the canopy flew off and the pilot ejected at 8,000 ft. The pilotless aircraft crashed into a sandbank just off the coast, its final resting place marked by a spiral of black smoke.

Graham's success was acknowledged with the award of a US DFC and an RAF promotion to squadron leader. He was also awarded the Queen's Commendation for Valuable Service in the Air, a new monarch now being on the throne. His combat successes continued into the new year of 1953, damaging a MiG on 27 January. He'd spotted the aircraft at 40,000 ft, and managed to manoeuvre onto its tail. "I nipped in behind him at .96, and hit him three times before he got out of range," he said afterwards.

By March, Graham was approaching the end of his tour in Korea. Keen to return home for the coronation, he had opted to forego an extension that would have taken him past 100 missions. On 13 March, he took off for his 95th mission. In the company of his wingman, Major Eugene Sommerich, they soon spotted a MiG nearing the Yalu River (the Yalu borders China and North Korea). Graham attacked, and had the satisfaction of seeing his bullets strike home. Pretty quickly the MiG began smoking heavily and lost speed, probably because of a damaged engine. Graham passed the MiG on its starboard side and then, inexplicably, turned to port and in front of the wounded enemy pilot who snapped off a quick deflection shot. He got lucky, blowing several feet off the Sabre's left wing. At the same time, Sommerich had started to shoot, his gun camera recording his leader's demise[6].

What happened next is unclear. Some reports suggest that Graham was seen to eject over the peninsula known as 'Long Dong' and was reportedly seen alive on the ground. A large but ultimately futile rescue operation was mounted as soon as weather allowed, but without any luck.

Squadron Leader Graham 'Blondie' Hulse DFC, one of the UK's least known but bravest fighter pilots, is still officially listed as 'missing in action'.

Graham Hulse was not the only ex-Halton apprentice to see combat in Korea. Roy Watson of the 49th Entry was also tempted by exchange duties with the USAF, forsaking his Vampire of 94 Squadron to train on both the F-84B and C at Luke Air Force Base. He survived and remembers arriving in the combat zone:

> "Clifford Meier[7], the CO, welcomed me to the 311th and I was given a camp bed, blankets and bed space. Additional furnishings could apparently be obtained from the supply officer with the aid of old packing cases, hammer and nails."

Roy's experience as a ground-attack pilot came in useful:

> "The first mission was a rail cut at Chaeryong County, an easy lead in. Then followed a rapid series of close air support and attacks on supply areas well to the north. After a while the really serious business began with attacks on big bridges at Sinanju. Fifth Air Force did not use their imagination on that series; they had us all going in at the same time from the same direction for three days running. We had to hand it to the opposition who sent MiGs in through their own flak to get us."

Flying a mix of combat air patrols and interdiction sorties, the US gradually amended their tactics from a four-aircraft flight to a two- or three-wing attack: "An important addition was the single mission night interdiction which consisted of an armed recce, a search for trains, or attacks on the repair work being carried out on previously damaged bridges."

Roy completed some 100 combat missions in Korea before being rested and considers the experience as being a very special period in his life:

> "Overall I was lucky I had previous ground-attack experience and that the CO gave me his support, making me C Flight commander. Also, the squadron was going through a very successful period helped by the F-84G Sabre – a fine combat aircraft which in many ways was ahead of its time."

15 WAR OPS: SUEZ

Mike Hines was late arriving at RAF Halton. Most of the 63rd Entry reported on 6 September 1949, but for some reason, Mike arrived on 20 September, in the company of another who was to distinguish himself in later life, Derek 'Min' Larkin. The two had met on the train between Baker Street and Wendover: "During our three years at Halton Min had almost as many jankers as anyone in the entry, and yet went on to achieve a higher rank than any of us," Mike recalls.

Originally from Wolverhampton, where his father was a dental technician, Mike moved with his family to Wales when his father embarked on a new profession as a policeman, eventually becoming assistant chief constable of the Mid-Wales Constabulary. The young Mike became fascinated by aircraft during the war through a favourite uncle who served as a ground gunner and was a keen model maker. Mike remembers particularly his models of a Lerwick, a Lysander and a Stirling. From that moment on, he never looked back:

> "After my school certificate, the headmaster filled out the forms to enable me to join the RAF as an apprentice, but it subsequently turned out that the completed forms were to join the Royal Navy as an artificer. Quickly the situation was rectified, and I went to RAF Hornchurch to take the requisite tests which I passed to be trained as an airframe fitter.
>
> "At Halton it was my first time away from home, and I was more than a little homesick, but the training all seemed so natural and interesting. Sergeant Bradbrook and Corporal Corbett were two NCOs I remember as being particularly alarming."

Mike's first task, like every apprentice, was to take the surface off a piece of mild steel with the use of a hammer and cold chisel. Most of his time, when not square bashing, was divided between the workshops and schools, one moment learning how to repair a tyre or stitch new Irish linen onto a frame, and the next creating engineering drawings or solving calculus equations. His contemporaries included

Mike receiving the Queen's Colour.

not only many of those who had come from their local grammar schools and technical colleges, but also the first apprentices from Pakistan who faced a tougher time than most because English was their second language.

After three years he passed out top of his entry as an airframe fitter in the new rank of junior technician. A few days before passing out he had the honour of receiving the Queen's Colour from the then uncrowned Queen Elizabeth on behalf of No. 1 School of Technical Training. Mike is believed to be the first non-commissioned serviceman in the RAF (and possibly in the other services) to receive a Royal Colour and to carry it on a ceremonial parade. It established a tradition in the RAF that the No. 1 SofTT Colour may be carried by an NCO on ceremonial occasions, as indeed it sometimes is to this day. It similarly remains the only royal colour to be awarded to a military youth training school in any of the services.

Others playing a crucial part that day included Flight Sergeant Apprentice (later Wing Commander) Lionel Parkin. Lionel was the escort squadron commander. After the presentation of the colour, the escort squadron had to perform a complete ceremonial parade in front of Her Majesty, Lord Trenchard, and many other high dignitaries. Lionel had the most nerve-wracking job of all. Memorising all the parade sequences and relevant orders was a severe test of the nerves for a 19-year-old. He remains the only apprentice to have commanded a parade for the Queen.

Perhaps more significantly, Mike was also one of two from the entry who were awarded a Cranwell cadetship. The other being Peter Papworth who later went on to Shackletons and subsequently became a wing commander and chief flying instructor at RAF Oakington.

Prior to flying training, Mike was 'graded' at Digby on Tiger Moths, to demonstrate he had at least some talent as a pilot, before training began in earnest at Cranwell on the ever-reliable Chipmunk, and then on the Merlin-powered Balliol.

Passing out as part of the 64th Entry (Cranwell cadet entry) in April 1955, Mike was awarded his wings by the commandant of Cranwell, Air Commodore

Henry Eeles[1], and distinguished himself further by winning the Sword of Honour, granted to the most outstanding student cadet of the entry. This was presented to him the day after receiving his wings by Air Chief Marshal Sir Arthur Sanders, the one-armed commandant of the Imperial Defence College.

Mike then progressed to 211 Flying Training School at RAF Worksop to convert to Meteors (the T4 and Meteor 8), and after a spell at Lindholme, observing bombing from the Varsity, he arrived at 231 Operational Conversion Unit (231 OCU) at RAF Bassingbourn to convert to the English Electric Canberra.

Mike had read about the Canberra and had learned something

Mike Hines pictured with a Tiger Moth after his first solo flight on 15 August 1952.

of its performance. First demonstrated to the public at Farnborough in the hands of the great test pilot Roland Beamont, the Canberra was not only economical on fuel, even at high cruising speeds, but it was also highly manoeuvrable. It was an instant success. Some marks of Canberra, however, were not without their foibles:

"Sadly, my first instructor, Flying Officer Jason Spokes, was killed in a tragic accident when the tail trim ran away on the Canberra he was flying and failed to eject. I had to complete my conversion in T4s with another student in the other seat. The Canberra was a delightful aircraft to fly; its only vice was if it was mishandled[2].

"It was some time before the flying course was started. Whereas there were plenty of pilots, navigators were in short supply. When I did finally crew up my navigator, Flight Lieutenant Russ Anderson, who'd won bombing prizes while flying in Lancasters, must have been delighted to have found himself with a sprog pilot."

Pilot and navigator were posted to RAF Binbrook in North Lincolnshire, joining 12 Squadron equipped with the Canberra B6. At the time, 12 Squadron was under the command of Squadron Leader William Donley DFC, DFM. Donley won his

DFM in 1941 with 49 Squadron and added the DFC with 78 Squadron in 1945.

Mike's first flight in the B6 variant was in the company of Flying Officer Harding, later to become famous as the chief of the Air Staff during the first Gulf War and as marshal of the Royal Air Force Sir Peter Harding.

With a crisis in the Middle East escalating, centred around the Suez Canal and the expansionist ambitions of the Egyptian General Nasser, the squadron found itself on a war footing. Mike flew to the airbase at RAF Luqa on Malta towards the end of September, but within days the squadron moved to the Royal Navy Air Station at Hal Far from where they would operate:

> "It meant flying with a full load: a three-man crew (pilot, navigator and bomb aimer), full tip tanks and, initially some 6,000 lbs of bombs. As the runway at Hal Far was only 2,000 yards long, barely long enough for a Canberra with 6,000 lbs of bombs, the bomb load was reduced to 4,000 lbs for our last raid."

While most of their bombing practice in UK had been with Gee-H, a highly accurate navigation and bombing technique, future ops would have to be visual. Despite the challenge of high temperatures, the ground crews worked above and beyond to ready their aircraft for action[3]. Every Canberra was painted with black and yellow 'invasion' stripes to make them instantly recognisable as friendly to the Israeli, French and British forces ranged against the Egyptians.

The air component of Operation Musketeer, as the Anglo-French plan to recapture the Suez Canal was called, was tasked with destroying the enemy's infrastructure and upsetting its supply lines. The Egyptian air force was identified as a particular threat, comprising some 48 Ilyushin 28 'Beagle' medium bombers and 110 MiG-15 fighters (as well as some older aircraft), and its airfields were therefore an obvious target. Things, however, did not get off to a good start.

On 31 October 1956, the squadron was tasked to provide crews for a raid on the airfield at Cairo West, as part of an attacking force of 24 Canberras and Valiants from the islands of Malta and Cyprus where some 150 Allied aircraft were now operating. It did not go according to plan, and 20 minutes into their flight, the 12 Squadron aircraft were recalled. American families were using the road running past Cairo West to evacuate the area, and the risk of injury was considered too great. Mike was in Canberra WH963, with Flying Officer Ian Ross as navigator and his regular nav, Russ Anderson, as bomb aimer. Mike remembers that when the recall order was received, it was particularly difficult to contact Squadron Leader Donley who was leading the squadron.

There was better luck the next day, 1 November, when Cairo West was finally hit. Mike was flying WH963 in the company of the other 12 Squadron crews. He landed safely after a round trip of almost exactly five hours.

A different target was briefed for a raid three days later on 4 November: El Agami Island. Mike was again flying Canberra WH963 with Flying Officer Ross and a new man, Flying Officer Frank Gorton, as bomb aimer[4].

Mike recalls:

> "On the run-up to the target, we were looking for the target indicators (TIs) from the marker force, but no sooner did we see them that they disappeared, and it was immediately clear that they had fallen into the sea and not onto the target. I decided to go around again, much to the crew's consternation, but we still couldn't make out the target. We'd been told that under no conditions were we to bring our bombs back, so on the way back to Malta we dropped them in the Mediterranean.
>
> "What we didn't know was that below us and waiting offshore was a Royal Navy submarine, which was strategically positioned to pick up any downed airmen. The submarine captain talking to us later about his part in the conflict said that he was very nearly hit by bombs from he knew not where. It certainly made a good story, and we didn't dare admit that we knew where they'd come from. It also shows how poor the communication must have been between the navy and the air force."

One other memory Mike has is that they were all issued with a .38 in case they were shot down: "Not all of us decided to load our revolvers, but Russ Anderson always used to make sure his was loaded with six bullets on the basis that if you needed it, you probably needed it very quickly."

The crisis ended almost as soon as it had begun. Political opposition at home and abroad eventually led to a ceasefire. The squadron was kept on readiness for the next few weeks until it was clear they were no longer needed, returning to RAF Binbrook in December. The squadron increased its number of aircraft and crews, and Squadron Leader Donley subsequently reverted to a flight commander on his own squadron when a change in policy required the squadron to be commanded by a wing commander. Wing Commander Alexander Blythe DFC took charge on 15 December[5].

Not long after his return, Mike was posted to Waddington for ground school instruction and 230 Operational Conversion Unit for flying instruction on the Vulcan B Mk 1. After a year as co-pilot, Mike qualified as a captain and took part in his fair share of 'Mickey Finns' and 'Kingsman' exercises in preparation for a nuclear war first with 83 Squadron and then latterly with 44 Squadron. In June 1962, on promotion to squadron leader, Mike was posted to No. 4 Joint Services Trials Unit (4 JSTU), as senior RAF pilot, spending two-and-a-half thoroughly enjoyable years at Edinburgh Field near Adelaide, South Australia, participating in the trials of the new Blue Steel missile[6].

Blue Steel was an air-launched, rocket-propelled nuclear-armed standoff missile built specifically by the Weapons Research Division of A.V.Roe to arm the RAF's V-Bomber Force comprising the Vulcan B Mk 2, and the Handley Page Victor B Mk 2. As such both types, as well as a Vickers Valiant, were available to fly and Mike as senior RAF pilot flew all three at various stages of his time on the unit. While not unique, it certainly makes him unusual. One incident he recalls in particular:

> "The Avro chief test pilot, Johnny Baker, was on a test flight in Victor XL161, the Victor assigned for Blue Steel trials when, at about 46,000 ft it developed a fault in the pitot static system giving a Mach meter reading of 1.02. A touch of nose-up to reduce the speed resulted in the aircraft going into a spin with the fully fuelled missile still on board. He was obliged to jettison it. A Meteor gave him an airspeed check, and when that became low on fuel, its place was taken by a Canberra. Baker managed to land the aircraft safely but later, Johnny refused to return home for the inquiry, with the result that the RAF was authorised to take over all the subsequent test flying."

Baker had indeed gone into a spin at 46,000 ft and finally regained control at 16,000 ft by streaming the brake parachute. The weapon was jettisoned over the army proof range at Port Wakefield. The Canberra was flown by Wing Commander David Glenn, the CO of the Australian squadron based at RAAF Edinburgh Field. With the Victor unable to dump its fuel, it had to continue flying until enough fuel had been burned off to reach a weight acceptable for landing without a brake parachute. Baker got down in one piece; the aircraft suffered only minor damage and was soon returned to flying. It went on successfully to launch several weapons both at high and low levels, as well as conducting many 'carryovers' and aborted attempts.

On returning to the UK in the new year of 1965, Mike attended Staff College at Bracknell before various spells at the Ministry of Defence. On the first occasion, he was appointed Victor tanker officer, despite knowing nothing about tankers and only having had very limited experience of Victors, and then only the B Mk 2. Between stints at the ministry, and promoted to wing commander, in March 1971 Mike received one of the most coveted of all operational postings to RAF Scampton, as Officer Commanding 617 Squadron, the 'Dambusters'.

> "At the MoD there had been no flying, which had been frustrating. Now, however, I had responsibility for one of the most famous squadrons in the RAF and given a sense of that responsibility when sitting behind the desk of the squadron's founding CO, Guy Gibson VC, and looking out of the window at the memorial to Gibson's faithful black Labrador."

The squadron flourished under Mike's leadership; V-Force had only recently given up its purpose as a 'nuclear' force, and the Vulcan B2s had now reverted back to a low-level 'conventional' role. While officer commanding he got to meet Barnes Wallis (designer of Upkeep – the 'bouncing bomb') and other wartime members of 617 Squadron, and was instrumental in developing the squadron association. It meant persuading Leonard Cheshire, one of his predecessors, that they needed to allow post-war members of the squadron into the association or else it would disappear, and eventually this was accepted[7].

After almost two-and-a-half years with 617 Squadron, Mike handed over the reins to Wing Commander Vivian Warrington and was posted to No. 2 Allied Tactical Air Force (2ATAF) at Rheindahlen in Germany. The unit was tasked with providing air support to NATO's Northern Army Group (NORTHAG) and comprising a host of British, Dutch, Belgian, German and US squadrons.

Mike found himself in the company of a Dutch wing commander who had been in the resistance, running contraband in the Netherlands during the war, and a German Luftwaffe group captain who assured Mike he had never flown in combat against the English. Among the German contingent was a pilot who had flown the F-104 Starfighter, and his successor, Gerhard Ille, who had flown the Messerschmitt Bf 109 in the defence of the Reich and had been shot down three times:

> "Gerd told me that on one occasion he had been attacked by Spitfires and put the aircraft into a spin to shake them off his tail but when he came out of the spin they were still there!"[8]

Once again returning to the UK and the MoD (including being given charge of a nuclear accident exercise that was eventually cancelled), Mike's last role was in defence equipment sales in Soho Square before taking premature voluntary retirement. He then embarked on a new career in antiques, taking a course in furniture restoration, and engaging with his former apprentices in the 63rd Entry and becoming the entry's association secretary. He also played a key role in creating and installing the first of the stained-glass windows in St George's Church at RAF Halton, dedicated to most apprentice groups and entries.

Mike's career took him from Halton to Soho Square, but it was his time at Halton that most influenced his later life. For a young man of today, would he still recommend a career in the Royal Air Force? He is adamant in his reply: "Yes of course. What could have been better!"

16 LIGHTNING REACTIONS

Many in the aircraft industry and thousands beyond have heard of the legendary story of the RAF engineering officer who inadvertently found himself airborne in a Lightning. The officer in question, Wing Commander Walter 'Taffy' Holden of the 47th Entry, became so frustrated hearing and reading his story told and retold with fanciful variations on the truth, he decided to record the definitive account of his very frightening experience to explain how he came to be in the cockpit of the Lightning in the first place.

Taffy was a qualified pilot, even though he was an RAF engineer branch officer. A Scotsman by birth but raised in Northumberland, Taffy arrived at Halton as an apprentice in 1943 and trained as a fitter IIE. It was at Halton that he acquired the nickname Taffy on account of his mixed Scottish/Northumberland accent being mistaken for Welsh! Passing out as a LAC he was awarded a technical cadetship which took him to Belfast University to read mechanical engineering. He also learned to fly Tiger Moths with the university air squadron. On graduating, he was given the option to continue with engineering or to follow a general duties (flying) career:

> "I chose the former path and the Air Ministry, at that time, considered that there was merit in allowing me to qualify to wings standard as a pilot, in the belief that an engineering officer with a pilot qualification could more easily see the pilot's point of view in aircraft maintenance matters. I too, thought this was a very good idea."

Taffy qualified on Harvards, but his early engineering duties only allowed him to keep up his flying hours on Chipmunks. At RAF Kinloss on the Moray Forth, he managed to get checked out on Airspeed Oxfords and on occasions assisted a qualified test pilot to air test twin-engine Lockheed P-2 Neptunes, the maritime patrol and anti-submarine warfare aircraft 'on loan' from the US. His only jet aircraft experience was as a passenger in the second seat of a Gloster Javelin T3 and again in the 'rumble' seat of a Canberra:

"In my service, one of my postings took me to 33 Maintenance Unit (MU) at RAF Lyneham where, as the commanding officer of a civilian-manned aircraft storage unit, I had Canberra, Meteor and Lightning types, which were gradually being prepared for despatch to various flying unit tasks. When the Meteor and Canberras had been cleared, the powers that be decided that the MU should close after the last Lightnings had been despatched.

"Up until the last Canberra, I had a qualified and current test pilot on my staff for those aircraft, but he was not a current Lightning pilot. When a Lightning needed test flying, I had to call for any available pilot with a current test pilot rating. Most times, I would find one who could be spared within a 24- or 36-hour period."

On the day in question, 22 July 1966, Lightning XM135, the first full production Mk 1 that had first flown in November 1959, was being prepared for despatch to a target facilities flight. It had previously seen service at Central Flying School (at Coltishall) and 74 Squadron. For several weeks prior, however, it had been giving the engineering team no end of trouble; every time it had been flight tested, the pilot reported that on the initial few yards of the take-off run, the inverter, supplying power to the primary flight instruments, would cut out and the standby inverter would have to cut in.

Lightning Mk 1As at Wattisham.

"Clearly this was an unsatisfactory state of affairs. Electricians were using every trick in their trade to establish the cause, each time thinking that they had removed, replaced and tightened every likely component. With nothing out of order, they would seek another test flight. It was a Boscombe Down pilot who next attempted to fly the aircraft, found the same problem persisting and refused to fly until a more positive explanation could be determined."

Going back to the drawing board, the electricians decided to devise some tests which might isolate the fault and indicate roughly where and which component was at fault. They intended to ask the next test pilot to switch in and out parts of circuits, using trailing wires from the likely circuits to temporary switches in the cockpit, and to do these electrical switchings before and after each few yards of a simulated take-off run, when the fault was manifest.

"The temporary wires from internal circuitry required the cockpit canopy to be removed and in this state the aircraft was made ready for another air test. Being a pilot, it was easiest for me, as CO, to request the services of a qualified test pilot, from wherever I could find one, but for the next test on XM135, no pilot was available for at least another week. With my unit closing down, many civilians being made redundant, a timetable of clearance being upset with this 'rogue' aircraft, there was much tetchiness and irritation amongst my staff.

"The intended Boscombe Down pilot, knowing I was a pilot, suggested I might try the test myself. He suggested using an out-of-use runway (runway 36 as I would only be using 30 or 40 yards at a time). He also suggested using a Land Rover to communicate with air traffic control (ATC) and to get their clearance for each movement of the aircraft. However, there was one remaining minor problem: I had only sat in a Lightning cockpit once before and I had no idea how to start its two Rolls-Royce Avon engines. The foreman of engine trades gave me a five-minute briefing on how to do this and XM135 was towed out to Runway 05 for my electrical tests.

"It was by way of extraordinary good fortune that my engine foreman explained that, although I would not be needing reheat, that reheat needed the throttles to be pushed past a reheat 'gate' and one had to feel for the gate keys, behind the throttle, to unlock. My only other knowledge of the Lightning was what I could remember from the pilot's notes. At each test flight by the qualified pilot, I would be in air traffic control with a copy of the pilot's notes, should he need any aircraft figures to be relayed to him. One or two figures stuck in my mind, namely that the undercarriage had a maximum speed before it should be retracted and I had an even vaguer figure of about 150 knots for a landing speed. Some extra knots would be required for each 1,000 lbs of unused fuel, but I did not need to bother with any such figures for the test which I was to undertake."

Taffy was duly strapped into the cockpit (seated on the *in situ* parachute and ejection seat) and after starting the engines and holding the aircraft static, on the brakes, he completed the necessary preliminaries for the electrical checks in the cockpit, checking the notes he had scribbled on a notepad which lay on the coaming in front of him. All seemed ready for the first test, and Taffy indicated to the Land Rover to obtain ATC clearance for use of the short 30 or 40 yards of runway.

"Holding the brakes, I gradually opened the throttles to about 90 per cent. My feeling at the time was the unexpected heavy vibration of Avon power held against the brakes. I did a quick check of the temporary electrical switches and circuitry lights, then released the brakes. That initial punch from the thrust was quite remarkable and I moved the expected 30 to 40 yards before I throttled back and applied the brakes."

So far so good. Taffy recorded his initial findings, altered some more switch positions, noted the on/off lights and prepared for the next test.

"This was done in a similar fashion and I was leaving the 'fault' diagnosis to my electrical staff who would have to interpret my notes. I needed to do one more test and ATC had noted that I had only used about 100 yards total, so they were quite happy to clear me for a similar short distance. ATC had also been holding up a fuel bowser and trailer with 3,600 gallons of AVTAG for a waiting C-130 aircraft refuelling; they decided to allow the bowser to cross the runway.

"On opening the throttles for that final test, I obviously pushed them too far, misinterpreting the thrust, because of the unexpected heavy vibration and they got locked into reheat. Yes, I did use some expletives but I had no time to think of getting out of reheat, because in front of me, the bowser and trailer had just crossed the runway, from right to left, so my thoughts were to make sure I was missing them by sufficient margin. No, I couldn't steer to clear them; reheat takes you in a straight path like a bullet out of a gun. The time between finding myself in reheat and just missing the bowser was less than half the time I have taken to record this sentence."

Taffy quickly found himself in trouble. Before his thoughts could compute getting himself out of reheat, the aircraft was gathering such speed that it was about to cross the main duty runway, where a Comet had just passed on its take-off run:

> "I then had no time to look for reheat gate keys, my eyes were on what next lay ahead. Two things, the end of the short runway 07 and just beyond was the small village of Bradenstoke, which I just had to miss. There was no chance of stopping, none whatsoever. I had gained flying speed (that is what reheat is for, short sharp take-offs) and I had no runway left. I did not need to heave it off the runway, the previous test pilot had trimmed it exactly for take-off, and only a slight backward touch on the stick and I was gathering height and speed. Then my thought was to get my speed back in case I should damage the undercarriage.
>
> "Incidentally, I could not have raised the undercarriage; the ground-servicing locks were in place for safety reasons. With only clear blue sky in front of me, I could then search and feel for those gate keys. Yes, I found them and thanked my lucky stars that my engine foreman had quite incidentally told me of their location and I was soon able to get the speed back to (I am guessing now) about 250 knots. My next thoughts were to keep Lyneham airfield in sight and where had the Comet got to, the one I had missed a few seconds ago? Then I asked myself, should I eject and where and when? No, I could not; the safety pins were in the ejection seat and safe for servicing, not for flying. My only alternative then was to attempt a landing, but how does one interpolate or extrapolate Tiger Moth, Chipmunk, Harvard flying to a two-engined, 11-ton beast like the Lightning?"

After regaining his bearings and a little composure, Taffy could see that the Comet was no longer an obstacle and decided to attempt a landing:

> "I was trying to combine all my limited flying experience into a few minutes of DIY flight 'training' on a Lightning. It wasn't easy, but I must admit that some of the elementary rudiments of my proper flying training and flight theory were coming in useful. I needed to get the feel of the aircraft, if I was to get it back on the ground."

Taffy's first approach was something of a disaster. He miscalculated every factor: speed, height, rate of descent, and alignment. The only option was to go around again, this time making sure that the throttles were well below reheat position.

> "A second approach was no better. As the duty runway 25 is on the lip of an escarpment, with a valley floor beyond, my rate of descent took me below runway height and I found myself adding power to get back to the right level. More power also meant more speed and I was trying to get to

something like 150 knots for landing, but the uncoordinated attempt was becoming a mess so I abandoned it, took myself away on a very wide circuit of Lyneham and decided to land in the opposite direction. This I thought would give me more time to get the 'feel' right and if I made a mess of the landing, I would overrun the runway and just drop (crash) into the valley beyond. In that direction, with a messed-up landing, I would have no fear of crashing into Lyneham village."

The long final leg of this approach gave Taffy the thinking time that he needed more accurately to gauge the speed, alignment, rate of descent, height and approach angle required.

"I plonked it down at about the right position off the runway threshold, but just forgot that I was in a nose-wheel aircraft and emulated my best three-wheelers in a Chipmunk or Harvard. The result was that I crunched the rubber block which encases the brake parachute cables. However, I had got down, but I then had to stop. I obviously knew the Lightning had a brake parachute, but where was the 'chute lever, button or knob? There, I found it marked 'brake chute' and I pulled it and I could then look ahead and concentrate on keeping straight and somewhere near the centre line."

Taffy hung on to the brake lever, but found that he wasn't slowing as much as he'd like:

"I had about 100 yards of runway left when I stopped and, even then, I didn't know that the brake parachute had dropped off as soon as it was deployed, because the cable had been severed as a result of my super tail-wheel three-pointer."

Relieved to be down in one piece, unharmed and in a comparatively unbroken aircraft, XM135 was towed back to the hangar and Taffy was taken to see the medical officer who gave him some pills to calm his nerves.

"I felt reasonably calm because I had almost killed myself on five occasions in that 12-minute flight, yet I had miraculously survived. What is more, I would see my wife and young family again. Two or three times in that same 12 minutes, I thought I would never ever see them again. My only priority was to save my own skin; I was not thinking about the non-insured loss of a Lightning Mk 1A aircraft. The minor damage to the aircraft was repaired with a new set of brake shoes and a new rubber 'chute block."

Although the tests Taff completed and the ensuing flight did not immediately provide a reason for the initial electrical fault, his electrical staff, with additional assistance from the aircraft's manufacturer English Electric, eventually did.

> "Apparently, in early versions of the Lightning, there was to be a ground-
> test button fitted into the standby inverter circuit. It was never fitted to the
> Mk 1A but the wires were left in the looms. It was one of these redundant
> wires which shorted on to the UHF radio as it moved on its trunnions when
> the aircraft nudged forward on take-off. Who would have thought I should
> risk my life to find it, in the way I did?"

Taffy's adventures could not go unnoticed, and an inquiry was opened to find out
what had happened and why, and to make recommendations to ensure it never to
happen again. As commanding officer of the unit, Taffy was responsible for his own
actions as well as the service actions of his staff:

> "I was not acting against any orders in the flight order book which I reli-
> giously kept up to date. But those orders did not cater for engineering officers
> doing investigative-type checks on Lightnings. They were later amended.
> After the unit inquiry I had to go up in front of the commander-in-chief.
> That was when I thought my career would be placed in jeopardy. I even
> thought that my coveted wings would be taken from me; I had no idea how
> the incident was being regarded by Command or indeed Air Ministry. But,
> as I stood in front of Air Marshal Sir Kenneth Porter (himself a former Brat),
> he read the proceedings, asked me if I agreed with his view that 'with the
> limited flying experience that I had, the test would have been better left to
> an experienced and current Lightning test pilot'. I agreed of course.
> "He then told me to remove my hat, sit down and proceeded to tell me
> some of his unfortunate flying incidents in Mesopotamia in the Middle East.
> I was thankful that nothing more was to become of the incident and that I
> still had a job to do back at 33 MU, Lyneham."

While Taffy was able to cope with the official communications regarding the incident, what he was not prepared for was for the story to be made public. He had
little or no experience of working with the press, and certainly none with any of
the world's broadcast media:

> "My Command Headquarters suggested I went away on leave before press
> releases were made by Air Ministry. This I did and took my family off
> camping to Jesola, in Italy. Imagine my complete surprise when, on the first
> day of camp, on my way to find some ice, someone shouted, 'Hello Taffy,

I've just been reading about your Lightning flight!' The world seemed a very small place.

"On returning to the UK I was overwhelmed to find that the incident was still frontline news. People wanted to write articles in newspapers, books, magazines, interviews on TV and radio and underhand attempts to hear my account of what had happened. Having admitted that I had made an unwise decision to do the ground tests, I decided that the unwanted publicity that I had attracted was in no way going to be for financial gain. I steadfastly refused offers other than for a two-page article in the *Sunday Express*; I requested the editors to make a donation to the RAF Benevolent Fund. Despite prompts, no monies were ever handed over and I became very disillusioned with all publicity media. Some friends thought I had gained reward for an article in *Mayfair*; it was written without my knowledge and authority, but, because it was factually correct, I had no redress from the Press Complaints Board. Nonetheless, I was extremely annoyed."

Some years after the incident, Taffy's hidden fears of high-speed flight came to the surface and he spent two periods in hospital; he had failed to acknowledge or come to terms with the emotional side of the drama.

"To return to my wife and family after five close encounters with death, was indeed a miraculous experience, but I had not been honest with myself, to accept it as such, so I needed psychiatric help. I could recall the technicalities of the flight without any hang-ups, but was unwilling to talk about that emotional side of the ordeal until I was placed under medical drugs and to bring those emotions to the surface. That was a rewarding experience and it gave me a much better understanding of people who might need that same kind of help, after similar unfortunate occurrences."

Taffy eventually retired from the RAF in 1981 as a wing commander. His last tour was at the MoD as staff officer for MT Maintenance and Repair having also spent time back at Halton as senior training officer which included responsibility for aircraft apprentice training. He later settled in Nantwich in Cheshire and died in December 2016 after a short illness.

Although he embraced his experience in the end, he never actively sought publicity for it. He did, however, keep the rubber block in the hope that one day it might be returned to XM135, which has been on display at the Imperial War Museum Duxford since being disposed of in 1974.

17 BY ROYAL APPOINTMENT

When Charles Owens arrived at RAF Halton in January 1938 as an apprentice engineer, he could little imagine how varied his subsequent career would become. Plucked from virtual obscurity at RAF Coningsby to assist in the assembly and testing of the Whittle power jet, he later qualified as a pilot and flew deep-penetration operations against the Japanese in the Far East. But it was after the war that he came to public attention, flying Her Majesty the Queen and her family on a royal tour of Turkey and Yugoslavia, and for being at the controls of a BEA Trident Two that treated the royal party to their first ever automatic landing at Heathrow – a landmark occasion in the world of passenger transport.

Born in Birmingham on 18 February 1922, and educated locally, Charles graduated from the 37th Entry at Halton in 1940 as a LAC fitter (E), and was posted to 106 Squadron at Finningley. Bomber Command was already starting to take its fight to the enemy, and Charles recalls one of his very first assignments as being to change an engine on a Hampden. He was still only 18 years of age.

The squadron moved to Coningsby in February 1941, and began re-equipping with the Avro Manchester, the forerunner to its more famous stablemate, the Avro Lancaster. It meant Charles exchanged working on Bristol Pegasus radial engines to the enormous and troublesome Rolls-Royce Vultures: "I am always amused by the 16-valve and 24-valve signs on some modern cars," he recounted later. "The Vulture had 24 cylinders and 96 valves!"

Quite why Charles was chosen for his next assignment has been obscured by time, though he often wondered if it had something to do with his insistence on becoming a pilot, rather than spending his war on the ground. As it was, he was posted as a corporal fitter to 'Power Jets', and told to report via the Air Ministry:

> "Everything was cloaked in a kind of exaggerated secrecy and this, coupled with the name 'Power Jets', could well have aroused more interest than was necessary. As I recall, I was merely given a railway warrant to London, where I found my own accommodation in the YMCA, and duly reported complete

with kitbag and full equipment to Kingsway."

From the ministry, Charles was sent to see Dr Roxbee Cox, an aeronautical engineer of some standing. Cox had been part of the engineering team for the ill-fated Airship R101 at Cardington before joining the Royal Aircraft Establishment at Farnborough and gaining a reputation for his work around flight safety. In May 1940 he had been appointed to the Ministry of Aircraft Production as deputy director of scientific research. Again, there was no explanation for Charles' appointment, but it was in meeting Dr Cox at Thames House in Millbank that he finally discovered what his posting was to be about.

> "He explained that Wing Commander Whittle (one of the apprenticeship's greatest success stories) was on the point of developing a successful gas-turbine engine which could affect the course of the war and certainly the whole future of aviation. It had been decided that four RAF fitters, all ex-Halton apprentices, should go to join the engineers at work at Power Jets. I heard later that this request for ex-apprentices stemmed from Whittle's own background in the RAF."

Whittle had fought hard to see his ideas come to fruition. The Air Ministry had turned down earlier attempts to build a gas turbine so he patented the idea himself and with the support of the RAF he launched Power Jets Ltd and began building and testing a new engine as early as 1936. Early designs provided inconclusive. When the Air Ministry at last conceded to finance his project, development work began again in earnest and by April 1941, the first of the new engines was ready for test.

Having been duly impressed with the need for absolute secrecy, Charles was despatched to Lutterworth, a village near Rugby, where he settled in at The Hind Hotel. Here he met his three colleagues – Martin, Love and Haswell.

> "To an airman in war time, accommodation in a pub like The Hind was marvellous but one had a feeling of unreality all the time. I never did have a pass for weekends or leave and cannot recall how I was paid. We seemed to be completely detached from the RAF and, apart from wearing uniforms, lived as civilians. In fact, all the RAF personnel were members of the local Home Guard in which we were eminently successful on manoeuvres because of our uniforms and ranks!"

The day after his arrival he reported to Power Jets. No-one asked him for any form of identification until several days later when he was first introduced to Whittle who asked to see his papers. Whittle, a diminutive man who had himself at first failed to gain entry as an apprentice on account of his small size, missed nothing. It was rumoured that he had once queried the colour of a man's eyes because, in his opinion, they did not match the description given on his identity card. Shortly after meeting Whittle, Charles met a jet engine for the first time.

"The introduction to a jet engine was rather impressive but not surprising. I had heard vaguely of such developments whilst at Halton; the device was structurally simple and easy to understand. What made a great impression upon me was the noise of the engine under test, and the apparent power developed which in fact was only a fraction of that produced by a modern engine. The Power Jets W1 produced about 850 lbs of thrust for a dry weight of 560 lbs."

Life very soon settled down to little more than routine 'fitting' and self-learning. No-one at any time attempted to instruct the four apprentices, and most of the learning was through practical, hands-on experience:

"The engine on test at that time was mounted on a cradle slung from the roof of the test house and anchored to a steel post in the floor by a simple scale which could measure thrust in pounds. Starting was effected by means of a small piston engine (I think from an Austin car engine) through a flexible drive in a similar manner to the old 'Hucks' starter. The engine test cell was separated from the control room by a thick wall with small windows. The senior engineers used the control room during test runs but I have a clear recollection of being in the test cell during runs, checking that all was well, feeling for vibration and so on. The fire system consisted of hand extinguishers in the test bay and at times I gained the firm impression that I was expendable!"

Other impressions that stayed with Charles over the years included the total lack of facilities (Power Jets was sited next to a foundry – not the cleanest of places), the great enthusiasm of the engineers, and the skills of the older civilian fitters. He recalls clearly the arrival of an engine for testing built by the Rover Company and the consternation which became evident when it was discovered that fibre lock nuts had been used on hot parts of the engine:

"As I remember it, we spent many hours fitting castellated nuts, and drilling bolts for split pins or locking wire to ensure security. I suppose that the progress made by the Rover Company in developing a suitable turbine engine for cars stemmed from their work at the time."

Charles does not over-state his part in the development of the Whittle engine, describing himself and his fellow apprentices as 'small cogs' in an otherwise larger wheel, though he imagines their work was useful. Although encouraged to go to Loughborough College and study for a degree in engineering, he had always joined the RAF with the intention of flying, and was inclined to ignore the authority's plea that it took three years to train an engineer, and only six months to train a pilot.

Shortly after Britain's first jet-power aircraft, the Gloster E28/39, took to the air on 15 May 1941, Charles was posted to Baginton (now Coventry Airport) to await a pilot's course, his perseverance finally paying off. His time was not spent idly; while there and at Honiley, he helped service a good many types, including Hurricanes, Beaufighters and Havocs, and supervised the assembly of half a dozen derelict Spitfires left behind by a Polish squadron: "With a motley crew of flight mechanics, we repaired all of them to be tested by the resident test pilot, Charles Turner-Hughes, and thence flown to squadrons for a return to active service."[1]

His time finally came at the end of 1941 when he arrived at ITW in Torquay via the traditional route of an aircrew reception centre (ACRC). Already schooled in the ways of the RAF, Charles breezed through Initial Training Wing and joined a large party of fledgling pilots on a ship to Canada, to be embraced within the Empire Air Training Scheme. Elementary flying training at the Royal Canadian Air Force base at Caron was followed by a commission, and an instructor's course at RCAF Vulcan, home to 2 Flying Instructor School. Further training duties followed at a service flying training school in Alberta, and a posting to RAF Penhold as an instructor on twin-engined Airspeed Oxfords.

By now a flight lieutenant and a flight commander, Charles agitated for an operational posting. His wish finally came true in the winter of 1944, when he went to Boundary Bay and Abbotsford in British Columbia to convert onto the North American Mitchell and Consolidated Liberator, the latter a well-armed four-engined bomber and stablemate to the Boeing B-17 Flying Fortress. After a brief stopover in the UK, he was posted to India, to join 159 (B) Squadron, part of South East Asia Command (SEAC), flying the very latest Liberator VIIIs on deep-penetration sorties in Japanese territory.

Charles and his crew were not formally posted to 159 at RAF Digri in Bengal until 23 June 1945. Command of the squadron had recently passed from Wing Commander Byron Burbridge to Wing Commander Lucian Ercolani DSO & Bar, DFC, and the squadron had only just started converting to the new mark. Ercolani's name betrays his Italian heritage, his father having come to Britain in 1910.

While the war in Europe against the Germans and their Axis allies had ended in May, the Japanese in the Far East were still clinging with increasing desperation to the lands and islands they had invaded four years earlier. The recently delivered Liberator VIIIs of 159 Squadron were being used to attack targets such as rolling stock and rail and communications in Malaya as well as minelaying operations to distant ports, including Singapore. This involved flights of up to 20 hours or more, testing men and machines to the full.

From early August onwards, and after the dropping of the atomic bombs on Hiroshima and Nagasaki by their American allies, the squadron flew missions of mercy, dropping food and essential medical supplies to the various prisoner-of-war camps across Siam and the East Indies, as well as the local Burmese who were starving. They also continued 'nickelling', dropping leaflets to those Japanese intent on continuing the fight.

On one particular sortie on 17 October, Charles was flying Liberator KL684 on a drop in good weather but struggled to find the drop zone (DZ). He spent more than an hour-and-a-half attempting to find the best, and in fact the only, possible approach. The DZ was surrounded by hills reaching up to 5,000 ft, and only by climbing with maximum revs and full boost was Charles able to avoid crashing. The relevant entry in the squadron's ORB states that the pilot 'experienced the utmost difficulty and considerable risk in accomplishing his duty'.

> "I flew about 20 operational flights before the end of the war and flew a number of special flights after the official end in connection with the French battles against the Viet Cong. The Americans were definitely not the first to become involved in post-war operations in that theatre."

A few weeks after the end of hostilities, Charles received a letter from a private soldier, Charles Ryan, a prisoner of the Japanese, expressing his thanks for the work of the bomber boys in the Far East:

> "No doubt you will be surprised to hear from a complete stranger, but I am one of the prisoners you 'entertained' on two occasions over Ubon with what we consider a very good air display. All the writing and talking on earth won't express our admiration for the bombing squadrons who were sorting out the yellow ____ in the Bangkok area and probably no people anywhere can speak with the same experience we can about the Allied bombers operating deep in the enemy territory."

Being a regular airman, and with his skills both as an instructor and as an operational pilot, Charles was understandably surprised to be demobbed so swiftly after the war's end, but by then he had already served eight years and was still only 24. A career in civil aviation was sought and eagerly adopted, first with Det Norske Luftfartselskap (DNL), which became part of SAS, as a captain of aircraft and then, in 1949, with the state-owned British European Airways (BEA) as a second officer flying the Vickers Viking, an airliner derived from the Wellington bomber.

Charles' abilities as a pilot were recognised with a promotion to company test pilot, undertaking test flying and de-icing trials on the Airspeed Ambassador before being promoted captain on Elizabethans (the name given by BEA to its Ambassador fleet) and then Vickers Viscounts. Further roles saw him oversee the introduction of the early passenger jets, the de Havilland Comet and the Hawker Siddeley Trident, becoming closely associated with the latter when appointed general manager of flight operations and specifically, commander of the royal tour aircraft to Turkey in 1971, and to Yugoslavia the following year.

It was an experienced crew that flew Her Majesty, the Duke of Edinburgh and Princess Anne out to Ankara on the BEA Trident Two G-AVFE, known as 'Foxtrot Echo'. Joining Charles in the cockpit was Captain Maurice Chick, from Truro, who had won the DFC and Bar while flying with 83 Squadron Pathfinder Force. He was the senior base training captain. History was made on Her Majesty the Queen's return to Heathrow, when Her Majesty had her first experience of an automatic landing. At the time, the *BEA News* (a newspaper for all BEA staff) trumpeted the success and significance of the flight: 'Currently such landings are made only in clear visibility conditions, but within two years it is expected regular landings will be possible in visibility conditions which would force poorer-equipped airliners to divert to fog-free airports.'

The fact that an automatic landing was possible at all was due in no small way to another Halton apprentice, Eric Poole. Eric was a close friend of Charles' at BEA, though the two had been several years apart at Halton. Eric, who was originally from Southend-on-Sea, had joined Halton in 1934 as part of the 35th Entry, and qualified as a carpenter rigger. He was identified early for pilot training, and upon gaining his wings was posted to 604 (Auxiliary) Squadron where he flew Gladiators (briefly) before converting to Blenheims in a night-fighter role during the Battle of Britain. He later flew Beaufighters under the command of one of the world's greatest night-fighter pilots, John Cunningham.

Eric damaged at least two enemy aircraft including one on the night of 12 April 1941 in combat over Holton Heath. His radar operator (Sergeant Kennedy) picked up a contact that proved to be a Heinkel 111. Eric was able visually to identify the enemy from its silhouette at 2,000 yards and eventually closed to within 200 feet whereupon the rear gunner spotted him and opened fire. Eric returned the compliment and the gunner was silenced. He continued firing until he was out of ammunition, by which point the port engine was smoking and the aircraft was steadily losing height as it turned out to sea. Throughout the attack, the gunners on the ground continued to fire.

After completing his tour, he was posted to the SBA school at Watchfield, and thence on to 59 OTU to convert to Hurricanes which he flew with 87 Squadron. Commissioned in 1943, Eric served in various roles, including interception, search and rescue and convoy work from the Scilly Isles.

On leaving the service in 1945 he joined the Associated Airways Joint Committee (AAJC), a forerunner to BEA. His appointments mirrored Charles', culminating in his becoming flight manager at Trident Development in 1961. In cooperation with BEA colleagues and manufacturers Smiths Industries and Hawker Siddeley, he progressed the work towards a fully automatic landing system, and on 10 June 1965 he made the first ever automatic landing of a scheduled passenger flight when BEA Flight 343 with 80 passengers on board and in-bound from Le Bourget Paris made a perfect touchdown at London Airport. To mark the occasion, every passenger was given a certificate.

From then on, Eric became something of a world expert in all-weather operations, further developing systems that enabled BEA aircraft to land when other airlines couldn't do so. In 1972 he was awarded, jointly with Captain Frank Ormonroyd DFM, the GAPAN's Cumberbatch Trophy – the award for an outstanding contribution to aviation safety – and in 1976 the Queen's Commendation for Valuable Services in The Air. He had flown more than 30 aircraft types during a 30-year career ranging from the Avro Tutor to the TriStar and including a Junkers Ju 52. He was closely involved in evaluating the TriStar, the DC10, and the BAC 211 (a paper aeroplane and never built).

Charles also qualified on the TriStar and continued his flying career into the late 1970s. As flight operations director of British Airways' European division, he was responsible for around 3,500 staff and an annual budget of some £120 million. He also held senior posts within IATA (as chairman of IATA Flight Operations Advisory Committee) and became a master of the Guild of Air Pilots and Air Navigators. His time with the royals was recognised by being made a Lieutenant of the Royal Victorian Order (LVO), an award which is solely in the gift of the sovereign to make.

In 1982, Charles wrote a technical book for Collins entitled *Flight Operations – a Study of Flight Deck Management* – and went into private business. Never wandering too far away from the world of aviation, Charles kept a foothold in it by acting as a consultant and occasional expert witness. His son, Robert, and nephew, James Gibney both flew British Airways Tridents, and his daughter became cabin crew.

18 GUEST OF SADDAM

Peter Goodwin has lived a charmed life. As a fighter pilot specialising in low-flying ground-attack operations in Aden, he survived a cannon shell punching an untidy hole in the wing of his Venom FB4; he is still slightly peeved that he never even received a thank you for bringing one of Her Majesty's aircraft safely back to base. On another occasion as an airline pilot, he just missed being hit by an in-bound Boeing 727 as it flashed across him while landing in the Bahamas. The Pan Am pilot in the other aircraft was subsequently fired. But undoubtedly his most astonishing piece of luck was in Kuwait, when he was captured, disguised as a woman, and taken to meet Saddam Hussein.

How Peter came to be in Kuwait is a long story deserving of a book in its own right. Originally from Kent, Peter survived a series of private schools in and around Tunbridge Wells before joining Halton as an apprentice in the 62nd Entry:

> "At 17 I was a little older than the rest. I had left school and was working as a comi-waiter in the Swan Hotel. I'd always been interested in aircraft, and Halton gave me an opportunity of learning a trade. I sailed through the entrance exam and set about becoming an electrical fitter."

Quickly promoted, Peter spent a thoroughly enjoyable if somewhat mischievous time at Halton, garaging his motorbike at the nearby Station Hotel and earning a little extra cash through loan sharking and charging 100 per cent interest. He worked hard at his studies for five days a week and harder still on his social life for the remaining two. The combination worked, for he qualified at the top of his particular trade and 11th overall for the entry.

Peter might have earned a cadetship, but an interview with the mercurial Don Finlay did not go well: "Telling an Olympic hurdler that my sporting prowess amounted to gliding and a bit of .22 rifle shooting did not impress him, neither did the fact that I didn't know where Cranwell was when he asked!"

Posted initially to RAF Thorney Island to work on Wellingtons, an application for aircrew training was swiftly followed up, for within only a few short months of leaving Halton, Peter was at Hornchurch undergoing his aircrew medical. A childhood problem with an eye resulted in an A1 G1 rating that in theory disqualified him from becoming a pilot. Fate lent a hand, however, for at grading school he so impressed the instructor that he was sent for another medical and blagged his way through by quizzing others on what letters were on the chart.

Peter had already accumulated a number of hours on Chipmunks at Halton, and as a glider pilot, and took to flying quite easily. A serious motorcycle accident in 1953 nearly ended his flying career before it had properly begun, but after a period of recuperation at Headley Court he was soon fit enough to resume flying training on Prentices and Harvards, gain his wings and be commissioned acting pilot officer. Before doing so, however, he had to bury his 19-year-old brother John, a National Service pilot, whose Meteor 8 had flown straight into the ground from 18,000 ft. It was one of more than 30 or so funerals he attended during his service life: "At one point it seemed like we were losing a pilot a week," he says.

After Flying Training School at Driffield, where an F-86 Sabre nearly crashed onto his car bonnet as he arrived, Peter progressed to 233 Operational Conversion Unit at Pembrey where he had another lucky escape. Taxiing out for take-off in a Vampire V, he looked down at the fuel gauges to see the needles flickering about and quickly realised that there was little or no fuel left in the tanks. The aircraft had not been refuelled, and the wrong Form 700 completed. It was a narrow escape.

In December 1955, Peter was posted to 32 Squadron in Malta at the time of the Suez crisis. His flight commander was Flight Lieutenant Joe Blyth, an exceptionally gifted and courageous ground-attack pilot who had been awarded the DFC in Korea[1]: "He was an unbelievable pilot," Peter recalls:

> "One of the very best. Ground-attack operations involved using our front guns, rockets, and bombs, and Joe always had the highest score in any competitions. The squash head rocket projectiles were particularly difficult but hugely effective. With the front gun you could see where you were aiming and the results, but with the rockets there was like a floating graticule in the sight which was really difficult to aim, and once you'd fired you had to break away to prevent being damaged by your own shot."

When Blyth was given command of 8 Squadron, Peter joined him (in February 1957) at Khormaksar, just at the time that trouble in the Aden protectorate was stirring once again. The squadron was equipped with the Venom FB4, the final iteration of the de Havilland type with a Ghost 103 engine, power-operated ailerons and redesigned tail surfaces. The FB4 also featured an ejector seat. Operations comprised convoy escorts, armed-reconnaissance sorties, and airstrikes in support of British Army units and the Aden Protectorate Levies (APL).

It was on one such airstrike against rebel insurgents that Peter's aircraft was hit by ground fire:

> "The insurgents would cross over the border to launch attacks on the APL and we would be scrambled. The air liaison officer (ALO) or the army on the ground would then direct us onto the target. We had Mosaic maps which made it very difficult to map read and we carried a Ghoulie chit just in case we were shot down and needed friendly help.
>
> "Usually a Shackleton would fly on ahead and drop leaflets telling the rebels to leave or they would be attacked. Then we would go in and shoot up literally anything that moved in the area. Men, camels, anything. There was no messing about. Along with our rockets and bombs we had 13 seconds of fire from four of our 20-mm cannons, and on one occasion one of our pilots managed to shoot himself down, or so it was thought, when flying too low and being hit by a ricochet from one of his own rounds. I was hit too, but by ground fire, which punched a large hole in my wing and damaged the undersides. Luckily there was no critical damage and I made it home, though no-one thanked me for it."[2]

With the publication of a government White Paper in 1958, Peter opted to leave the RAF for a career in civilian flying as the civil aviation sector was short of pilots. Remarkably, and despite his experience, Peter failed his instrument rating ("I was

8 Sqn Venom FB4 on start-up.

test flying a Dove for BOAC!") but was offered a job at the fleet requirements unit at RAF Hurn in Dorset, where he managed to take a turn in a Sea Hawk and a Sea Fury: "I was just given the pilot's notes and told to get on with it," he says.

> "While I was strapping myself in I said to the airman 'how do you start this thing' and he thought I was joking. I was a jet jockey but here I was with an aircraft with a propeller and a tail wheel. The three-stage supercharger was magnificent and the 2,500-hp engine gave it real power, I used to enjoy beating up warships and carriers and I was sorry to leave."

After a brief period selling encyclopaedias, something of a low point in Peter's life, he married (a high point) and the very next day returned to flying as a test pilot at the Royal Aircraft Establishment at Farnborough. He was despatched to Llanbedr in Wales and tasked with testing the Meteor U15, an early pilotless aircraft experiment where the aircraft was 'flown' by telemetry from the ground, but still required a pilot in the cockpit lest control should be lost. The experiment was not without its mishaps, including a spectacular accident which saw a Meteor hit the roof of one hangar before eventually coming to a halt inside another. The pilot, 'Johnny' Johnson, emerged miraculously unscathed and went on to enjoy a successful career as a civilian airline pilot.

Still a civilian, Peter re-joined the RAF in March 1960, and was appointed Flying Wing adjutant at RAF Leuchars, much to his new wife's frustration. All seemed well when he joined 25 Squadron at Waterbeach, closer to home and friends, only to find a few weeks later that the squadron was to move again – to RAF Leuchars.

The plus point of his new squadron posting, however, was the chance to fly the RAF's latest all-weather interceptor, the Gloster Javelin. For this he needed a navigator, and recalls the 'crewing up' procedure when at 228 OCU (RAF Leeming) with some humour:

> "There were seven pilots and seven navigators and after ground school we all went to the pub to sort the crews out amongst ourselves. There was a great deal of questions like 'how many hours have you got' and that sort of thing. In my case, with experience in day-fighter/ground-attack squadrons the conversations did not last very long!
>
> "At the end of the evening, the WingCo Flying said: 'Peter this is your nav.' I said, 'Hang on a moment, I haven't chosen yet,' to which he replied, 'You are the only two left in the bar!' As it was it couldn't have been better. John Galley had not only done a tour on Meteor night-fighters but had also been at Halton (53rd Entry). What a lucky break. We sailed through the course with no problems."

Night-time practice interceptions, Peter recalls, were particular fun:

> "A Javelin would fly 800 yards ahead of the aircraft behind and then switch its lights out. If you were the aircraft behind, you would then try and keep on the Javelin's tail ahead. The chap in front would twist and turn and do the occasional half roll and we'd be right behind them."

Once a year a 'standardisation team' (colloquially known as 'Trappers') would visit the Javelin squadrons to ensure their readiness for war.

> "The timing of any visit was not given to the crews – but we would normally find out – and if the 'Trappers' came anywhere near the squadron, there would be an empty crew room PDQ, even hiding in flying suit lockers."

Peter's time on Javelins was an enjoyable one; the FAW9 had two Bristol Siddeley Sapphire engines capable of 11,000 lbs thrust and 13,390 lbs with reheat. It had a top speed of 620 mph at 40,000 ft and could climb to that height in less than six minutes.

But flying any new type of fighter was a challenge:

> "We had no simulators and so it was not without its dangers. I remember

Javelin ejector seat installation.

my first time in a Venom FB4 and finding myself in a loop that turned into an inverted spin from which I couldn't recover and thought of ejecting. Then it recovered itself, but it was frightening at the time. Many were killed for failing the art of asymmetric flying, or understanding that when coming in on only one engine you needed to keep the power on and only when you were absolutely convinced you'd get it down did you pull the power."

Peter left the RAF for a second time in February 1965, after a pleasant tour in Geilenkirchen with 11 Squadron (including time in the 11 Squadron formation aerobatic team) and joined BEA. He spent 15 years as a civilian pilot, including spells with Dan Air (as a captain on BAC 111s) and Boeing 727s before joining Singapore Airways as a captain on an early Airbus type, the A300-B4[3]. He then turned to a stint of private flying as personal pilot to Maharishi Mahesh Yogi (of Beatles' transcendental meditation fame) before joining Kuwait Airways flying both the 727 and HS 125 on VIP work.

He arrived in Kuwait to temperatures of 40°C and impressive sandstorms. This was more than compensated by a financial package that included three months' leave, free luxury accommodation in Faheel, 15 miles south-east of the city, and no tax. His flying extended from Bombay to London with some good night stops including Baghdad. As an added bonus, Kuwaiti customs officials were wont to turn a blind eye to the odd bottle of booze brought into the country.

Peter's wife, Dorothy, worked for the British embassy, and the pair were surprised one morning (Thursday, 2 August 1990) to be woken by the vice consul to be told that the Iraqis had invaded Kuwait. Looking out from the window of their apartment they could see tanks rumbling down the road and surrounding their tower block. Peter was not immediately concerned:

> "As an ex-pat working in Kuwait I did not think that the Iraqis would be interested in us so I drove to the airport where I was due to take an instrument rating test. On my way the Iraqi soldiers seemed friendly enough, but this was not the case as we neared the airport where firing could be heard, so I returned to our apartment. Local phones were working but not the international lines. Many cars were travelling south towards Saudi Arabia, including my next-door neighbour who was with the CIA. As my wife was a warden, responsible for the British ex-pats in our area in cases of emergency, we decided not to leave immediately."

For the first few days of the occupation, Peter did not perceive any particular threat. He stocked up on food from the local supermarket and withdrew cash from the

ATM. Then disturbing rumours began to reach him of hijacked cars, looted shops, and the arbitrary arrest of British and American citizens. It was time to leave.

> "In a convoy of about 100 cars we took off for Saudi, five days after the invasion began, but after just a few miles we were turned back by the military. The threat of being rounded up was increasing so another escape was planned, this time by the army liaison team (they were British Army seconded to the Kuwaitis, ironically, to teach them how to be soldiers!)."

Ten days later, at 03.00 hours, and this time in a much smaller convoy comprising only five, four-wheel drive vehicles, they made their break. It did not last long. An Iraqi tank pursued them and opened fire.

> "We were herded back towards Kuwait City with an armed escort at the front and rear of the convoy. There was also an armed Iraqi soldier in each car except mine since there was no room for more than me, my wife, my next-door neighbour's wife, her daughter and their two cats. Going through a town called Jarrah, the convoy opened up and I saw a chance to turn off into a side street, did so, and drove back to my apartment!"

Peter and his wife spent the next three weeks in hiding, making the most of a false ceiling to avoid any searches. The Iraqis intensified their efforts, and with provisions running scarce and the danger mounting as soldiers looked for enemy snipers, they decided once again it was time to leave.

> "Dorothy had a passport belonging to a friend called Mary Price and so the plan was to dress me up as a woman with the aim of getting to Baghdad and the sanctuary of the British embassy. We shaved my arms and the back of my hands, and I donned a wig, jeans, and a well-filled bra beneath a lovely blouse. There was one last coach for women and children only departing for Baghdad, and I was to be on it."

All went well with the first few check points; the Iraqis conducted a cursory head-count and examined their passports. Just south of Basra, however, the passengers were ordered off the coach and taken into a side building where each of their names was called in turn. As the name 'Mary Price' was called, Peter stepped forward, attempting to look as feminine as possible. His disguise was simply not good enough:

> "An angry Iraqi officer started waving a gun in my face and I was hauled into an adjoining room and roughly handled. My wife raced forward with

my correct passport to prove my real identity, while they peered down my bra and tugged at my wig to confirm I was a man. They also started taking snap shots of me in various states of undress. Dorothy was ordered to return to the other passengers and the coach left without me. I was taken to Basra police headquarters where I was interrogated and accused of being a spy. I was not physically beaten, but one of the men was pacing up and down with a long, flexible wire rod, and the threat was very clear if I didn't answer their questions to their satisfaction. That evening I was put on a train with a member of the secret police and travelled overnight to Baghdad."

Peter was taken to the Mansoir Melia Hotel to join a group of fellow ex-pats who were to be used as 'human shields' – a vain attempt by Saddam to prevent the coalition forces from bombing certain strategic military targets. Together with two married British couples, he was first taken to a power station at Al Zubayr near Basra, a journey of some ten hours. The group was put into a bungalow inside the security fence, moving a few days later to the power station's main control room. Three weeks later, Peter was moved to Martha, another power station 30 miles to the north. After ten days he was moved again and taken to Basra airport for a flight to Baghdad.

"They put me on a Boeing 727, in a window seat, with just a single armed guard for company. For the briefest of moments I wondered whether I could overpower him and get to the cockpit, but any thoughts of hijacking the aircraft quickly disappeared when a group of about 50 soldiers climbed on board!"

In Baghdad, Peter was loaded onto a truck with around a dozen handcuffed Arab prisoners and driven to a prison in the centre of the city. This was in effect a compound with rooms off to the side with no doors and a small roll of carpet as a bed. There were around 50 prisoners in all, including two Germans and two Norwegians who were charged with attempting to leave the country without a visa. The Arabs were accused of everything from theft to murder. Peter was not in the prison long before he was moved, along with the two Norwegians, to a high-security centre where conditions were far from ideal:

"We shared a cell, from which it was impossible to see out, with four Indians. We had just a single bucket between us and were only allowed out to shower once a day. Food was a lump of bread and a foul-smelling brown liquid with sometimes a lump of cheese. We could hear, and sometimes see, through a crack in the door some of the Arabs being tortured with wooden planks and this did not help one sleep at night.

"After two weeks the Norwegians and I were taken to the Central Criminal Court to be tried for our various escape attempts. The Norwegians had an Iraqi lawyer but for some reason the British embassy refused to get me one but luckily the Iraqi said he would act for me as well. While we waited some fairly hefty sentences were meted out to the Arab prisoners and our legal man tried to boost our morale by saying that the most we would get was 15 years but that the majority of that would be suspended given the time we had already served."

Peter faced a court of three judges, but as the trial was all in Arabic, it was difficult to follow the exchanges between the prosecuting and defence councils:

"Previously there had only been gloom and doom but now they were all smiles and there was even some laughter, especially when they were looking at the photographs of me undressing from my disguise. The end came with much hilarity when the defence council informed me that dressing up as a woman was unusual in Iraq but not against the law. As for escaping, Kuwait was now a precinct of Iraq and, as I was travelling to Baghdad, I was not therefore trying to escape. The judge pronounced 'not guilty Mrs Goodwin!' and again there were smiles all round. I was not smiling myself, however, as the prosecution lodged an appeal and so I was taken back to prison. A week later I was finally released into the hands of the secret police and taken back to the Mansoir Meila Hotel where, much to my surprise, my wife was waiting for me.

"Dorothy had managed to arrange for the wives of the other hostages to travel to Baghdad in an effort to obtain our release and had also arranged meetings with the Women's Federation of Iraq, the deputy prime minister, and had many TV interviews. Eventually we were much relieved to hear that we were all to see the president himself, Saddam Hussein (see photo). For this we were transported in a blacked-out bus to one of his palaces where the meeting was impressive and, with the press looking on, we were told that we would at last be going home. We could first go on a tour of the country if we liked, but we politely declined."

19 BRITANNIAS, TANKERS AND SNOOPY

Alan Kidson enjoyed a long and varied career in the RAF, as an air engineer on Hastings, Britannias and VC10s. But it was his tours with the C-130 Hercules, and one aircraft in particular called 'Snoopy', that was perhaps the highlight of almost 40 years of service.

Educated at Queen Elizabeth Grammar School in Faversham, Alan's instinctive desire to fly came from watching the birds soaring over the Kent countryside. With three cousins passing out in the 37th, 52nd and 56th Entries, it was perhaps inevitable that Alan would follow his contemporaries to Halton. It was virtually a family tradition!

> "I was 16 years and seven days old when I arrived at Halton as part of the 78th Entry and I was incredibly naive to the point of being immature. I had a sister, but she was nine years older than me, and so I had little experience of life. I remember packing my suitcase and my mother crying, but once you got to Halton you got to know people and make friends pretty quickly, and you always had six weeks in which you could change your mind!"

Alan, however, did not change his mind. Nicknamed 'Lank' on account of his remarkable height (he was almost six feet three but only ten stone), Alan enjoyed his time training as an engine fitter (servicing). After three years of schools and workshops, he was due to take his final examinations in June but his mother died and he ended up having to take his exams with the Brats of the 79th. It did not put him off, and he finished in the top ten of the entry with a 74 per cent average.

By a strange quirk of fate, he therefore never actually 'passed out', but finished his time as a junior technician. His initial postings followed the traditional path of maintenance units, including what Alan describes as a 'misadventure' at an oxygen production unit at Faldingworth, followed by a posting overseas. At his first MU (32 MU at St Athan) he worked on Canberras, a type he went on to service during a two-year spell at RAF Akrotiri between 1961 and 1963.

"For major servicing of Canberras there was a 'Man A' and a 'Man B'. 'Man A' was in charge, and usually a senior aircraftman (SAC); I was 'Man B'. The best thing about working on Canberras was that the engines were generally easy to get at. The worst part was when you had to crawl up inside the jet pipe to inspect the turbine blades for cracks or dents.

"Unlike Halton, at St Athan we had tremendous freedom. Given my height, I was a keen goalkeeper, and played in the Welsh League including the

Alan Kidson receiving his brevet.

Welsh Cup. By the time I was posted to Akrotiri – my first posting overseas – I had been promoted, and so now I was a corporal. I settled in very quickly, even though I knew nobody when I arrived. On a station, there were several senior NCOs and the quicker you realised they were in charge, the better."

Life on the beautiful island was hard but rewarding. Work began at 07.00 hours and ended by midday, given the intense heat of the summer months. While in Cyprus, Alan helped to devise a new way of removing the seal on the Avon engine without having to lift it: "It was quicker, easier and cheaper, and the sergeant in charge of the team received the British Empire Medal," he recalls.

A desire to fly, however, led him to apply for the air engineers' course, Alan describing an AE as effectively being a 'rebranded' flight engineer[1]. The course, however, was still undertaken at St Athan, at least initially, and the aircraft type was the Handley Page Hastings. Alan loved the aircraft from the start: "It was certainly more exciting than Shackletons," he says. A happy two years with 36 Squadron at RAF Colerne, and a promotion to sergeant, was followed by a posting to 48 Squadron at RAF Changi, by which time he had converted to another type, the C-130 Hercules: "The Hastings featured mainly wartime technology but the Hercules was rather more sophisticated. Being American, it was designed such that a trained monkey could have flown it."

Alan was right in at the beginning of the Hercules' RAF career in 1967, qualifying as part of No. 2 Course and being again promoted flight sergeant. It is somehow fitting that he should return to the type for his final posting, 20 years later, but in-between he began an affair with probably his favourite aircraft, the Bristol Britannia.

> "It was a superb aeroplane and probably one of the finest aircraft I flew in. It was the first 'fly by wire' and the engines were controlled electronically. Electrically it was all rather complicated, and you learned to be flexible in your responses to any problems that occurred. The inverters, for example, were prone to get rather sticky, and so the engineer would go to the back of the aircraft and jump up and down until it started working again. Not everything was covered by the book, but if you knew the system, you could work it out. Like the story of the experienced plumber and the boiler. It was the experience of knowing where to hit it that was important and what you paid for, not the time that it took."

The Britannia had joined the RAF fleet in 1959, giving Transport Command its first turboprop transport aircraft. Its four Bristol Siddeley Proteus 255 engines gave it a cruising speed of 360 mph and a range (with maximum payload) of around 4,300 miles. With a typical crew of five (captain, co-pilot, navigator, air engineer and loadmaster), it could accommodate more than 100 troops or more than 50 stretcher cases. With a full load of passengers, another loadmaster and two stewards would be added.

Alan trained on type at 242 OCU at Brize Norton, and spent four years with 99 Squadron flying the aircraft until it was finally retired from service, with the squadron disbanded shortly afterwards. By this point, Alan was a master engineer, and spent almost all of his career as a B or C-rated AE: "As a B-rated engineer you were entitled to fly VIPs and police dogs."

A brief period at 10 Squadron, in charge of loadmaster tasking and learning operations, was followed by a more challenging posting to B Squadron, A&AEE at Boscombe Down where he was reunited with both the Britannia (the 312F) and all marks of Hercules. His logbooks are peppered with references to a number of other interesting types, including the Armstrong Whitworth (later Hawker Siddeley) Argosy C1 (a distinctive twin-boom, four-engined transport), the Basset CC1 (a twin-engined 'light executive' aircraft), and the VC10 C1 and K2.

An incident in an Argosy transport/cargo aircraft he recalls with some amusement:

> "We were conducting various parachute trials and after completing the necessary external checks I climbed up inside and took my seat. As I caught sight of the pilot I said 'Hello Reg' and the rest of the crew froze. He was a

senior officer, a wing commander in charge of A Squadron, and I was a mere NCO. What they didn't know was that Squadron Leader Reg Hallam had been a contemporary of mine at Halton."[2]

The test pilots at Boscombe were an eclectic bunch. One of the more noteworthy who had been through Empire Test Pilots School was Squadron Leader Tony Banfield – later a regular pilot with the Battle of Britain Memorial Flight. "We called him 'Banzai' Banfield because the joke was that he was particularly gung-ho."

Tony had actually completed tours as co-pilot and captain flying the Vickers Valiant with 49 and 543 Squadrons, before becoming a qualified flying instructor on Gnats and Jet Provosts. After a staff tour at HQ Training Command he flew Victor tankers at Marham on 214 Squadron as a QFI and pilot leader before returning to instructing as OC Standards Squadron at RAF Linton-on-Ouse. By the time he joined the BBMF in 1985, he had more than 7,500 flying hours and had flown 38 types of aircraft.

Up to that point, Alan had managed to avoid any conflict with which the RAF had been involved in the modern era. Indirectly, however, he was to perform an important cameo role in a row several thousands of miles from home in the South Atlantic.

At the beginning of 1982, and with the Argentines declaring 'Las Malvinas' as their own, B Squadron A&AEE was put on something of a war footing. Trials of the Mk 3 Hercules, which were then underway, were put on the back burner, as was a trial to fire a Very pistol from the rear Para door of the Herc to throw off a heat-seeking missile, and new trials accelerated on the newly converted Hercules tanker C Mk 1 (K) which had a probe fitted for inflight refuelling.

> "We spent time doing trials on the C Mk 1(K), tanker. We also spent time trialling the Hercules C Mk 1(R), 'receiver', which had the probe fitted for in-flight refuelling. We also flew behind various tankers including the Victor, the Douglas DC-10 and the Lockheed TriStar. A converted Vulcan was also later included.
>
> "I found operating the receiver quite exciting and it was surprisingly difficult to connect up the probe and drogue. With the Victors, because of the difference in speed, we had to carry out what was known as 'tobogganing'. This meant both aircraft going into a slight descent while the refuelling was going on so that the Hercules could keep up with the faster jets."

The manoeuvre was devised by Squadron Leader John Brown, another of Boscombe's resident test pilots. Two major problems arose with the tanker conversion: the tanks fitted in the freight bay of the tanker and the switching on the drogue recovery system.

"The extra fuel tanks fitted within the freight bay were four of the type designed for the Andover aircraft. The Americans would not supply us with purpose-built tanks so the MoD decided to fit what was available. The main problem was that the tanks were not fully compatible with the aircraft. We were plagued with leaks which at times left aviation turbine fuel (AV-TUR) splashing around the floor of the aircraft. When these points were put to our masters at MoD we were told that we were not trialling the tanks but the system – so effectively, wind your necks in!"

The refuelling system was a standard hose reel as supplied by the Flight Refuelling company. This consisted of a hose and drum system fitted to the aircraft ramp and door at the rear which were specially modified to take it.

"Flying with us on the trials was a technician from the company. Controls for the system were on the flight deck and controlled by the air engineer. To trail the hose, we simply released the electric brake and the hose reeled out to its full length. On the wind in, an electric motor operated to wind the hose in. When full in a micro switch stopped the wind-in and automatically applied the brake to the drum. We had a problem on one occasion when, on the wind-in, the contact kept bouncing off the micro switch. This meant that the lock did not apply and the hose would start to reel out. As soon as this happened the wind-in motor engaged to bring the hose back in, and so on. This continued to happen and it felt like the whole unit was going to rip itself from its mounting."

No amount of resetting the switch would stop the problem. There was no off switch, only a reset, nor was there a fuse or circuit breaker to isolate the system.

"The only way round the problem was to land with hose trailed. This was done successfully, and it transpired that a later trial would have required us to do this anyway. We were ahead of the game. My report was such that the control was then wired through a circuit breaker and a switch position for off was incorporated. After the completion of the receiving trials the tanker trials continued with Harriers, Phantoms, Nimrods, Buccaneers and a Vulcan being re-fuelled. It was all very useful to me on the long flog from Ascension to the Falklands many years later."

After the excitement of Boscombe Down, Alan's subsequent postings to fly VC10 C1s and then the Mk 3 version of the C-130 seemed somewhat benign, but it was by no means the end of the excitement. His final posting to the Meteorological Research Flight (MRF) introduced him to a very special operation in a very special kind of aircraft: Snoopy.

It was during the departure of Saddam Hussain's Iraqi troops from Kuwait in late February 1991 that his engineers carried out, what was for them, a tremendously successful operation to set fire to hundreds of oil wells. From the Allies' point of view, however, it looked like being an environmental disaster of huge proportions. Some 600 naturally pressurised oil wells were now burning around 1.5 million barrels of oil a day sending a smoke plume some 18,000 feet into the atmosphere.

Throughout the Gulf War campaign, the Meteorological Office at Bracknell had monitored weather patterns in the area to give information to the allied forces. Now it became imperative that scientists find out just what environmental effects the smoke could have. To this end, the Met Office was able to task its own special duties flight to travel to the Gulf to take measurements of the smoke and its contents.

MRF was a lodger flight at RAE Farnborough and operated a much-modified C-130 Hercules designated Wmk2. The aircraft (nicknamed 'Snoopy' because of its likeness to the famous Peanuts character and its role in 'snooping' around) was prepared for the task by the six RAF crew as well as the scientific staff. The crew comprised two pilots, two navigators and two AEs.

> "As one of the AEs, we had to organise such things as ground-engineering support from Lyneham, catering in Bahrain (where we were to be based), arranging protective nuclear, biological and chemical (NBC) kits for the crew and our 'passengers', and giving desert survival lectures to the scientific staff. Added to this we liaised with the Institute of Aviation Medicine about preparations for crew and staff and agreed to take a medic with us. We then worked out our load details and organised the aircraft in preparation for loading."

The aircraft was loaded on 20 March for departure the next day.

> "With Akrotiri being so busy we flag-stopped at Iraklion (Crete) and arrived late in the day in Bahrain. The following day was spent offloading and organising. We were to fly every day for ten days with the navigators operating one day and flight planning the next. This meant that both engineers would fly every day."

Alan's first flight into the smoke plumes started early in the detachment. As the smoke may have contained dangerous particles it was decided, in conjunction with the aviation medic, that the crew would wear full NBC protection kit.

> "This meant that we were probably the only crew to operate in the conflict

Snoopy departs Fairford..

area wearing this kit. The pattern of flights was similar to those normally flown by the aircraft except that, for calibration purposes, we flew one leg into sun and one across. At low level the aircraft was depressurised to take scientific measurements. While we were at low level over the Gulf it was noticeable how much oil was spreading across the water and being deposited on the shores causing the death of much of the area's wildlife."

For the very first profile through the smoke plume there was some understandable apprehension among the crew and scientists:

"As we entered the plume it got progressively darker until we were unable to see even the base of the aircraft's barber pole nose. The solar radiometers, which measure light, were reading zero. As we emerged from the plume, however, and realised that it had not affected the operation of the aircraft or its engines we all felt much happier."

One of the biggest problems the crew encountered was the overheating of the scientific equipment in the aircraft freight bay. To overcome this problem, the air engineers uplifted several kilos of dry ice and placed it immediately on and above the equipment. The trips continued with minor variations over the next week. They did, however, dispense with the use of the full NBC kit after clearance from their medical advisor, and simply wore masks.

To keep fit, and despite the heat that could reach up to 40°C, Alan elected to run to and from the airport daily. He was scheduled to run in the London Marathon before his training had been interrupted. He also found time when off-duty to relax with the crew. It was on one such expedition when partaking of a cold beer that they were approached by the well-known BBC TV reporter, Jeremy Bowen:

> "He wanted to know what precautions we were taking to protect ourselves during the flights. He said he was worried about the effect of the smoke on the populace in Kuwait. We decided that discretion should be our watchword and refused to disclose any technical information. It was only then that we learned that he had been tasked by the BBC to enter Kuwait himself."

As a crew, they were congratulated personally by the senior British officer in the region, General Sir Peter de la Billière, when he visited the aircraft. On their way home, they also found time for a day off in Iraklion – the first in 12 days for the engineers – and they both got thoroughly drunk. They also flew the aircraft to Lyneham for a good wash: "I have never seen such a dirty aeroplane," Alan adds.

Once all of the dust had settled, literally and metaphorically, Alan's skipper – Squadron Leader Martin Lampitt – was awarded a Queen's Commendation for Valuable Service in the Air. Alan was proud of what was, in effect, a royal thank-you to the crew. He was similarly proud when the flight applied for, and was granted, an official RAF crest: "The main design was the work of our senior nav, who was once a draughtsman, and I managed to find an appropriate Latin motto. So I left a little mark there."

After completing 39 years less one week in the Royal Air Force, Alan finally retired. By that time, he had accumulated 10,500 flying hours and visited 95 different countries. He initially worked in a motorcycle dealership before taking a 'resettlement course' and becoming something of an expert in health and safety, launching his own consultancy. Today he remains actively involved with his local RAFA and looks back on his career with great fondness: "I had so much fun," he says.

20 THE HISTORY BOY

As a youngster, Wally Epton dreamed of flying. He particularly wanted to fly one of two iconic single-seat fighters: the Hawker Hunter or the Supermarine Spitfire. He even wrote to the Hawker Aircraft Company telling them of his future ambition to fly their fast jet and was thrilled with the brochure they sent him by return. It is ironic, therefore, that while the former at one stage looked more likely, it was the latter that became a reality.

Wally's journey to the cockpit of arguably the world's favourite aeroplane as part of the RAF's Historic Aircraft Flight was far from traditional. His father was a coal miner in the Chislet Colliery in Kent and married a maid of Kent in Herne Bay. As a schoolboy commuting to Queen Elizabeth I Grammar School in Faversham, Wally joined the Herne Bay air cadets with a single ambition of following his brother into the Royal Air Force. A less than glittering school career, however, obliged Wally to look at more creative ways of getting to fulfil his dreams and so he became an RAF apprentice:

> "To fly, the first thing I had to do was get into the air force. I attended an apprentice recruitment session and decided to join the Supply Branch in the 35th Entry with the eventual aim of becoming an air loadmaster. However, I soon realised it was all forms, forms and more forms and knew I had made a ghastly mistake. When the school moved from Credenhill in Hereford to Bircham Newton in Norfolk I put in a general application for a transfer from the Administrative Apprentice Training School to the Technical Training School at Halton. I was told in no uncertain terms that no-one ever transferred from admin to technical training – it was always the other way around. TT failures went to admin!"

Luckily for Wally, under Queen's Regulations 'gen apps' could not be refused and so he was called to RAF Halton for interview:

"They sent a Standard Vanguard staff car to collect me and drive me to Hunstanton railway station. When I arrived at Wendover, I was met by a sergeant who drove me to the camp and introduced me to Squadron Leader Candy who was in charge of electrical trades. I was given a tour of the workshops and schools, and after lunch was asked whether I had made a decision about which trade I wanted to join. I felt very special as a 17-year-old receiving such top-class treatment. I opted to become an aircraft electrical fitter and so swapped my green hat band for a yellow hat band and became part of the 92nd Entry at Halton."

Wally remembers his time at Halton with great affection, especially marching back and forth to schools and the workshops behind the Wing band. It was one of the greatest true examples of early social mobility.

"Trenchard offered mothers the opportunity of taking their sons, feeding, clothing and housing them, training them and even paying them. Most of the boys at Halton sent money home to their parents and we even had a compulsory savings scheme. Many of the boys were from broken homes or fractured families as indeed happened to me, and the air force became their father."

The first few weeks were spent acclimatising and getting to know his fellow intake. Eating irons and mugs became valuable commodities, often bashed and broken 'accidentally' by the more senior boys as they passed on their bicycles and dislodged them from the unsuspecting junior apprentice's swinging arms. Privileges became greater as they progressed through the apprenticeship; trades and entries were originally mixed with each of the three wings taking new recruits as each entry enrolled replacing the graduating senior entry in each wing. This changed during Wally's time with entries forming squadrons in each wing divided into their respective trades into separate accommodation.

Sport was important to Wally, as it was to nearly all of the young apprentices, and he also kept a motorbike in a rented lock-up in Amersham:

Hunter in the workshop.

"I had a Douglas 350cc flat twin considered to be a hot machine but on one occasion I was a little over-exuberant with an emergency stop and broke the chain. I swapped the Douglas for a more reliable Lambretta scooter which was good enough to get me into London or to visit my mother in Herne Bay. Once when I was late back from Kent, I had to hide the scooter in some nearby woods and secrete it back to Amersham later in the week."

Wally passed out in May 1962 after a three-year course and was the last of the warrant officer apprentices to command a graduation parade. He credits some of his promotion to his parade ground voice: "I remember early in my time at Halton one of the drill instructors saying that with a voice like mine I would get to the very top! Command and leadership were important qualities in the air force."

Finishing as a top apprentice, Wally was offered a cadetship to the RAF College Cranwell, which offered that opportunity towards his dream of becoming a pilot. While waiting for the course to start, he was posted to RAF Technical College Henlow to catch up on his academic shortcomings, and within eight weeks crammed two A levels in physics and mathematics. He also learned how to fly:

"They had a Chipmunk and a very kind instructor called John Law who took me up a few times unofficially giving me flying lessons and then asked me what I was doing in the holidays. He suggested I should stay with him and his wife in their married quarters – the college was closed for the summer break – and promised to get me off solo. He was a real mentor. My first solo was at RAF Henlow in July 1962."

Wally arrived at Cranwell to discover that the first year of training was a non-flying year; they were there to learn how to become officers, and study theory. Limited flying instruction was provided on Wednesdays:

"Flying training started in earnest in our second year and so I went solo for a second time. The instructor realised I could fly but I had kept it quiet. It was not something to shout about, but he did ensure my flying logbook was brought properly up-to-date.

"Cranwell were very clever in their selection of instructors and choosing the appropriate instructor for each pupil pilot. I was considered a steady type: capable and reliable, and I learned a great deal while I was there."

Wally did not always, however, endear himself to his peers. When asked by Air Commodore Neil Cameron (later MRAF Baron Cameron of Balhousie), the commandant at Cranwell at the time, what he thought of the new carpet in the front hall of the main building, Wally told him he preferred the old one!

Jet instruction was provided on Jet Provosts (Mk 3 and Mk 4s) which Wally remembers were prone to icing:

> "We used to refer to them as constant thrust, variable noise, and with relatively small air intakes and stator blades they could easily ice up. It could be very unpleasant, especially when coming into land, to push the throttle forward and not get any thrust. Once when landing with the throttle open and in the glide path I decided just to leave everything as it was and landed somewhat apprehensively!"

After around 135 hours flying time, Wally was awarded his wings and posted for advanced flying training on the Folland Gnat at 4FTS RAF Valley. This comprised a further 90 or so hours of training in preparation for an operational aircraft.

> "I really enjoyed my time on Gnats but it was very hard work. Then came the selection process. We could express a preference, but it was down to the RAF where and what we flew. I saw this as my chance to fly Hunters, but it was not to be. The powers that be felt I would be more suited to an aircraft with a crew, and so I was posted to Canberras. It could have been worse: some of the boys were posted to Vulcans or Victors. I recall one or two pilots on receiving V Force postings deciding to leave the RAF there and then!"

Wally was assigned to the English Electric Canberra getting his first taste of the aircraft at 231 OCU at Bassingbourn. He and his newly formed crew were then posted to 6 Squadron at Akrotiri – the so-called 'Shiny Six' to fly the operational B15, an updated version of the B2 with underwing hardpoints for bombs or rockets for its nuclear and conventional weapons role in strike/ground attack: "It had taken the RAF the better part of seven years to train me, and now at last this was my turn to deliver some of that investment back."

While on the squadron, Wally found himself on the wrong end of the OC's attention and seemed to be always 'in the dwang'. On more than one occasion he would find himself in serious trouble, though it was later explained to him that it was for his own good. Wally was prone to be reckless in

Wally at Cranwell in 1963.

pressing home rocket attacks to 600 ft rather than the proscribed 1,000 ft, and his commanding officer felt he was a danger to his crew. Wally admits to a few frightening incidents, but as he has discovered since at squadron reunions his escapades were no more or less than any others experienced by young officers at that time.

It was in Akrotiri, however, that Wally was able to indulge in a passion he had first taken up at Cranwell: rowing. Although a comparative novice he helped set up the RAF Akrotiri Rowing Club and continued to row throughout the rest of his RAF career and beyond. He competed at Henley in the RAF first VIII as well as some years later when rowing for his Australian Melbourne club, taking part in the first ever World Masters Games in Toronto.

After his tour on the Canberra ended, he hoped to move on to Phantoms or a posting to Central Flying School, but the RAF determined to keep him on multi-engine types. He was sent to Thorney Island to convert to the C-130 Hercules. At the end of the course, he was called in to see the OC, Squadron Leader David (Dave) Parsons:

> "The OC and a group of senior officers were all there and Dave started to berate me for my progress on the course. He said it would be a total waste of time and money to send me to 24 Squadron as a co-pilot, and that they were going to give me another chance. I was to fly with the instructor, nav leader, engineering leader and Wing Co flying and be given further training. I thought at that point I'd failed the course but then he said, 'if you do all right, we'll re-course you to captain immediately'. Captains at that time were meant to have completed a tour on transports of at least two years before being given command of a Hercules but I went straight to Lyneham as a captain."

Wally thoroughly enjoyed his time flying the mighty Hercules and jumped at the chance of a tour with 48 Squadron in Singapore. Training flights and landings on half-prepared fields were punctuated by flag-waving trips to Australia and Japan. They supported relief efforts during the catastrophic floods in the Ganges Delta caused by one of the most devastating cyclones of all time and played a part in preventing a dangerous oil spillage from becoming an environmental disaster when the hull of the SS *Ennerdale* (sister ship to the *Torrey Canyon*) was breached. This involved landing a Hercules on the beach in Mahe Island, Seychelles long before the current airport was built. Wally can also claim to be captain of the last 48 Squadron C-130 to have (officially) flown out of Changi before they closed it down.

On his return to the UK, Wally was posted to RAF Coltishall and put in charge of the general duties flight, making him responsible for, among others, the service police. Coltishall was also home to the RAF Historic Aircraft Flight, under the command of Wing Commander Dave Seward, and Wally spied a chance to fulfil an impossible childhood dream – to fly a Spitfire.

> "Dave said that if I could fly the Chipmunk and land it better than he could, then I was in. I did quite well, much to his feigned annoyance, and he promptly sent me to Boscombe Down to fly the Harvard. My instructor there was Flight Lieutenant Wackett, and he taught me everything there was to know about flying older aeroplanes. I also quickly learned for myself that you never knew which wing would drop first in a stall."

The RAF Historic Aircraft Flight at that time comprised four Spitfires (P7350, AB910, PS853 and PM631), and a single Hurricane (LF363). New pilots would usually fly the Hurricane first because it was easier to take off and land and had a more robust undercarriage but in early 1972 LF363 was having a prop change, so Wally was allocated to P7350 – the 'Baby Spit'.

'Training' initially comprised ground instruction, sitting in the cockpit of the Spitfire in the hangar with the aircraft on jacks, a hydraulic rig working the undercarriage up and down and operating the flaps with air. Wally was taken through the instruction by the flight's lead pilot Peter Gostick. Only when Peter was satisfied, was Wally allowed to take his first solo, an event he remembers well.

> "I was both thrilled and satisfied in equal measure. It met all of my expectations in terms of its handling qualities. I'd read before that pilots felt that it became part of them, and they were right. It was effortless. You'd think you wanted to turn to port and you turned; it just happened.
>
> "I was very aware that I was being given responsibility for an iconic piece of British history. It also gave me enormous respect for the pilots who had flown the Spitfire in combat. While sitting on a runway, waiting to take off for a display, I would think about that 92-gallon fuel tank and the 1,000 hp + Rolls-Royce Merlin in front of me, and try to empathise with those fighter pilots in 1940 who used the aircraft as a weapon of war.
>
> "In my time on the Historic Flight in terms of flying displays, we were not allowed to do aerobatics as it was considered it would put too much stress on the aircraft. Victory rolls were also banned, until the CO pointed out that a roll pulled less G than the flat turns that were part of our regular displays. Permission for a 'V' roll was granted."

Wally's first practice attempt at a victory roll over the Norfolk Broads was something of a fiasco:

> "I pulled the nose up by about 12-15 degrees and commenced the roll at which point I promptly fell out of the sky. The engine almost stopped, and

I went into a dive. I recovered and tried again, this time pulling the nose up to about 30 degrees and the same thing happened. On my third attempt, I tried 50 degrees and the aircraft rolled beautifully. When I landed, I discussed the issue with one of the other pilots, Jimmy Jewell, and his response was 'Didn't anybody tell you that?'"

The RAF Historic Aircraft Flight (which later became the Battle of Britain Memorial Flight with the addition of the Avro Lancaster in 1973) was much in demand at air displays and official ceremonies. Wally remembers one occasion at RAF Leuchars when a Mk XIX Spitfire gave him trouble:

"Every time I started pulling G the engine would run rough. Our chief engineer flying in my escort Bassett investigated. On the ground run the engine ran perfectly, but in the air, during the display, and on our way back to Coltishall it was running rough again. Over Newcastle, I began losing height and decided to land immediately at Acklington. Ultimately chiefy found the fault; the spark plug connectors had not been tightened properly and kept popping off each time I pulled G."

Wally also recalls an unfortunate landing in AB910 – a Spitfire Vb – his favourite aircraft:

"I came into land at the end of my first flight in AB910 with a moderate crosswind and ran off the side of the runway and put the Spitfire on its nose. It was not an uncommon accident, but it hit my confidence badly. My CO was very understanding and I continued to fly with the flight but it took a year or so to put the aircraft back in the air and I did everything I could to help, using the skills I had been taught at Halton and fetching and carrying parts. My contribution must have been appreciated because at my farewell party the engineers presented me with part of the broken propeller, polished and varnished, and with a brass plate inscribed with the serial number of the aircraft and date of my mishap."

Wally's time with the flight came to an end in 1974. On his promotion to squadron leader, Wally took command of the Dominie squadron that formed part of 6FTS at RAF Finningley. The Dominie – the RAF's name for the Hawker Siddeley HS 125 – was primarily used as a navigation trainer. He left the RAF in 1978 to move into business aviation, a conscious decision that would enable him to continue flying the HS 125. He flew for a firm in Switzerland for two years before joining Shell and setting up a new flight department for them in Australia and moving with his family to Melbourne. He later returned to the UK as chief pilot for Ready Mix Concrete.

He was re-acquainted with the Dominie in 2011 when the last aircraft were retired from RAF service and a number were sold to a friend who needed them ferrying from Cranwell to Kemble.

> "We moved six in two days, dropping the aircraft off and flying back in a Piper Lance. Five years later I flew two of them again to Humberside where they are now at BAe Systems' apprentice training school. I was pleased to help modern apprentices to experience similar training to myself."

Wally in 1977.

Wally continues flying today, with two regular private clients and plenty of freelance work, undertaking post-maintenance flight checks before returning the aircraft to their owners: "There are not that many of us who are happy to stall an aircraft deliberately, or de-pressurise an aircraft deliberately to test systems," he jokes. "Some companies insist that one of their pilots should fly with me in the co-pilot's seat. Typically, if they are ex-military men, they enjoy it; if they have always been civilian pilots then they are not so comfortable."

A member of the Honourable Company of Air Pilots (formerly GAPAN) for over 30 years, he was recognised with the award of a Master Air Pilot Certificate and became the former Guild's Master in 2011. He is proud to have been through the full spectrum of craftsmanship laid out by the liveried companies of the City of London. From apprentice through freeman and liveryman to master of the craft, he now describes himself as a journeyman pilot plying his trade in the sky. The City of London has provided many rewarding experiences and Wally recalls an amusing incident at a livery dinner when he was introduced to HM the Queen who said she was very fond of the Air Pilots: "I responded to Her Majesty's remark by saying that her son, the Duke of York, Prince Andrew was our grand master and an enthusiastic aviator. 'Oh yes,' she replied, 'he always has been fond of those gadgety things!'"

At the time of writing Wally has around 17,000 flying hours to his name, from fast jets to historic warbirds continuing to fly his beloved HS 125 nearly every week. He instructs on light aircraft and is an active chairman of two committees for the British Business and General Aviation Association. Wally continues to lead the Historic Aircraft Association (HAA) as its chairman, whilst also undertaking the restoration of his own Tiger Moth: "Retirement is not an option," he laughs.

21 THE NUCLEAR OPTION

Lawrie Haynes has never been conventional, at least not in the usual sense. It is unlikely that many, if any, of his contemporaries or instructors at Halton would have imagined the career that would evolve for the young apprentice, principally because it has come as something of a surprise to Lawrie himself. To be one of the country's most well-respected business leaders on the main board of Rolls-Royce Plc and now chairman of the board of trustees of the Royal Air Force Benevolent Fund seems an unlikely result for a small boy whose sole passion in his early life was to join the RAF, and who revelled in his time as a junior technician on a front-line fighter squadron.

Born in Scunthorpe in 1952 as the youngest of three boys, it was perhaps inevitable that Lawrie would seek a role in the armed forces. His father had been wireless op aircrew in Bomber Command and 2TAF, and his mother an LACW teleprinter operator. After the war, his father had taken a job as a foreman electrician in the local steel works and his mother trained as a seamstress before teaching others the art of dressmaking.

The family moved from their council house in Abbey Road to an old property in the village of Amcotts on the Isle of Axholme, where they set about turning a rather tumbledown house into a home. Lawrie also found time to keep pigs and became something of an expert as a registered pig breeder. It was perhaps the first sign of the unconventional path that he has chosen to follow.

While Lawrie was set upon joining the RAF, he was beaten to the race by his eldest brother, Chris: "He was 17 when he was accepted for pilot training and later awarded a commission," Lawrie explains. "He flew Chipmunks, Provosts, Gnats and Hunters, and gained his wings at RAF Valley. It was very exciting to think I had a brother who was a fighter pilot."

Stuart (but he preferred to be called David), his middle brother, had similar ambitions, but chose instead to apply for Halton and was accepted as part of the 208th Entry. Then at last it was Lawrie's turn. But there was a hitch – his eyesight:

Top: *A. J. 'Boy' Gooding. A recently discovered photograph of one of the youngest ever members of the RFC (at 14 years and one month) and one of first to pass through Halton's doors.*

Middle: *Two Brats at work on a Fairey IIIF of 8 Squadron in Aden.*

Bottom: *Brats consider the next steps in returning this ground-looped aircraft to its feet.*

Top: *One of the most famous aircraft to pass through the Brats' hands was the Fairey Long-Range Monoplane. Only two were built and this one crashed in 1929.*

Middle: *A Fairey Gordon comes to grief while serving with 14 Squadron in Aden in 1935.*

Bottom: *Halton airfield in the 1930s. These aircraft would not look out of place in a scrapyard!*

Top: *Inspecting the damage. A spanner, an oily rag, and the Brats will soon have this aircraft back in the sky.*

Top right: *J9060 Fairey III seaplane of 47 Squadron. Brats were often placed in 'gangs' when serving overseas to service particular aircraft types.*

Middle left: *Fairey Gordon SR1178 in flight over Aden.*

Middle right: *A Handley Page Heyford of 97 Squadron at Leconfield in 1934. One of the last of the RAF's biplane bombers.*

Bottom right: *Brats served on land and at sea, and in no-man's land that included flying boats such as this Saro Cloud.*

Top: *A line up of Avro 621 Tutors in 1937 on what appears to be an open day, given the little girl just visible centre foreground.*

Middle: *Brats could often be called upon to lend a hand to strange visitors, including this early airliner of Imperial Airways at Hinaidi.*

Bottom: *Engine problems: fixing an engine the hard way, beneath the blazing heat of the desert sun, with pith helmets at the ready.*

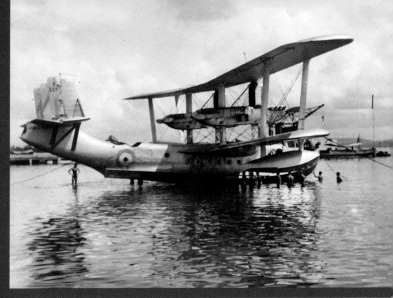

Top: *A Short Singapore. Inspecting a damaged float or hull often meant taking a dip.*

Middle: *A Flight, 51 Squadron at the start of the war. On many of the early raids, Brats would volunteer for service as air gunners.*

Bottom left: *Harry Clack of 39th Entry, the youngest apprentice to die in the Second World War while still only a teenager.*

Bottom right: *Guard Duty. Every Brat was expected to take his turn, though not all had time to pose for the camera like this 36 Squadron apprentice in Madras!*

Top: *A Wellington of 135 MU Egypt, 1943. Brats tended to prefer serving in operational squadrons to maintenance units.*

Middle: *Brats working on a late mark Spitfire in Allahabad in 1945 towards the end of hostilities.*

Bottom left: *An unknown Brat navigator's snapshot of a formation of Mosquitoes from 84 Squadron taking part in the VJ Day flypast.*

Bottom right: *Don Finlay leads the VJ Day march past while Mountbatten takes the salute.*

Clockwise from top left:

One of the more unusual types encountered by apprentice airmen was the Canadair Sabre, a variant of the North American F86. This is a snapshot of a 20 Squadron aircraft.

Ivan Whittaker, Dambuster of the 38th Entry (third from left), survived the raid and the war, winning the DFC and Bar.

Passing out with the Queen's Colour.

Taking the salute. Lord Trenchard with MRAF 'Peter Portal' (second from right).

18-year-old Sgt A/A G. Bryan barks orders at the passing-out parade. He was awarded a prize as the best fitter armourer.

Top left: *Mike Hines flew the Gloster Meteor 8 at Flying Training School. This particular Meteor F8 was written off in an accident in June 1955.*

Top right: *Venom WR340 of 249 Squadron in Amman in the summer of 1955. The aircraft was written off the following year. As Pete Goodwin found, looping a Venom was a dangerous thing to do.*

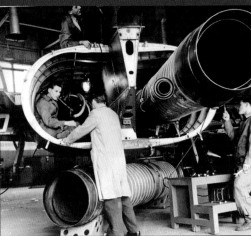

Middle left: *Ahmed Sheikh of the 69th Entry. As Halton's reputation spread, The Royal New Zealand, Pakistan, Ceylon and Rhodesian air forces and the Burmese and Malayan air forces all sent boys to Halton to train alongside British apprentices. The Venezuelan air force also sent boys to train at Halton in the 1950s.*

Middle right: *An inside job! Brats learn the ins and outs of engine maintenance.*

Bottom: *Brats ready to fledge. The proudest day for any Brat is the passing-out parade and awards ceremony.*

"I was knocked back on the medical but my father wrote to the RAF and explained I was already in the air training corps and that I was very keen to join and so I was given another chance. This time my father gave me a tip. He said to memorise the test card and in particular the fourth line as that was the one that they tested you on. I did as he suggested, and I passed."

With David already at Halton, he was able to tell his younger brother what to expect from the tests they would be given at RAF Stafford prior to being formally accepted. It required the discipline of learning and practice, especially sums, and his endeavours paid dividends. In October 1968 he arrived at Halton as part of the 216th Entry, remembering well the excitement of queuing to be kitted out with their uniform and the yellow hat band that signalled the newest of new boys. "We were well fed, given three meals a day, but still made our way to the NAAFI for beans on toast with a fried egg."

Lawrie settled quickly into service routine, the cleaning, polishing and general 'bull' that goes with being a new recruit and that gave him the essential grounding that was so important for his later career:

"We marched everywhere, usually behind a brass band, and they used to hold up the traffic to allow us to march across the main road that dissects the camp from the barracks to the workshops and schools. There was always someone with a witty remark or joke, even though there was no talking in the ranks. Humour played an enormous part in my life, and still does."

The camaraderie, Lawrie explains, was second to none:

"Of course as teenagers there were the occasional disagreements but we all genuinely looked after one another. It taught me the importance of being part of a team, and some of the basic training at Halton I was still using in 2018 at Rolls-Royce, especially when it came to recognising leadership on the factory floor."

With his fellow craft apprentices, Lawrie learned to file, drill and ream, as well as study the more complicated engineering subjects such as hydraulics and pneumatics, and how they applied to undercarriage and oleo legs. He well remembers the thrill of working on real aircraft – albeit ageing piston-engined Provosts – for the first time.

At sport, Lawrie became an active member of the camp hockey team, and later played at a senior level and for the RAF, but recalls one incident that backfired spectacularly when called for a cross-country:

"We studied PI in batches – three weeks of boxing, three weeks of cross-country and so on – and I was never that keen on cross-country. I knew that if I went sick, I would never get away with it so decided to go dental sick instead. The dentist was delighted to see me (I don't think he ever got much trade) but when he looked into my mouth it all went wrong. He discovered I had four impacted wisdom teeth that all had to come out."

Another amusing incident involved his eldest brother, Chris, who was by then based at RAF Coningsby flying Phantoms:

"I was invited to a Battle of Britain 'dining in' night at Coningsby and Chris said that if I brought a dinner jacket he'd get me in. To be at Coningsby by 6.30 p.m. meant leaving Halton early, by 3.00 p.m. I had to see my flight sergeant, who was God, and ask permission. I stood to attention in front of him and asked him if I could go. 'How long have you been in the RAF?' he said. 'I want you to leave my office, and come back in. And when you do, I want you to say to me that your grandmother has died, and you need all of Friday off for the funeral.' I duly obliged him, but when I asked for the whole day off he refused: 'No,' he said. 'But you can have from 3.00 p.m.'"

A similar incident occurred while in Germany, after he had passed out:

"I had met a girl at Laarbruch, where we were based, and she was in a band that was playing at Gütersloh and I wanted to see her play. Our chief technician was 'Slim' Coleman, an enormous armourer/plumber. I asked if I could leave early and to my surprise he said yes, as did my immediate boss. As I was packing my bag, the corporal armourer drove up in a Land Rover and said Slim wanted to see me. 'I'm sorry Haynes,' he said. 'But we need you to fetch some parts from Gütersloh, so you'll need to take the Land Rover and make sure you have some civvies with you.'"

On passing out, Lawrie's first posting was to 228 OCU but on the encouragement of his brother he joined a fighter squadron, 41 Squadron, a band of "reprobates and discards who won every NATO cup going" as Lawrie describes them.

"We were all misfits in a way but fiercely loyal to our squadron. It was another lesson I was to take with me into the commercial world when dealing with leaders of separate business divisions who were all part of the same group. I would say to them that in the RAF you could be loyal to your squadron, but your first loyalty is to the RAF. The same goes in business: you can be loyal to your division, but your first loyalty always has to be to the company."

Lawrie's previously carefree life was turned upside down on 21 November 1972 when his brother Chris was killed in an air crash. The 6 Squadron Phantom he was piloting along with his navigator Flight Lieutenant Martin Smith, was performing a low-level abort procedure in very poor visibility when their aircraft struck Scarrowmanwick Fell in Cumbria leaving the two men no time to eject. More tragedy befell the family the following year (on 13 November 1973) when his middle brother, David, was killed in a motor accident by a drunk driver.

On both occasions, the support that the RAF gave Lawrie, and in particular the kind words of his squadron commander, Wing Commander Brian 'Dink' Lemon, has stayed with him throughout. The tragedy prompted Lawrie to re-evaluate his life, giving him a new perspective, living in and for the moment. After six years in the air force he was still only a junior technician; promotions had passed him by because the minimum criteria of attending 80 per cent of ground school classes to qualify for a promotion exam could not be met as the squadron was constantly on the move. On one occasion the squadron moved to Singapore where their aircraft were painted in RAAF colours to convince the Chinese that the Australians had Phantoms on their doorstep. A posting from 41 Squadron to RAF Waddington to work on Vulcans ("Most of the aircraft were older than me," he says) finally made him decide that the time had come to move on.

Purchasing his discharge from the RAF he went to college in Edinburgh, getting a distinction in his Scottish National Certificate in Business Studies, and earning a place at Heriot Watt to read Business Law, a career inspired by a godfather who had a practice in Scunthorpe. He viewed study in logical terms, devoting 40 hours per week to the books and the rest of his time to leisure, primarily hockey. He did, however, also find the time to get married, although even their courtship was unconventional: "I met Carol whilst playing hockey at the Edinburgh Easter Festival (in 1978) and we only saw each other on five occasions before we married. She was a driving force in encouraging me to go to college then to university."

Graduating in 1983 with a BA (Hons), Lawrie joined the contracts/commercial law division of BAe Systems:

> "I'd applied to join the aircraft division but despite being in the RAF I was rejected and found myself, instead, in BAe's Space Systems business. I remember my starting salary as being £8,157 compared to the £2 I'd received on starting with the RAF."

It proved to be a fortuitous outcome, working in the very high-tech world of satellites and space modules. Within five years he was running the commercial/legal department and was then closely involved with a new joint venture formed to bid for a new personal communications network licence awarded by the government. The JV comprised firms in the UK, US and France, coming together as Microtel

Communications which subsequently emerged as Orange.

His senior and mentor, Sir Graham Day, asked Lawrie to join the business as its legal director. Sir Graham was in turn being advised by Dr Charles Bahn, and an incident on a train led to a further step up the career ladder:

> "I was travelling from Bristol to London with Charles and I had a first-class ticket and he had a standard class ticket. I said I would join him in his carriage. Two weeks later, Sir Graham's PA called me and said that Sir Graham needed to see me the following morning at 5.30 a.m. When I arrived, he greeted me and said that he'd been hearing good things about me from Charles. I did not have an opportunity to say yes or no to what followed. He told me that at 9.00 a.m. it was going to be announced that I was taking over as managing director of Microtel, and to get all of the PAs together and tell them first. Then they would all be on side."

Lawrie's relationship with Sir Graham endured through some difficult times, including a two-year spell back at BAe (Sir Graham was the then chairman) as project director of British Aerospace PLC overseeing a raft of mergers and acquisitions. "I had good support from both the finance director and the HR director, and air cover provided by George Simpson (Baron Simpson of Dunkeld)," he adds.

An approach from a headhunter led Lawrie to take his career in yet another different direction, a role that he at first turned down. It was as chief executive of a new organisation called the Highways Agency. Lawrie explains:

> "I did not see myself as a civil servant but it transpired that Sir Graham had put me up for the role and advised me to take it. He said that it would mean experiencing how to run a £2 billion business and learning the machinations of government and Whitehall – both of which, he told me, would be crucial skills to have for the future."

Three days of interviews culminated in a brief meeting with the Secretary of State, John MacGregor in 1994.

> "As I was shown in to meet him, my escort addressed me by saying 'young man the minister will see you now'. (I was then 42.) When I came out, the same man said to me, 'I realised I called you young man and have also realised I am now working for you.'"

As CEO of the Highways Agency, Lawrie learned the direct correlation between traffic growth and economic growth. He had a balance sheet of £55 billion and a business run on cash accounting. In effect this meant attempting to manage 20-year projects on an annual budget. Among the first changes he made was to bring in an accruals accounting procedure and make swingeing changes to procurement rules to prevent costly over-runs. They introduced design, build, finance and operate contracts as well as a new 'toolkit' to help those previously constrained by the Highways Manual. John Prescott, then his boss, wrote the foreword, providing the new document with immediate credibility and high-level support. The use of hard shoulders and variable speed limits on motorways were all introduced during his tenure, and he regularly attended Transport Select committees and Treasury Select committees to explain and support his actions.

> "Here I was, standing in front of a succession of Secretaries of State – John MacGregor, Brian Mawhinney, Sir George Young, John Prescott – at these important meetings wondering how I ever got here. I was still a mere junior technician at heart!"

After six enjoyable and professionally rewarding years at the Highways Agency, Lawrie decided to move on, and after a brief appointment at PWC he was again approached to lead a team at the Lattice Group, initially as group managing director telecoms, reporting to Sir John Parker. His first task was to lead a half-a-billion-pound project to install fibre across the UK, at the time of some of the worst flooding the country has ever seen, and hampered still further by an outbreak of foot-and-mouth disease that seriously restricted access to farmland where the cable was being laid. Despite these hurdles, the project was completed within budget and on time.

A decision to merge the business with the National Grid – a decision taken over one Easter weekend and coming as a complete surprise to the market – effectively meant Lawrie was out of a job, but was immediately headhunted to join BNFL as a main board director, and with specific responsibility for the British Nuclear Group.

> "BNG was a high technology group responsible for managing and operating major nuclear sites and involved in the decommissioning and clean-up of legacy nuclear waste, and with joint control and oversight of the UK facilities at the Atomic Weapons Establishment (AWE). As you can imagine, it was a very responsible job working within Sellafield, Magnox and the AWE, as well as working across Europe and the US, and I was immediately impressed by the quality and skills of the people they employed.
>
> "I was able to look at what were obviously very complicated facilities and units with the eye of a basic professional. At Halton and at 41 Squadron, flight safety had been drummed into us – the risk of foreign object damage for example – and the same focus on safety was evident within

BNG. They had 'shadow boards' for their tools, like we did, so if you took ten tools out you made sure you took ten tools back, and the shadow boards helped you to identify if something was missing."

His responsibility was brought home to him one day when there was a major nuclear incident at one of the sites involving a broken pipe: "The public relations director called me and asked me what I intended to do and I said I would go straight to the site to which he replied, 'correct answer!'"

Eventually, and with the planned break-up of BNFL, Lawrie resigned owing to what he calls "a difference of opinion between me and the Secretary of State on policy". He was not out of work for long, joining White Young Green (WYG) as chief executive shortly after. WYG was an international engineering and project management business that worked across both the public and the private sectors in equal measure, but when plans to sell the business were not enthusiastically embraced by the exec, Lawrie eventually accepted an overture from Rolls-Royce on 1 February 2009 to join its leadership team.

Initially appointed to run the company's nuclear business, where he worked closely with the Royal Navy, Lawrie was again impressed and comforted by the quality of the designers, engineers, fitters and technicians within the workforce. His success in leading the nuclear business was recognised with his appointment to president of Land & Sea, the division comprising two further businesses, Rolls-Royce Marine, and Rolls-Royce Power Systems, based in Germany. To give some idea of scale, in 2014 the Land & Sea division turned over £5.1 billion in revenues, and its 21,000 staff helped deliver some £450 million in profits.

While Lawrie's post-RAF CV reads like a 'Who's Who' of some of the biggest names in British business, his roots as a junior technician who has 'walked the walk' have never left him. Neither has the importance of humour. Both qualities have enabled him to navigate through a myriad of challenges, not least his negotiations with the union firebrand Mick Cash during his time at Network Rail where he was a non-executive director and chairman of the safety committee:

> "I invited a union rep onto our safety committee, and although it raised an eyebrow or two at the time it seemed the obvious thing to do. As I said to Mick, he had 44,000 members; I had 44,000 staff! Having Mick on my board was a great success."

A visit to a site in Norway with Rolls-Royce Marine also proved a talking point:

> "Walking the floor, one of the engineers was using a vice that had no protection in the jaws which you need when working with some of the softer metals to prevent them from being damaged. I discussed it with him, and

sure enough the jungle drums were beating around the factory in no time."

Since 'retiring' from full-time executive work, Lawrie has taken on a number of non-executive roles, including a spell at Louis Berger, a global engineering-led business, as the only 'Brit' on the board. He was particularly delighted recently to have been made an honorary doctor by his alma mater, Heriot-Watt – not bad, he says, for an old Trenchard Brat. More recently still he was appointed chairman of the nuclear decommissioning authority subsidiary, Magnox.

Lawrie's appetite for learning has never left him: "Whether at Orange, the Highways Agency, BNFL or Rolls-Royce I was always having to learn," he concludes. "I acquired the habit of learning as an apprentice."

Lawrie at Halton.

Lawrie as he is today. (Oliver Dixon/Imagewise)

22 THE ACCIDENTAL AIRMAN

Graham 'Dusty' Miller never particularly meant to fly. Neither did he intend to join the Royal Air Force, for that matter. The former came to him by chance; the latter was driven by his mother and family circumstances. But having found himself as part of the RAF 'family' he took full advantage of the opportunity it presented, rising from a craft apprentice at Halton in 1967 to retire at the end of a distinguished career forty years later as Air Marshal Sir Graham Miller KBE, deputy commander, Joint Force Command.

Born in Winchester in 1951, the middle of three children, Dusty's father was an architect with the New Towns Commission and the family moved to Crawley to follow his father's work. Sadly, his father was diagnosed with a brain tumour when Dusty was only seven, and died three years later, placing tremendous strain on his mother.

When Dusty was 15, and – in his words – on a path to outstanding mediocrity at school (he did enjoy the sciences, however, and especially physics), he attended the RAF Youth Selection Centre in Stafford at his mother's instigation, after she'd written to the RAF careers office in Brighton and he'd attended a first interview. It was, Dusty says, the best idea she ever had:

> "At Brighton I was tested and then there were more detailed tests at Stafford, after which I was offered a choice of two apprenticeships, either as an airframe fitter or a cook. It was also where it was incontrovertibly confirmed I was red/green colour blind, something I was aware of much earlier and has been a complication all of my life."

Dusty arrived at the unfamiliar world of Halton as part of the 210th Entry still two months short of his 16th birthday.

> "My first impression was 'oh my god, what have I let myself in for?' Everyone seemed to be much bigger, hairier and older than me. I'd had a

comparatively sheltered upbringing, and the first six weeks were pretty tough going. I wasn't the only one. A number walked out or later bought themselves out, but I had nothing to go back to and so leaving wasn't really an option. I also knew how disappointed my mother would have been, so I put my head down and got on with it."

As an apprentice airframe fitter, Dusty quickly learned that there was no such thing as 'good enough'; it was either right, or wrong. Familiarity with hand tools was the first lesson: he was given a lump of metal and told to file it, then file it flat, then file it flatter still, all to a uniform depth. He learned the mysteries of hydraulics, pneumatics, wheels, and tyres, almost everything except the engines, weapons and electrics. "We knew where the engine was, of course, but that was 'owned' by another trade."

Even the smell of a workshop today transports Dusty back to Halton:

"On an official visit to St Athan when I was AOC Training Group, I was watching a trainee working on a piece of aluminium but could not recognise the piece he was producing from the drawing he was meant to be following. When I asked him what he was making he answered as quick as a flash: 'Scrap metal, Sir.'"

Joining the RAF had never been Dusty's idea, but once part of the service he began to consider his options.

"I wasn't unhappy being in a trade, but neither was I that comfortable either. My trade skills were OK, but my rivets were always crooked, and I realised it probably wasn't the career for me. Becoming an officer, however, would broaden my horizons and so I set about ensuring I made the minimum rank (corporal apprentice) to be considered, and went to night school to improve my education and get the six O levels needed at the time."

Dusty's hard work at Halton paid off; he made corporal and in his final term was promoted sergeant apprentice along with Mick King:

"Mick and I were vying to make sergeant apprentice and they chose us both. At the passing out ceremony, Mick took the parade and I carried the colours. We were also both selected for officer training at RAF Henlow along with Harry McNeil, who had passed out first in our entry."

Towards the end of his time at Halton, Dusty decided upon becoming a supply officer, and it was only at the end of the selection process at Biggin Hill that he was asked why he had not wanted to fly:

> "My interviewer asked why I had not considered becoming a pilot or nav-
> igator and it was simply because I hadn't really thought about it. I prompt-
> ly asked to train as a pilot, and not a supply officer, and shortly after took
> my first air experience flight. For a brief moment again I thought 'what
> have I done?' but there was also the thought that if it didn't work out I
> could always go back to being a supply officer."

As it was, Dusty fell in love with flying from the start. Indeed, he nearly messed
up while flying the Chipmunk from Church Fenton, simply because he spent too
much time marvelling at how wonderful it all was and not really concentrating on
what the instructor was saying. On Jet Provosts at Leeming, a course of eight pilots
was quickly whittled down to two, and since the CO decided he would not hold
a Wings Parade for two people, Dusty was asked whether he wanted to join the
course ahead and catch up, or wait for the course below. Always one who likes to
be pushed, he opted for the former. From the Provost he progressed to the Gnat
at RAF Valley, and quickly realised that if he finished first or second on his course
he would take one of the two Harrier slots available. It was a dream that was
thwarted at the last: "I finished first in my course, by which time they had changed
the postings, and whoever came out on top went to Central Flying School. I had
somewhat overplayed my hand!"

Flying was fast becoming second nature, and Dusty graduated from Little Rissington as a qualified flying instructor in December 1971, returning to Leeming to
instruct on Provosts. Like all instructors, Dusty had his fair share of hairy moments.

On one occasion, while coming in to
land, he instructed the student pilot to
respond to a simulated engine failure.
The student, who was having a particularly dull day, pulled the stick back,
stalled, and belly flopped the aircraft
in from 100 ft, causing considerable
damage to the undercarriage and
wings: "It was a very one-sided interview with the AOC," Dusty recalls. "He
told me it was a good job I was only a
flying officer and inexperienced as an
instructor, because if I had been more
senior, I would have been in more serious trouble." The student, it is believed, went on to fly helicopters.

Dusty about to start flying training in January 1970.

He was later posted to the tactical weapons unit at RAF Chivenor to convert onto the Hunter (his favourite aircraft), followed by conversion (at 226 OCU) to the Jaguar. He was then posted to 14 Squadron at RAF Brüggen in Germany.

> "Until I arrived in Germany I had never really thought about defence, but in your first briefing you're suddenly aware that the enemy is only 160 miles – a few minutes flying time – to the east. Your life is one of respirators, combat kit, live weapons and bombing exercises on the Nordhorn Ranges – every waking moment was focused on operations and I enjoyed every second of it."

Dusty remembers long periods of sitting in the cockpit on immediate readiness, waiting for the code word to launch, and then having to do some rapid calculations to make his allotted bomb strike time:

> "When we first started, it was all a bit chaotic, with everyone getting in one another's way, but in time we got it all down to a fine art. In Sardinia we dropped bombs and strafed with the 30-mm cannon, and in the evenings drank copious Deci Red (named after the Decimomannu air base). It was all very competitive.
>
> "Most of the flying was at low level (250 ft) and sometimes, just to keep up the flying hours, they flew high altitude routes at night. Sometimes they flew even lower.
>
> "At 100 ft flying at 500 mph, it's amazing how focused you can be. But when you are comfortable, rehearsed, and current, you can even look around. Later, the Tornado, with auto pilot and terrain-following radar, flew itself and you could look out and glimpse the hills and mountains above you, even in the dark."

After two years in Brüggen, his experience as an instructor stood him in good stead when Dusty received the dream posting for any fast-jet ground-attack pilot to become a qualified weapons instructor (QWI). An important part of his training was being taught how to teach.

> "It's about taking a student from the known to the unknown and doing it in blocks based on the individual student's capacity to absorb information and develop new skills. You learn that your own demonstrations have to be convincing, to give the student a model of what you want them to do. You want them to learn the right technique to get the bombs on the target and the wheels on the concrete, all at the right time.
>
> "You also learn how to analyse results and talk a student through any

faults he has. You focus on the major faults – those that have the most impact on the results. You tell them what you need them to remember."

Every pilot, Dusty says, is guilty at some stage in their lives of TLAR – that looks about right. But there is no substitute for the right technique and accurate flying.

Dusty returned to Brüggen and 14 Squadron twice more, until in May 1984 he was posted to Headquarters 1 Group:

> "I was by now 32 and a squadron leader, and about to commence a staff tour. It was the first occasion that I tasted failure and I didn't like it. My written work was particularly poor, and I really struggled. 'Hoppy' Granville-White took me under his wing in a fatherly way and showed me how to do staff work properly. Several years later, Hoppy introduced me to offshore sailing and we remain firm friends to this day."

A short course at the Joint Services Defence College was followed by a posting to High Wycombe, headquarters of Strike Command, in charge of Plans 6, the airfield hardening programme which Dusty describes as a tour of 'Boys Own' interest.

After some six years on the ground, Dusty began wondering if squadron command would come his way. He returned to RAF Brawdy for a refresher course on Hawks (the only challenge being the use of red/green indicators for the undercarriage) before converting to the Tornado in preparation for taking command of 17 (F) Squadron. With a crew of two, Dusty had to get used to having someone in the back:

> "Until then I had done everything myself, but in the Tornado I had someone behind me and it took a little getting used to. As the squadron boss I flew with one of the senior flight commander navigators and told him that if I was walking towards a cliff edge to tell me. Later I would fly with more junior or problem navigators – those who were perhaps not progressing as fast as they should – and usually the jolt of flying with the commanding officer was enough to get them back on track."

The differences between the Tornado and the Jaguar were marked, as Dusty discovered during one night-check with the Wing QFI:

> "The Jaguar had small wings, which meant minimum lift, and very little power. We used to joke that the only reason the Jaguar got off the ground was that the curvature of the earth meant the ground dropped away. It could also go from controlled flight to uncontrolled very quickly. With variable wings and greater engine power, the Tornado could get you out of most trouble, but it still had its foibles. The spin and incidental limitation system

(SPILS) had to be switched off for gun firing and that could catch you out."

The invasion of Kuwait by Saddam in 1991 saw the squadron divided into two components, one half despatched to the Gulf and the second – which Dusty commanded along with half of 9 Squadron – remaining in Brüggen, on stand-by to replace aircraft and crews as required.[1] With the conclusion of hostilities, Dusty's contingent was deployed in theatre to maintain a British presence.

It was while in command in Brüggen that 17 (F) Squadron adopted its own mascot to match those used by rival squadrons on the base, notably 'Arris, a large stuffed teddy bear belonging to 31 Squadron. Initial plans for a set of bagpipes and even a racehorse were ultimately usurped by the introduction of a Trabant, which had previously served as an advertising hoarding for a double-glazing product. The squadron aircrew, using the facilities of the local maintenance unit, returned the vehicle to good working order, painting it in squadron colours and adding the legend 'Dusty and Lesley' in a visor strip across the windscreen to complement the furry dice.

The 'Trabby' became a key feature of squadron life, being used as the 'carriage' to whisk the CO and his wife away to the summer ball, and even – occasionally – to collect Dusty's children from school. Keeping the Trabby safe, however, and free from malicious damage was a constant challenge, and shortly before Dusty handed over the keys to the squadron, the Trabby was stolen. To be more accurate, 31 Squadron staged a carjacking, and a full two days of negotiations were required to secure its return for a crate of beer that was well past its sell-by date. Dusty's boys soon had their revenge, however, kidnapping 'Arris, the 31 Squadron bear, and overseeing its demise. The tit for tat continued, the Trabant being stolen for one last time, crashed into a tree and deliberately set on fire. But by then, Dusty was at the MoD as a group captain, looking at the weapons equipment requirements for the RAF for the next 25 years. Then he was given command at RAF Lossiemouth.

> "It was like all of my birthdays coming at once. We had Jaguars and Tornados, as well as a couple of Sea Kings. I managed to acquire around 100 hours on the Sea King plus around 350 hours on the jets during what was probably my favourite tour and the last time we were all together as a family.
>
> "We had eight wing commanders at Lossiemouth and all were destined for higher rank. I got to know the lads very well – both aircrew and ground crew alike – and we became a very close team."

Promoted air commodore in 1998, Dusty spent a tricky but interesting five months in Sarajevo as part of NATO's stabilisation force, with a particular focus on re-opening the Bosnian air space to commercial flights. The Bosnian Serb air force, however, still had some weaponry and air power at their disposal, including napalm, posing a potential threat to the ongoing peace: "It meant breaking bread with the Bosnian Serb general," Dusty says, "and getting his people to work with us." It also meant the opportunity to fly yet another aircraft type: "The Slovenians provided me with a helicopter, so we'd take off from Sarajevo, then put down somewhere, swap seats, and I'd take it from there to Banja Luka."

On his return from the Balkans in the summer of 1998, Dusty returned to the MoD during the period of smart procurement (Better. Faster. Cheaper), looking at future offensive air systems which in effect was a competition between Boeing and Lockheed Martin. The latter was successful, the result being the F-35 that is now coming into service today.

As Air Commodore Offensive Operations with 1 Group, Dusty – along with Peter Ruddock (later Air Marshal Peter Ruddock CB, CBE) – found himself "in charge of all the pointy aircraft in the air force". It was on his watch that 9/11 occurred, and the build-up of US forces for Operation Enduring Freedom to counter the Al Qaeda and Taliban threat in Afghanistan. He joined the Joint Task Force – South West Asia (JTF-SWA) at Prince Sultan Air Base for Operation Oracle.

> "We were keen to help in any way we could and were deploying for exercises in Oman so had plenty of kit in the region. The US Air Force were already deploying many bombers so we concentrated our efforts where we were most needed and could add greatest value, namely photo reconnaissance, airborne early warning (AWACS), and tanker refuelling, along with a Nimrod."

He was made Commander of the British Empire in 2002 for his work during this period.

On his return to the UK, Dusty was promoted to air vice-marshal and became AOC Training Group, waking up one morning to find he was in charge of 600 aircraft. He was AOC for 17 months and achieved the remarkable feat of flying all eight training aircraft in a single day, thanks to some skilful co-ordination and organisation from his team. These were the Squirrel, Tutor, Dominie, Hawk, Vigilant, Tucano, Jetstream and Griffin.

> "Very early on I was invited by the physical education officers to their annual dinner, and while I cleverly thought I had managed to work into my speech every sport or physical activity they were involved with, I failed to mention parachuting. As a matter of honour, therefore, I went to Hereford to do a parachute jump, but the weather was too poor, and I ended up watching the special forces being trained. The PEOs didn't forget I owed them a jump, which I achieved in tandem with a huge warrant officer strapped to my back at Weston-on-the-Green."

Dusty (right) may have been contented to see out his days in training but had one last 'hurrah' in Naples, as the deputy commander of Joint Forces Command.

> "It was a great tour to end on, with never any worry about budgets or costs, and running day-to-day operations because the US commander, a four-star US Navy admiral, was frequently out of office, and I had fully delegated powers in his absence."

The tour was not without its issues. Any decisions had to be cleared with the North Atlantic Council but getting them to agree on anything was a challenge. It coincided with the training mission to Baghdad to establish the 'Sandhurst in the Sand' and the huge cultural challenges this presented.

> "We had to train basic Iraqi soldiers to guard the camp but the guards would sometimes arrive on duty with no ammunition because they had sold it in the market in order to buy food. On one occasion the guards simply never reported for duty, and when we investigated, we found that their commander had been kidnapped and there was nobody to give any orders."

During his final year in Naples, Dusty seized the opportunity to fly in the back seat of a US Navy F-18 Super Hornet from the deck of the USS *Enterprise* when she was visiting the Mediterranean.

> "As carriers go, *Enterprise* is a big ship, but the deck still looked tiny from the approach to land – we had fair weather and a flat sea, and I can only imagine the skill required to operate successfully at night and in bad weather."

Dusty was knighted in the 2007 New Year's Honours list for 'total commitment to his military calling'. He was delighted with the award for the simple fact that:

> "My wife, Lesley, who had supported me throughout my career, brought up our children often single-handed, and cared for the men and women who had worked with me, as well as their families, gained the title of Lady Miller – a small recognition for the time and effort she had also devoted to the service."

Since retiring from the RAF as an air marshal, Dusty has continued to involve himself in service life, and indulge his passion for sailing. He was previously the commodore of the RAF Sailing Association and a pilot with 8 Air Experience Flight flying just over 1,000 air cadets before age finally clipped his wings. He is currently one of two vice patrons of the Halton Apprentices Association. His brother, Clive, followed him into Halton as part of the 219th Entry and retired as a warrant officer. Dusty attended the ceremony to see Clive presented with the Meritorious Service Medal.

So what does Halton mean to Dusty? He answers the question by reaching into his pocket and pulling out the original brass wheel he was given upon becoming an apprentice: "You must never forget your roots."

23 VIGNETTES

Halton prides itself on the training it provides to its apprentices, not just at a practical level, in a Brat's ability to fashion an improbable repair from the seemingly impossible, but also at a personal level, preparing them for life beyond the services. There are those who win their spurs in more unlikely environments, including the police, the civil service, or the clergy, or who follow an arguably more 'traditional' path but still find themselves pressed into an unusual service, on land, sea and in the air.

Take the example of Robert Yaxley of the 20th Entry. Yaxley, who was born in Bath and educated at King Edward VI School, came from a military family; his father had been in the Somerset Light Infantry and his uncle in the RAF. Enlisting as an apprentice in 1929, Robert passed out as fitter (AE) in the rank of LAC. One of the few to be granted a cadetship to Cranwell, Yaxley passed out a second time, but this time as an officer cadet, winning the Air Ministry prize for Aero Engineering. Posted to the Middle East, Yaxley served with the RAF's No. 2 Armoured Car Company and was closely engaged in the Arab Revolt in Palestine for which he was awarded the Military Cross. The citation made mention of his 'gallant and distinguished services in connection with emergency operations in Palestine during the period 15 April to 14 September 1936'.

First and foremost a pilot, however, Yaxley joined 252 Squadron and in December 1940, became its commanding officer. The following autumn he took command of 272 Squadron flying Bristol Beaufighters and was awarded the DFC for raids on enemy aerodrome and seaplane bases in support of the safe passage of convoys through the Med. The DFC was quickly followed by a DSO (a contemporary newspaper cutting claimed this to be the first during the campaign in Libya). The citation states that his squadron had been responsible for destroying 46 enemy aircraft in six days of fighting: 'Much of the brilliant success can be attributed to the courageous leadership and determination played by Wing Commander Yaxley.'

Yaxley continued to fight in the desert, as CO of 117 Squadron, but on 3 June

1943 he was killed while piloting a Lockheed Hudson over the Bay of Biscay en route to North Africa. Among his passengers was the fighter ace Osgood 'Pedro' Hanbury DSO DFC & Bar.

Yaxley was certainly not the only Brat to receive a bravery award for actions on the ground. Pilot Officer Arthur Cork, a carpenter rigger and high-flyer within the 11th Entry, was similarly awarded the MC when in charge of a party of 37 Squadron airmen embarking on the SS *Dumania* from Alexandria to Greece. They had four Lewis gun positions to defend themselves. Their vessel soon came under attack both on the route out and on the journey home. The citation for his MC reads:

> 'Throughout all these attacks, which were made either by dive bombing or torpedoes, Pilot Officer Cork controlled and used his guns continuously, manning individual gun positions in turn himself, although in an exposed position on the upper deck. His splendid leadership inspired the gun crew to resist the enemy with vigour and accuracy.'

In all, some 6,000 rounds were expended and at least two enemy aircraft damaged.

Not every ground action required engaging with the enemy directly. Sergeant Ernest Russell, who'd passed out of the 23rd Entry as a metal rigger, won his Military Medal for bravery under fire during the Norwegian campaign and as part of the ground-servicing team attached to 263 Squadron. His father, a former soldier in the Middlesex Regiment, would have been very proud. In the recommendation for his award, the words make mention of considerable courage and devotion to duty: 'Much of his work was on re-arming the squadron aircraft and was performed whilst subjected to enemy bombing and machine-gun fire.'

A bravery award to a Brat in a very different war went to Muhammad Akmal Khan, and resides in the Trenchard Museum collection. Muhammad was an electrician, part of the 63rd Entry. He recounted his part in the war that broke out between India and Pakistan in the first week of September 1965:

> "I was stationed at PAF Station Badin, which was about 40 miles south-west of Karachi and 20 miles from the Indian border. At about 08.00 hours on 17 September, Indian Air Force (IAF) Hunters attacked the station as the prelude to a ground assault by Indian commandos. I was entrusted to look after the security of the powerhouse and two radar units.
>
> "When the air attack was over, I came out of my trench to look around for possible damage. Both radar units were on fire and PAF fire fighters were trying to extinguish the flames. As I started looking around the radar towers a burst of machine-gun fire came towards me. I immediately jumped into a trench. The gunfire continued and after a few minutes I heard foot-

steps approaching. I readied my Sten gun with my finger on the trigger.

"The approaching Indian commandos first threw a grenade, then, as they were crossing over my trench towards the power-house, the bullets from my Sten gun hit them. Two of them fell headlong into my trench with three lying dead outside, like wooden planks. After two hours a siren sounded; the Indian attack had been repelled with heavy casualties."

Muhammad Akmal Khan.

Muhammad was one of a number of trainee apprentices from Pakistan, several of whom went on to distinguish themselves in the India/Pakistan war. Some achieved high rank, including Air Vice-Marshal Mohammad Younis[1]. Younis was born in Gordaspur (on the India/Pakistan border), and joined the air force as a sepoy. Winning a place at Halton, he passed out as a fitter (AE), reaching the rank of sergeant apprentice. A hugely popular figure, he also graduated from Cranwell, and claimed to be the first Pakistani pilot to shoot down an Indian spy plane in Rawalpindi in April 1959.

In the war of 1965, Younis was a squadron leader who flew several operations behind enemy lines. The official history puts his achievements in the context of the aircraft he flew which, it suggests, had limited capability, poor navigational aids, and outdated weapons systems.

'Squadron Leader Younis repeatedly pressed home his attack by night on enemy communications in the face of fire from the ground and successfully damaged two trains and blew up a small ammunition vehicle. This success is attributed to his offensive spirit and hunting eye which enabled him to spot the enemy movements in spite of black-out and poor light conditions.'

For his bravery in combat, Younis was awarded the Tamgha-e-Basalat, an operational award for acts of bravery, and later went on to become AOC Northern Command during the Soviet war in Afghanistan. On leaving the air force, he became head of Civil Aviation Pakistan. He died in 2014.

Brian 'Manx' Skillicorn was another former Brat who distinguished himself in a post-war conflict. Originally from the Isle of Man, Brian was part of the 93rd Entry and joined Halton from Douglas High School in the Manx capital. Qualifying as an airframe fitter, despite having to retake one of his exams, Brian learned to fly at Luton where he obtained a private pilot's licence.

Obtaining a commission, Brian exchanged fixed wing for rotary aircraft, becoming an accomplished helicopter pilot, initially with 225 Squadron, when he was mentioned in despatches. He joined 103 Squadron in November 1965 and was praised for landing a helicopter in a jungle clearing after a tail rotor failure and for landing safely on a beach after the engine failed.

On 10 August 1966, Brian was captain of a Whirlwind helicopter on an operational flight in Sarawak. The citation for the Air Force Cross that followed tells its own tale:

> 'As he reached a point about 250 yards on final approach to a hilltop landing site in trees on top of a hill at a height of 1,400 feet above the nearby plain, there was a loud bang from the engine followed by complete loss of power. He quickly turned the helicopter away from the hill, recovered the rapidly decaying rotor rpm and established an autorotative descent towards the plain, which was covered with a mixture of primary and secondary jungle relieved by only a few very small patches of swamp and primitive cultivation.
>
> 'Flying Officer Skillicorn selected a clearing within his limited range and began his circuit. He then discovered that the clearing was obstructed by fallen trees and at almost the last moment had to change his approach to reach an even smaller clearing, about 75 yards long and 25 yards wide separated from his first choice by a screen of trees and limited further by a stream which cut it in two. Despite this setback and the fact that the whole incident, from engine failure to landing, occupied little more than one minute, Flying Officer Skillicorn transmitted clear correct distress calls and adjusted his approach to reach the second clearing.
>
> 'He cleared the screen of trees, but to do so had to manoeuvre the helicopter between two taller trees so close that the tips of the main rotor blades were slightly damaged. On landing, it was found that the ground was soft, and the front wheels dug in, pitching the helicopter forward and breaking off the tailboom. Neither Flying Officer Skillicorn nor his co-pilot were injured.
>
> 'A pilot without Flying Officer Skillicorn's qualities of determination and

skill would, in the circumstances he encountered, have had to accept a crash-landing, with severe injuries or loss of life for his crew being the normally inevitable result, but, by his cool, courageous and skilful handling of the situation, Flying Officer Skillicorn ensured the safety of his crew and, but for the treacherous nature of the ground would have saved his aircraft even from the damage it sustained.

'In a force whose bravery and professional expertise have aroused general admiration, his own record has been second to none. His fine example

Drawing of Freddie Lanham.

has been an inspiration and an encouragement to his fellow pilots, all too well aware of the hazards of flying single-engined aircraft over this inhospitable terrain.'

Bravery comes in many forms; it is not always demonstrated on the battlefield. Some examples of the most exceptional heroism were shown by those Brats who found themselves prisoners of the Japanese after the fall of Singapore and the collapse of the British and Commonwealth Forces in the Far East.

West Country-born Sergeant Freddie Lanham of the 24th Entry is just one example of quiet heroism that more often than not goes unrewarded but is nonetheless remarkable. He'd passed out as a metal rigger and was captured after the fall of Singapore. As the senior prisoner in a Japanese POW camp, Freddie had to supply a given number of men as slave labourers each day. If he failed to do so, he was beaten with the length of bamboo which he had to carry at all times as his badge of office. One of his fellow prisoners, for whom Freddie had endured many beatings because he was too sick to work, drew a portrait of his senior in September 1942 (see above) which hangs in the Trenchard Museum alongside the piece of bamboo in which the drawing was hidden.

In total, more than 5,100 RAF men were recorded as Far East prisoners of war (FEPOWs). Of that number, more than 1,700 died – a figure of more than 40 per cent compared to the 5 per cent that died in German prison camps. Of the 224 FEPOWs who were Halton apprentices, 76 (34 per cent) failed to make it home, victims of illness, malnutrition, or the barbarity of the Japanese and Korean guards.

Freddie was one of the lucky ones. After VJ Day he was still in prison at Batavia but managed to get a letter sent to his mother. It reads:

'If this should reach you in the near future it will relieve your mind of any anxiety you may have concerning me as I am sure that the casualty lists being issued are far from accurate. I am one of the fortunate ones originally taken prisoner here who is still alive. At the moment my weight is 105 lbs and I am not too clever, but that will change by the time you see me. We are still in jail and very little better off. Food is still scarce and poor in quality. Hoping to get back before many months have passed.'

Bravery can also be shown in overcoming adversity, and Douglas Park certainly had to go through more than most. Part of the 29th Entry, not long after passing out as a fitter II Douglas was involved in a serious motorcycle accident and had to endure several operations before a decision was taken to amputate his left leg. A tough man in mind and body, Douglas literally fought his way back to fitness, overcoming his disability by taking part in heavyweight boxing bouts.

With the onset of war, he volunteered for aircrew, qualifying as a flight engineer and commencing a tour with 35 Squadron at Graveley in July 1942. With the elevation of 35 to Pathfinder Force, Douglas' crew was at the vanguard of some of the heaviest raids and most fiercely defended targets, including Cologne, Essen, Frankfurt, Hamburg, Mannheim, Munich, Stuttgart and, of course, the 'Big City' itself, Berlin.

Posted to 156 Squadron in June 1943, Douglas completed a further five operations before his crew was tragically killed in a flying accident near East Wretham on 3 September 1943. His pilot was a Canadian Flying Officer Clifford Foderingham DFC. Douglas was not at his pilot's side that day and survived his operational tour to be awarded the DFM. The citation makes specific reference to Douglas' bravery in facing everyday life:

'This NCO has taken part in 40 operational sorties against targets in Germany, Italy and the occupied territory. Five of these sorties have been on Pathfinder Force duties. Flight Sergeant Park came to this squadron with a very high reputation as a flight engineer. This reputation he has consistently maintained. He has always shown the utmost courage, determination and tenacity of purpose in spite of the fact that he has an artificial leg and is constantly suffering from inflammation of the stump of the leg which gives him intense pain. By his qualities of grit and devotion to duty, Flight Sergeant Park has earned the admiration and respect of his fellow members in the squadron.'

Douglas was later commissioned and retired from the RAF as a squadron leader.

Throughout every one of his 40 operations, as well as the countless number of training sorties and flight tests, Douglas knew that his chances of abandoning a

34th Entry conducting engine running tests.

crippled aircraft with an artificial leg were slim. He knew also that even if he had made it out, he was likely to be seriously injured once he hit the ground. Despite this, he kept on flying, a fine example of the indomitable spirit of Halton.

Edgar Harold (Harry) Jenkins of the 34th Entry found himself as ground crew within 12 Squadron of the Advanced Air Striking Force (AASF) at the start of the war and caught up in the chaos of the retreat that followed its ignominious thrashing at the hands of an all-conquering enemy.

He recalls the squadron's arrival in France and being billeted in a hayloft at Berry-au-Bac, bedding down in straw and washing and shaving in freezing water. The only positive was being rationed by the French, which meant a daily allowance of red wine, and a milky coffee served in the evening by the farmer's daughter.

In terms of servicing in the field, Harry recounts a particular issue that was not widely reported at the time or since: "I recall the problems with repairs that were caused by the non-interchangeability of airframe parts, the Fairey Battle components having been made at different factories."

Moving with the squadron as it deployed to different airfields, Harry was detached to a garage in Guignicourt (to the north of Rheims), sleeping on wooden beds and enjoying the warmth of a coke stove:

"Our job in the workshop was to do top overhauls to Merlin engines; one of my jobs was to grind the valves in a machine that Le Patron showed me how to use, such luxuries not forming part of the Halton equipment. We also made the mounting kits for the under-mounted rearward-firing Vickers machine guns and turned out many sets of bomb-delay gear – sets of vanes that fitted around the bomb tail to slow down their rate of fall. We were told that some Battles had been hit by their own bombs which ricocheted up during low-level attacks."

In May, their workshops detachment was evacuated to Troyes, travelling separately from the rest of the squadron: "The rumour at the time was that we were lucky to get away, having been forgotten until a three-tonner which was collecting gear from the officers' mess in the nearby chateau thought of us."

Such was the pace of the German advance, and the chaos that ensued, that Harry and his fellow airmen moved twice more in quick succession from Échemines to Le Mans, being strafed by Luftwaffe fighters en route. They moved again to the outskirts of Brest on 16/17 June and were told to abandon their kit and march to the quay to disembark. Back in the UK with only the clothes he stood up in, Harry was transported to RAF Locking and given a period of leave. He re-joined the squadron at Finningley, and with the threat of invasion looming, spent time in the cockpit of a Battle manning the rear Vickers K gun as part of the airfield defence.

Moving with the squadron to Eastchurch and then Binbrook, his overriding memory of these times – beyond being bombed by the Italians – was of spending many hours trying to bleed air from the Battle's hydraulic system. He left the squadron on promotion to corporal, and a posting to 44 Squadron at Waddington.

Harry was commissioned in May 1942 and enjoyed an impressive career in the Technical (now Engineering) Branch of the RAF, being honoured with the CBE and retiring in 1973 in the rank of air commodore.

Edinburgh-born James McGregor of the 41st Entry spent most of his war years in India with 99 and 215 Bomber Squadrons, having left Halton in 1942. On his return to the UK in 1946 he served at Boscombe Down before being posted to Hong Kong in 1951. A keen and useful footballer, James played for the RAF against the Royal Navy at Wembley and represented the Hong Kong National team for two years between 1951 and 1953. It was in 1953 that he finally left the RAF to join the Hong Kong government civil service.

Demonstrating excellent business, administrative and leadership skills, James quickly rose through the civil service ranks to become deputy director of Trade and Industry and deputy commissioner for Customs. He was awarded the Imperial Service Order in 1973 and appointed to the Most Excellent Order of the British Empire in 1975. Various other senior appointments followed, including his election to the Hong Kong Legislative Council. In 1995 he was appointed to the executive council to advise the governor of the colony, Chris Patten.

For his long and distinguished career in public service in Hong Kong he was knighted by HRH Prince Charles in June 1997, during the transfer of the colony to China. He was the last person to be knighted in Hong Kong, and the only former apprentice not to reach air rank before becoming a knight. Sir James McGregor KB, OBE, ISO died in Canada in 2014.

Whereas Sir James could claim a 'last', an apprentice from the 56th Entry could boast a 'first', as the first ex-Brat to become a divisional commander in the Kenyan police. Charles Long fell in love with Africa while flying training in Southern Rhodesia. Indeed, he loved it so much that on his return to the UK he resigned from the RAF to join the Kenya Police as an assistant inspector in October 1953 at the height of the Mau Mau troubles.

His Halton training stood him in good stead for he was quickly promoted through the ranks. By 1963 he was a superintendent in Nairobi Area Headquarters and ultimately given command of the North Coast division which stretched from Mombasa to the Somali border. There was rarely a dull moment:

> "The North Coast was the most interesting division, with armed raids by the Somali 'Shifta' into Kenya, various tribal raids such as the Wakamba into the Orma areas, and the Pokomo Tribe versus the Waboni, as well as armed poachers killing game in the Tsavo Game Reserve. This was in addition to the usual police activities following assorted murders, rapes, burglaries, thefts, car accidents and drunken tourists, all controlled by my eight police stations in the area.
>
> "I was awarded a medal by President Jomo Kenyatta for operations against the Shifta after independence which goes nicely with the one I got for opposing the Mau Mau before independence."

Another who might claim a 'first' among Halton's illustrious alumni is Squadron Leader Albert Rumble AFC of the 9th Entry. Holder of the RAF's air gunnery record, Albert could, with some justification, claim to have been the power behind the world's first true 'Top Gun' school.

Passing out as a carpenter rigger in the summer of 1926, Albert fulfilled an ambition to fly only four years after leaving Halton, and after gaining his wings was posted to 32 Squadron at Kenley. A gifted pilot from the off, Albert took part in the Hendon Air Display of 1936 and 1937, thrilling crowds with synchronised aerobatics in the squadron's Bristol Bulldogs. He followed a flying instructor's course with a further course in air gunnery, becoming something of an expert. On 14 May 1937 he put theory into practice, breaking the RAF's air gunnery record with an astonishing 90.1 per cent hits. He also made the first interception using the experimental 'high-frequency direction-finding' equipment.

Retiring from the RAF in the summer of 1938 and being placed on the reserve, he re-enlisted on the outbreak of war as an instructor, and in December 1941 became a test pilot and air combat instructor at the Air Fighter Development Unit (AFDU) at Duxford. It was here that Albert devoted his time to devising new air-fighting tactics for both Fighter and Bomber Command, tactics that no doubt saved hundreds of lives in the years of fighting that were to follow. His experience was gleaned from testing and evaluating captured enemy aircraft, including a Bf 109 seized by the French during the Battle of France. It was while flying this aircraft on its last flight before being shipped to America that Albert nearly came to grief, intercepted and attacked by Spitfires of 308 Squadron. He also flew the Italian Fiat CR.42 biplane fighter that is now on display at the RAF Museum at Hendon.

Albert was seconded to D Napier & Sons at Luton in the summer of 1942, helping to develop its new 24-cylinder engine installed in two test-bed aircraft, a converted Fairey Battle and the unusual Folland 43/37, an aircraft specifically designed for engine testing. Six months later, and by now a squadron leader, Albert joined de Havilland Propellers as chief test pilot with which he saw out the war. He survived a crash on 28 February 1946 in an Avro Lincoln when all four engines failed shortly after take-off and Albert needed every ounce of his skill to glide the bomber down into a snow-covered field. He was awarded the AFC.

A good many former apprentices found themselves serving – not always completely voluntarily – at sea, responsible for the aircraft of the Fleet Air Arm. His Majesty's Ships *Anselm*, *Avenger*, *Dasher*, *Hermes* and *Nabob* are just some of those vessels that became 'home' to the brave band of 'seaborne Brats' before, during and after the Second World War. Among them was W. J. Burnett of the 11th Entry, posted to the FAA in December 1928 in preference to the Aircraft Depot in Karachi. Since a posting to India meant a five-year unaccompanied stretch, and an attachment to the FAA only two-and-a-half years, to Burnett the choice was obvious! He was posted HMS *Glorious*, a former battlecruiser that had been converted into a carrier and could carry up to 48 aircraft.

> "Joining HMS *Glorious* during the settling down period I was in a complete maze of new and exciting experiences. We were dubbed 'Crabfats' by the RN and Royal Marine lads – crabs become fat from eating the paint covering the ships' hulls, which was grey blue in colour similar to our uniforms. Well, that was the naval explanation. I remember the chief petty officer remarking, 'The only thing that flies around here my lad is the dust – so get cracking!' Not a spectacular introduction to 'life on the ocean wave'."

Initial sea trials and testing the safety and security equipment began in the spring of 1929 in Scotland:

"Testing the safety nets, designed to prevent landing aircraft from toppling over the side, was left to the dockyard engineers and the RAF. No hooks or hookwires were fitted at the time. The trial aircraft were post-First World War DH9As. They were prepared for normal flight, but the controls were set so as to prevent actual take-off. Cords attached to the throttle and ignition controls were taken to the rear of the tail section, chocks put in position and the engines run up to a pre-determined throttle setting. As the chocks were removed, the ignition was cut, and the aircraft was left to veer to port and enter the nets.

"This was fine in theory, but we lost three aircraft over the side until it was decided to reduce the throttle setting. Crude systems they may have been, but the designers were able to re-assess safety measures and many a pilot's life was saved."

Burnett stayed with the carrier for its spring cruise, a visit to France, Italy, Greece, Yugoslavia (as it was then) and Egypt. Their first port of call was Gibraltar for provisioning, and then out into the Med. Disaster struck, however, on 1 April 1931, when entering a fog bank. The captain had reduced speed as there was an eerie silence as they crawled slowly through the nothingness that surrounded them. The carrier's aircraft were already aloft. Then there was a sickening crunch and the ship shuddered to a halt. It had collided with a French emigrant ship, the SS *Florida*, bound for the South of France. Such was the impetus of the *Glorious* that it scythed through the smaller ship and into its hold where most of the emigrants were accommodated. Twenty-four passengers and crew and one member of the *Glorious*'s crew were killed.

"During later years I witnessed many examples of death and mutilation, but none has left its mark so indelibly on my mind as that dreadful 1 April. As for the aircraft, they were instructed to land wherever they could. Some made it to Spain, some ditched alongside our accompanying destroyers, and others alongside *Glorious* herself, to be hauled aboard by crane or whatever means were to hand. The *Florida* became a floating hospital and mortuary, whilst the uninjured survivors were brought aboard the carrier before transfer to other ships. Eventually *Glorious*, with badly damaged bows, limped into Gibraltar for temporary repairs, all thoughts of our spring cruise long forgotten."

Surtees Elliott, known to family and friends in his home town of Washington as 'Stan', was part of the 29th Entry and trained as a fitter rigger. He was also an outstanding athlete, being awarded a Barrington Kennett medal and competing in the AAA Junior Championships at White City.

Close up of damage to aircraft in Aden.

After serving as a fitter with 102 Squadron, Stan was posted to Aden in June 1938 where he joined 8 Squadron equipped with Vickers Vincents. Like most ex-Brats of his vintage, he quickly volunteered for flying duties, manning the Lewis gun mounted in the rear cockpit.

On 15 January 1941, Elliott was detailed to fly as the crewman in Vincent K4716 on a routine flight carrying spares to a detached flight in the Hadhramaut region of the Aden Protectorate. Lashed to the starboard wing was a spare wheel being delivered to an army unit. Some way into the flight, the lashing on the wheel worked its way loose. The slipstream forced the tyre up against the hot exhaust of the engine where it caught fire, sending molten rubber against the fabric fuselage sides and the wing.

Elliott immediately saw the danger and attempted to climb on to the wing, in an action reminiscent of a future VC, Norman Jackson. He was hindered by his parachute, which he was forced to remove. Once on the wing he pulled the wheel clear of the exhaust and attempted to re-secure it to the wing strut. With a very precarious hold, this difficult operation took him over 30 minutes. The severe turbulence merely compounded the problem. Eventually, he managed to lash the wheel down and return to the safety of his cockpit before the pilot made an emergency landing.

Some weeks later, it was announced that Leading Aircraftman Surtees Elliott had been awarded the Air Force Medal for his gallantry. The citation recorded that 'he undoubtedly saved the aircraft from catching fire and the crew from serious injury'. The air officer commanding-in-chief, Middle East Command had recommended the award of the George Medal, a higher award, but the RAF Awards Committee in London felt differently.

It was by no means the end of Elliott's gallantry. In early 1942 he remustered to flight engineer/air gunner and later joined 265 Squadron in Madagascar to combat the increasing number of German U-boats and support vessels operating in the Indian Ocean. On 20 August, Elliott and his crew set off for their 18th anti-submarine patrol. Previous patrols in the Catalina flying boats had been long and arduous, some lasting up to 18 hours.

On that day they got lucky and spotted a U-boat (U862) on the surface. His skipper dived out of the sun to attack but presented a steady target for the German gunners who opened up with their 3.7-cm and 2-cm flak guns. The bow gunner in the Catalina (quite possibly Elliott) opened fire just as the aircraft received a direct hit in the starboard wing and engine, which set the aircraft on fire. The pilot continued to fly straight at the U-boat, even when the flak started to register hits in the cockpit area. The U-boat manoeuvred violently as it appeared that the burning Catalina would ram the submarine. The aircraft just missed and crashed into the sea a mere 50 yards away where it exploded. There were no survivors.

Stan and his twelve crewmates are commemorated on the Alamein memorial.

Of those former Brats who achieved fame and celebrity after leaving the RAF, perhaps the best known was the broadcaster Cliff Michelmore CBE. Cliff was a typical apprentice in many ways; his father died when he was two, leaving his mother to bring up six children on her own. After briefly flirting with the idea of becoming a Methodist minister, Cliff arrived at Halton as part of the 32nd Entry, passing out in 1938. Recruited to join the British Forces Network radio in Germany, he became a regular presenter of *Forces Favourites*, and was initially put off joining the BBC on account of not being the right class. Unperturbed, he focused on the 'new' medium of television, later becoming the anchorman of *Tonight*, described as the first nightly television programme to blend current affairs with light entertainment, and which ran for eight years from 1957. He covered three general elections, as well as the Aberfan mining disaster, but is perhaps better remembered as the long-serving presenter of the BBC's *Holiday* programme.

He had only the highest praise for Halton, and the start it gave him.

> "Once you left Halton, you had this tag on you that you were an ex-Brat, and that was a caché. That was something very much in your favour, because engineering officers, COs and so on would say 'he's an ex-apprentice, by definition he knows what he's doing'. And that, in a way, was a responsibility."

24 GERMAN GENERALS, OILY RAGS, AND MRS CHIANG

On 12 September 1921, W. S. Reed[1] took part in what can only be described as an epic flight. An aircraft of 55 Squadron had crashed while defending local levies from attacks by rebel tribesman in the Mosul area of Iraq. Our Brat, a corporal Fitter observer, was to fly in a second aircraft tasked with locating the crashed machine and any surviving crew. He packed the DH9A with as many bombs and as much additional ammunition for the guns as they could carry, as well as the usual 'forced-landing' provisions which included a spare undercarriage wheel.

Arriving over the village where the aircraft had been attacked, they bombed and strafed the immediate area and then flew lower in order to find their missing friends. Locating the burned-out wreckage of the aircraft, his pilot opted to land, first firing a Very cartridge to confirm the wind direction. Luck and providence were on their side, for despite landing in a rock-strewn valley, their aircraft came to a stop with all parts still in place. Including the undercarriage!

They found the downed pilot and his observer, both badly injured and burned, and both clearly requiring medical attention. The captain of the levies, now on the scene, agreed to take the pilot to the nearest levy post, since he was considered too ill to fly. The unconscious gunner was taken to the waiting aircraft, with its engine still ticking over, and strapped into the rear cockpit, prompting the levy captain to enquire of the pilot where our intrepid observer would sit. His own words tell the story:

> "My pilot replied, 'Oh I'll take him on the mainplane. I think I can get off all right and he won't fall off'. It was with a sinking heart that I lay across the top surface of the lower mainplane on the port side, curled my arms around the front strut, and hooked my legs around the rear strut."

The Brat waved a tender farewell to the levy captain, tightened his hold on the strut, shut his eyes and prayed.

"Getting into wind the pilot grinned at me to see if I was ready for the take-off. I managed to give a sickly smile and a feeble wave, and with my heart in my mouth, prepared for the worst. The pilot opened the throttle, and away we went, missing large stones by inches, any one of which would have brought about disaster had we hit it, and I received a good volume of exhaust gases and carbon from the open exhaust pipe."

After what seemed a lifetime, the jolting ceased and they were airborne, making 67 miles back to base with our Brat hanging on, literally, for his life. The landing by his pilot was exemplary ("Never have I experienced such a smooth landing."), and on halting, the pilot told his observer to hop off. "Sir," he replied, "I've travelled 67 miles in this position, and I don't intend to get off and walk from this side of the airfield to the hangar." His pilot taxied the aircraft to the hangar curtains at which point the Brat fell from, rather than dismounted, the aircraft.

Reed was black with exhaust smoke and had lost a good pair of flying goggles. A Form 664B action was taken later. When the returning aircraft was inspected subsequently, a bullet hole was found close to where our Brat had been lying. It had passed through the port side, near the plane root fittings, and carried away three ignition terminals from the port side Delco Ignition Distributor.

The injured gunner recovered, only to be injured again by a water buffalo, after an hilarious evening in Mosul. The story has unfortunately been forgotten in time.

On 21 October 1937, a delegation of senior German Luftwaffe officers visited Halton as part of a high-level German air force mission led by General Erhard Milch. The RAF chief of the Air Staff was under no illusions as to what was afoot and recognised the Germans would be assessing not just the quality of the training provided, but also the status of the boys' morale. A letter from the CAS to the Halton commandant made it clear his desire to impress upon the German mission the RAF's state of preparedness and efficiency. Questions were to be answered forthrightly, and the mission should be allowed to see (as it were, 'casually') apprentices undertaking physical training. He also wrote: 'It has been decided that the Nazi flag will not be flown but that, as a small compliment to the German air force, small Nazi emblems (which appear to give pleasure) may be displayed on the luncheon tables.'

Howard Balchin of the 38th Entry travelled to the Middle East in November 1940 for the start of almost three years' service overseas. He was promoted to become the senior NCO in charge of all aircraft servicing and repairs in Eritrea. On one memorable occasion, a strange four-engined aircraft landed unexpectedly – a Boeing Stratoliner – and with an American civil engineer, Howard marshalled it into a suitable parking area. Opening the door and peering inside, they were confronted by a sea of Chinese faces, from which a lady's voice could be heard saying: "Good morning gentlemen". The lady was Soong Mei-Ling – better known as Madame Chiang Kai-shek – wife of the famous wartime Chinese leader.

As a staging post, there were strict orders that the OC should be immediately notified of the arrival of any VIPs but the man in question lived out and took some time to convince that it really was Madame Chiang on his station. While they waited, Howard ordered one of his men to fetch tea and doughnuts from the canteen for the visitors.

Their departure was a different affair altogether, with a cavalcade of 20 or so cars and BOAC officials in their finery to see their guests safely on their way. As Howard was to remark later, few Brats will have been able to claim that they'd shared canteen tea and wads with Madame CKC!

Frank Tams of the 22nd Entry flew convoy escorts with 217 Squadron from St Eval in Cornwall – dull, routine sorties in the vain hope of spotting a U-boat on the surface. Returning from one such sortie in his Avro Anson Mk 1, Frank's wireless operator received a signal that St Eval was fog-bound, and it was impossible to land. Low on fuel, Frank dropped as low as he dared to find safety and was rewarded with the sight of a long and potentially smooth beach on which to land. Making a quick pass to ensure there were no obstructions, Frank came in for a near perfect landing. Switching off and clambering out of their aircraft, the crew found themselves confronted by a small boy who began firing in questions about the Anson. It soon became clear that he knew as much if not more about their aircraft than they did. When asked where he had gleaned such detailed knowledge, the boy replied simply: "From my cigarette cards".

A bowser arrived next morning, and with the bombs removed, the Anson took off and returned safely to St Eval.

Experience can never be taught; it has to be learned. No-one knows this more than Neville Jack BEM of the 40th Entry. At 37 MU Burtonwood he spent many weeks cleaning drip trays and sweeping hangars. His chiefy's orders were quite explicit: "Look, learn but don't touch." Sadly, Neville didn't listen.

During his second week at Burtonwood, a Miles Magister landed late one afternoon with a pretty Air Transport Auxiliary (ATA) pilot at the controls, Lettice Curtis. Chiefy gave Neville responsibility for marshalling the aircraft to dispersal. Full of enthusiasm but devoid of knowledge, Neville guided the 'Maggie' to a parking slot, jumped up to help the pilot out of the cockpit, and put his foot straight through the port wing. Nobody had told him the Magister had wooden wings.

Happily, Neville was not court-martialled, though he did receive a deserved rocket. Chiefy detailed a corporal rigger to work all night to repair the damage. It was the best lesson Neville ever learned in man management.

The story of the Lightning engineer is a famous one (see Chapter Sixteen). But it is certainly not the only occasion that an apprentice has taken to the sky when they shouldn't have. On 29 November 1940, AC1 Jeff Amer, a rigger on 421 Flight at RAF Hawkinge, clambered into the cockpit of a Spitfire IIa, started the engine, and tried to take off in the misguided hope of convincing his superiors that his application for pilot training should be accelerated. He had been determined to be a pilot since passing out of the 38th Entry and spending the first few months of service at 65 Squadron at the height of the Battle of Britain.

His attempt to take off was little short of shambolic. At the moment the aircraft should have come 'unstuck', the starboard wing tip struck the ground and was torn cleanly off. Momentum sped the rest of the Spitfire, minus one wing, further along before finally coming to rest in a cloud of mud and filth. Luckily it did not catch fire. Jeff was court-martialled and found guilty of 'trying to take off in a Spitfire without authority and the necessary qualifications, thereby crashing it and causing damage of not less than £20'. He was sentenced to six months in the glasshouse but the morning he was due to start his sentence he absconded, enjoying a meal at a local pub in Bexhill and then fleeing to London where he was apprehended by the RAF police at Marble Arch underground station. He received a further 27 days onto his sentence. Jeff became a media sensation, and some officers felt his punishment should have been more lenient since he had shown 'the right spirit'.

Jeff never did become a fighter pilot but did forge a career in air traffic control.

Group Captain John Manning OBE of the 57th Entry has established his place in apprentice folklore. He was the last flight sergeant aircraft apprentice to command a passing out parade in front of the school's revered founder Lord Trenchard. Before the parade, John was briefed that Lord Trenchard liked to talk to his apprentices, and if this happened, he was politely to ignore him and a carry on. John's worst fears were realised at the end of the parade when he approached Lord Trenchard to request permission to march off. The great man started to chat. Nervously wondering what he should do, John listened for a while until Lord Trenchard paused for breath at which point he saluted smartly, returned to his post and marched off the 57th.

John thought his career had ended there and then. Not a bit of it. He was commissioned in the then Technical Branch in 1953 and served his first tour in Singapore responsible for repair and salvage during the Malayan emergency. He spent many detachments in Malaya recovering crashed aircraft often in difficult and uncomfortable circumstances. As a flight lieutenant, John was posted as OC Tech Wing on secondment to the Royal Rhodesian Air Force and served again in Singapore as a squadron leader OC Engineering Squadron and again as OC Engineering Squadron at Wittering. In 1968, he was the engineer who managed the ground support for the RAF Harrier which won the *Daily Mail* Transatlantic Air

Lord Trenchard inspecting apprentices.

Race to convince the Americans it was an aircraft worth buying.

Air Marshal Sir Kenneth Porter enjoyed a distinguished career at Halton (as part of the 17th Entry) and at Cranwell (he was awarded a cadetship in January 1931), and served on the carrier HMS *Eagle* in the Far East until sustaining a severe injury to his foot that left him crippled for life; his right foot was almost severed from the leg by a drogue cable. Sir Kenneth enjoyed a distinguished war in Signals (for a time he was chief signals officer at 11 Group) and immediately after the war was the CSO at Bomber Command as an air commodore. He was three times mentioned in despatches. It was as AOC-in-C Maintenance Command and head of the Engineering Branch, however, that Sir Kenneth achieved arguably his finest hour.

Taking questions after a lecture at the RAF Staff College in 1969, certain young graduates somewhat arrogantly suggested that the future belonged to men of their calibre, and not those pilots – like Sir Kenneth – who were 'yesterday's men'. Sir Kenneth listened patiently and politely to their views before responding.

Before they set their sights on his job, he said, they had a great deal to learn. He advised they listened to their senior NCOs and airmen, particularly former Brats, and learned from them, especially around the difficulties of servicing aircraft in the field. At the end, and with his voice rising to a crescendo, he virtually shouted: "You give me an ex-Halton apprentice with a spanner and an oily rag and I'll build you a fucking aeroplane!"

He sat down to thunderous applause from the pilots and aircrew present.

Shackleton crews on 205 Squadron at Changi in the early 1960s could expect to serve seven or eight two-week detachments at RAF Gan during their tour in Singapore. Gan, situated at the bottom of the Maldives archipelago in the Indian Ocean, was a staging post for RAF and other aircraft flying between Aden and Singapore. The squadron detachments provided vital search and rescue (SAR) cover for the vast area of ocean between the two.

Whilst at Gan the crews had a pretty easy time compared with the hectic activity of squadron life in Singapore. With two crews always in residence, work schedules were not especially onerous. A 24-hour stint on SAR stand-by, followed by 24 hours relaxing and enjoying the golden sandy beaches, and a wealth of sporting facilities available on an idyllic tropical island.

'Min' Larkin, a commissioned air electronics officer of the 63rd Entry, remembers a formal dinner night for his off-duty crew in the presence of the AOC Air Forces Middle East Air Vice-Marshal Andrew Humphrey:

> "Just before midnight our crew retired to our accommodation in a noisy alcoholic state. We had an inkling that the duty crew, who were hacked off because they had drawn the duty straw for that night and had to remain abstemious, might have some unpleasant surprise for us on our return. We were not disappointed. As we were about to enter our rooms (all at ground level) they sprang out from the dark carrying buckets of water which they hurled over us. They raced back to the ablutions to recharge their buckets while we found our own buckets and a fire hose to fight back. A water battle ensued with each of us discarding our wet clothes as we battled on until we were stark naked and soaked to the skin – typical high jinks for young aircrew."

After 20 minutes or so the battle petered out and Min made for his bed.

> "As I tried to enter my room there were howls of laughter from the duty crew. I had stupidly left my key in the lock when I went to the dinner but they all denied having it. No problem, I thought, I can outwit this lot and belted off to the mess where duplicate door keys were kept in an open cabinet in the mess foyer.
>
> "I burst through the swing doors at the entrance to the mess, confident that nobody would be around at such an early hour in the morning. I was wrong. There in their full mess dress were the AOC and OC RAF Gan. My disciplinary training kicked in. I automatically stood to attention just look-

ing at them while desperately trying to think of some kind of explanation for my naked state. For a brief moment they just stared back at me in total silence until the CO enquired: 'Can we help you?'

"'I have come to collect the key to my room,' I replied nervously. 'Carry on', he said, without missing a beat, while the AOC continued to stare blankly ahead. I dashed to the key cabinet, grabbed my key and beat it out of the mess like lightning. (I would love to have known their subsequent conversation.) Back at the accommodation building the crews had dispersed, kindly leaving my old key in the door. I lay on my bed not quite believing what had just happened. All I could think about was what sort of punishment might follow the next day. I don't think I slept a wink. As it was, I never heard another word about it.

"I claim therefore to hold a unique service record in being the only officer or even airman to have appeared at attention in front of his commanding officer and AOC soaking wet and stark bullock naked at the midnight hour."

Michael Armitage joined the RAF as a Halton Apprentice in 1947, he won a cadetship to Cranwell and was commissioned as a pilot in 1954. He served tours of duty in Hong Kong, the UK, Germany and Malta. He later became director of Forward Policy in the Air Force Department of the Ministry of Defence. In 1982 he joined the Defence and Intelligence Staff, and three years later became the first chief of Defence Intelligence. He was the Air Member for the Supply and Organisation in the Air Force Department followed by two years as commandant of the Royal College of Defence Studies. He retired as Air Chief Marshal Sir Michael Armitage having been knighted in 1983.

But it was as station commander at RAF Luqa in Malta that he faced arguably his most memorable challenge – helping to negotiate the release of almost 300 hostages from three terrorist hijackers.

It was 25 November 1973 when KLM Flight 861 left Amsterdam en route to Tokyo via Beirut[2]. It was over Iraq that the hijackers made their move, and after various adventures, the aircraft diverted to Malta. Sir Michael recalls:

"I was just leaving the office to go back to the married quarter and I got a call from the air traffic control tower who said, 'We've got [the pilot of] a hijacked aircraft on the air and he wants to land here'. I thought tell him to shove off and go to Catania in Sicily, we don't want a hijacked aircraft here thank you very much. 'Oh that's no use,' said the pilot, 'because I've got the chaps up the front on the flight deck and they're holding a gun to my head and they're insisting on landing in Malta.'"

Fortunately, Sir Michael had considered the possibility of a hijack situation (they were not infrequent in the 1970s) and put his emergency plan into action:

> "We had ambulances standing by, and buses converted into ambulances all at the ready. We also had the Royal Marine commandos from army head-quarters on the alert in case it came to some sort of shoot-out. In due course the aircraft landed on the airfield – a very good piece of flying by the pilot (the runway was unsuitable for landing such a large aircraft), and I got on to headquarters down at Valetta."

Shortly after, Dom Mintoff, the then prime minister, arrived on the station and was escorted to the control tower: "Mintoff and I sat there, all night, bargaining with these terrorists, getting passengers off in return for fuel, which took a long time."

After tense negotiations, 225 passengers – mostly Japanese – were released: "The terrorists were very difficult about the whole thing and it took a long time to pacify them."

During the night, the Egyptian consul arrived to offer his support. A plump, rather silly man, he struck something of a comic figure:

> "He came trundling up to the control tower and said: 'Tell me what I can do to help.' So we got on to the hijackers who were speaking through an interpreter in the aircraft, and said we had the Egyptian consul with us asking if he could help in any way. 'Ah,' said the chief hijacker, 'send him out to the aircraft and we'll release some more hostages.' We told the con-sul this and he collapsed on the floor. We had to carry him out!"

Happily, all of the passengers and crew were eventually released unharmed.

APPENDIX ONE
APOLOGIA AND NOTE ON SOURCES

Former Halton apprentice Chaz Bowyer, writing in *Bomber Barons* (William Kimber, 1983), felt obliged to explain why so many other notable bomber pilots and aircrew had not been included in his book. I feel a similar obligation.

There will undoubtedly be those who question why other notable Brats such as Hamish Mahaddie, Sir John Lapsley, Peter Wykeham, and George Lott are not included, as well as the likes of Roy Ralston, Wally Lashbrook and Jamie Pitcairn-Hill. They may also question why more recent airmen such as Cliff Spink or Sir Keith Williamson, the former chief of the Air Staff, have not featured, or why the stories are weighted so heavily in favour of Halton over Cranwell.

A simple explanation is space; a more complex answer is that I have endeavoured to choose examples of men who have not necessarily been written about extensively before. I have also deliberately tried to include 'ordinary' Brats, and not just those who achieved high rank or high awards, as well as including stories from different theatres of war and in different decades. More than this, I have attempted to demonstrate that the genius of Halton is that it prepares boys for life beyond the service. Success comes in many guises.

In terms of sources and referencing, since this is not written as, or intended to be, a heavy reference book, I have used endnotes in the text to provide additional detail or context within a story where appropriate. I have occasionally used a similar technique to highlight a document or published source from where the story/information has been derived when I think it useful in terms of further reading. I am conscious that too many references, while evidencing the depth of research, can be distracting for the reader. Others may disagree; I like to write books how I like to read them!

The sources for chapters ten, eleven, fifteen, eighteen, nineteen, twenty, twenty-one and twenty-two are the memories, logbooks and personal correspondence and archives of the individuals interviewed over an 18-month period. Official records (operations record books and specific TNA documents) were also consulted where appropriate and are easy to access.

For the chapters on the Rajah of Sarawak (chapter six) and Special Duties (chapter thirteen) I am fortunate enough to have acquired the logbooks of both

Francis Brooks and Bob Lewis, and these provided the framework to their stories. Francis left a written testimony which I consulted, with particular reference to his later tour on B-25 Mitchells, and the incident with 180 Squadron referred to in the text. Bob Lewis also wrote a detailed, first-hand account about his special duties, as well as leaving a recorded interview with a local journalist which I similarly own and have had transcribed.

The principal source throughout the book is the Halton Archive. This includes a box file on every entry since the school was founded. They vary, of course, in the level of information they contain, but invariably have the relevant order of merit and exam results for each entry. Occasionally there are rolls of honour, and in certain cases, there are privately published 'yearbooks' with reminiscences from various former apprentices. These have been especially useful for chapters twenty-three and twenty-four, as have back issues of the *Halton Magazine* and the more recent *Haltonian*. The RAFHAA website is also an incredibly useful starting point for any research into Halton, with a list of decorations for bravery that is constantly being updated as new information is discovered.

Every so often a box file reveals a 'gem', as in the case of the letter from Ian Muirhead's sister to the archive a decade or so ago seeking further information about his time as an apprentice. It revealed a number of personal anecdotes and insights that I have included to help bring Ian's story to life.

In terms of further reading, there are surprisingly few books about Halton. *Son of Halton*, by Charles Kimber, is probably the best known, as well as *The Poacher's Brats*, and both are worth a read, as is John Clements' book *The Electronic Airborne Goldfish*. Chapter eight, the story of Gerry Blacklock, has been sourced from Gerry's unpublished autobiography entitled *Half a Life. Half Remembered*. This is just one of dozens of memoirs kept at Halton which are worthy of further investigation, should ever a sequel be in the offing!

APPENDIX TWO
AWARDS AND COMMANDANTS

Below is a list of the apprentices awarded knighthoods (including Halton, Cranwell and Flowerdown apprentices). Sir Walter Dawson is variously reported as being a boy mechanic and an apprentice, so is included in the list.

MRAF Sir Keith Williamson GCB, AFC (50th Entry)
ACM Sir Alfred Earle KBE, CB (11th Entry)
ACM Sir John Rogers KCB, OBE (49th Entry)
ACM Sir Michael Armitage KCB, CBE (56th Entry)
AM Sir Herbert Spreckley KBE, CB (3rd Entry)
AM Sir Norman Coslett KCB, OBE (13th Entry)
AM Sir Kenneth Porter KCB, OBE (17th Entry)
AM Sir John Lapsley KBE, CB, DFC, AFC (27th Entry)
AM Sir Peter Wykeham KCB, DFC, AFC (28th Entry)
AM Sir Eric Dunn KBE, CB, BEM (48th Entry)
AM Sir John Fitzpatrick KBE, CB (56th Entry)
AM Sir Dusty Miller KBE (210th Entry)
AVM Sir Thomas Shirley KBE, CB (8th Entry)
AVM Sir Colin Scragg KCB, AFC* (10th Entry)
AVM Sir Bernard Chacksfield KBE, CB (17th Entry)
Air Cdre Sir Frank Whittle OM, KBE, CB (8th Entry)
Sir James McGregor KBE, OBE, ISO (41st Entry)

ACM Sir Walter Dawson KBE, CBE, DSO (Boy mechanic 1919)

Below is a list of the commandants of RAF Halton.

AVM F. R. Scarlett CB, DSO – December 1919 – February 1924
AVM G. L. Lambe CB, CMG – February 1924 – March 1928
Air Cdre I. M. Bonham-Carter CB, OBE – March 1928 – September 1931
AVM N. A. K. MacEwen CMG, DSO – October 1931 – December 1934
Air Cdre J. T. Babington CB, DSO – January 1935 – July 1936
Air Cdre G. R. M. Reid DSO, MC – July 1936 – August 1938

Air Cdre G. B. Dacre CBE, DSO – August 1938 – August 1939

AVM Sir O. Swann KCB, CBE – August 1939 – July 1940

Air Cdre G. B. Dacre CBE, DSO – July 1940 – October 1942

Air Cdre M. G. White CBE, DSO – October 1942 – January 1946

Air Cdre J. F. Titmas CBE, DSO – January 1946 – February 1949

Air Cdre N. Carter CB, AFC – February 1949 – January 1951

Air Cdre J. G. Elton CBE, DFC, AFC – January 1951 – February 1952

Air Cdre J. G. Weston CB, OBE – February 1952 – January 1954

Air Cdre G. N. E. Tindal-Carill-Worsley CB, CBE – January 1954 – May 1956

Air Cdre E. D. McK Nelson CB, ADC – May 1956 – April 1958

Air Cdre T. N. Coslett CB, OBE – April 1958 – July 1961

Air Cdre B. Robinson CBE – July 1961 – December 1963

Air Cdre D. M. Strong CB, AFC – December 1963 – March 1966

Air Cdre A. C. Deere DSO, OBE, DFC March 1966 – November 1967

Air Cdre H. P. Connolly CB, DFC, AFC, AFM, ADC – November 1967 – December 1968

Air Cdre R. H. G. Weighill CBE, DFC, ADC – December 1968 – April 1973

Air Cdre B. Hamilton OBE, DFC, AFC – April 1973 – June 1975

Air Cdre M. P. Stanton CBE – June 1975 – November 1977

From November 1977 the post of commandant RAF Halton was discontinued and replaced by a station commander at group captain rank. Four ex-apprentices returned to command the station:

Group Captain M. Evans (70th Entry) – September 1981 – November 1983

Group Captain I. Blunt (84th Entry) – December 1988 – January 1991

Group Captain R. Brumpton (106th Entry) – January 1991 – January 1993

Group Captain G. Burton (100th Entry) – January 1993 – February 1995

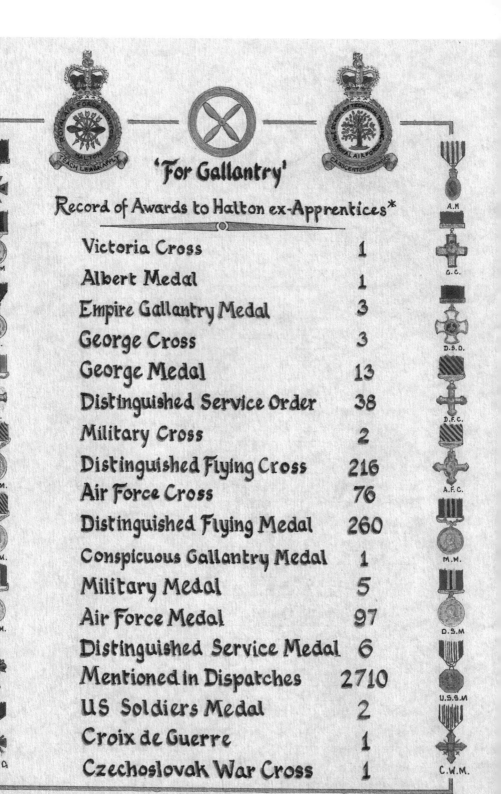

'For Gallantry'

Record of Awards to Halton ex-Apprentices*

Victoria Cross	1
Albert Medal	1
Empire Gallantry Medal	3
George Cross	3
George Medal	13
Distinguished Service Order	38
Military Cross	2
Distinguished Flying Cross	216
Air Force Cross	76
Distinguished Flying Medal	260
Conspicuous Gallantry Medal	1
Military Medal	5
Air Force Medal	97
Distinguished Service Medal	6
Mentioned in Dispatches	2710
US Soldiers Medal	2
Croix de Guerre	1
Czechoslovak War Cross	1

Medal labels (left column): V.C., E.G.M., G.M., M.C., D.F.M., A.F.M., C.G.M., MiD, C. de G.

Medal labels (right column): A.M., G.C., D.S.O., D.F.C., A.F.C., M.M., D.S.M., U.S.S.M., C.W.M.

* Collated from the records of the 40,000 Apprentices who graduated between 1920 – 1993

Clive Brookes C93
2020

APPENDIX THREE
THE APPRENTICES' ASSOCIATION

There had been an Old Haltonians' Association from the earliest days of the Halton apprenticeships in the 1920s. It was founded by Lieutenant Colonel Alexander Caldwell DSO in 1925. The purpose of the association was to stimulate interest and comradeship between all ex-Halton apprentices. It was also to provide information on the progress and activities of former Brats and of those apprentices still under training and increase the range and circulation of the *Halton Magazine*.

The association re-energised in the 1970s with the Golden Jubilee in August 1970 and the publication of Charles Kimber's book, *Son of Halton*, in 1977. (Charles was in the 18th Entry.) Charles became part of a group led by Douglas Henning (37th Entry) who organised a reunion at Halton in October 1978 with the help of Squadron Leader Jim Skerrett (35th) who was serving at Halton at that time. Almost 180 former apprentices gathered in Henderson (No. 1 Wing) mess, and the guest of honour was Group Captain John Downes, the then Officer Commanding RAF Halton.

Along with Douglas and Charles, a wider group of former apprentices including Maurice White, Arthur Bint (50th Entry), Les Anderson (51st Entry) and Bill Marsland (34th Entry) helped with organising a further reunion in September 1980 which attracted an estimated 3,500 ex-Brats. It was strongly supported by the station commander, Group Captain Owen Truelove, and set the pattern for all future reunions. During the day, the RAF Halton Aircraft Apprentices Association was formed at an inaugural meeting chaired by Douglas Henning. A constitution was adopted, and a management committee formed. Bill Marsland was appointed vice chairman, and Ed Stonor (54th Entry) volunteered to take over from Maurice White as treasurer. Group Captain Don Dormer (41st Entry) became secretary. Others on the committee included Hector Stallworthy (11th Entry) and Flight Lieutenants John Harris (55th) and Alan Rainbow (34th Entry), the latter providing the vital link to the station as the Halton liaison officer. There was even, at the beginning, Chief Technician Apprentice Carden, to represent the current generation. Owen Truelove was appointed the first ex-officio president of the association and all succeeding station commanders have been delighted to accept this position to this day.

Within weeks of the reunion, the first of what was to become a network of regional branches was set up. Other groups were established based on the order of entry, and these have formed the heart of the activities of the ex-apprentice community ever since. Bill Marsland took on the role of co-ordinating the branches, a post he continued for almost 20 years.

The association was instrumental in resurrecting the *Halton Magazine*, now rebranded the *Haltonian*, as a means of keeping current and former apprentices aware of planned events and meetings, as well as the latest news. One of those news items included a focus on the return of Lewis, the fifth incarnation of the famous goat mascot, present for the passing out of the 131st Entry in April 1981. In August 1985, production of the magazine was taken over by Bill Kelley (55th Entry) and published in a new format.

The first annual general meeting of the association was held on 19 October 1981. It was attended by 125 members, including the association's patron, Air Vice-Marshal Michael Armitage (56th Entry) and the newly appointed president, Group Captain Mike Evans (70th Entry), who had taken over as station commander three weeks earlier[1].

One of the major items discussed was a resolution to support a campaign to reinstate the apprentices' 'wheel' badge. The right to wear the wheel had been lost under the 1974 revision of the arrangements for the treatment of young airmen and apprentices under training. The resolution was transmitted to all appropriate authorities with the particular support and involvement of the patron with his access to the higher echelons of the RAF. The wheel was reinstated in time for the graduation of the 134th Entry in September 1982.

In more recent times, the association's constitution has been revised and updated and annual and life membership subscriptions created.

At the 2010 AGM it was proposed and accepted that the name of the association should be changed to drop the word 'Aircraft' from the title and thenceforth be known as the Royal Air Force Halton Apprentices Association (RAFHAA) and to be informally known as 'The Old Haltonians'. Today the RAFHAA is a registered charity and has around 2,500 members. It holds a major reunion at Halton every three years. The next one is scheduled for August 2020 to celebrate Halton's centenary year.

Current vice patrons are Air Marshal Sir Dusty Miller and Air Marshal Cliff Spink (104th Entry). The latter was the former station commander at RAF Coningsby who served as the Tornado Detachment commander during the Gulf War. He is also a noted Spitfire display pilot.

The official contact details for the RAFHAA are as follows:
ROYAL AIR FORCE HALTON
APPRENTICES ASSOCIATION
Building 412
RAF Halton
Aylesbury
Bucks HP22 5PG

Telephone: 01296 696896 (with answerphone)
E-mail: secretary@rafhaa.co.uk

ENDNOTES

INTRODUCTION

1. Two returned as an air commodore, the other four as group captains after the post was down-rated in the 1970s.

CHAPTER ONE

1. His contemporary report appears in a 1932 issue of the *Halton Magazine*. Goffe was later commissioned and retired as a flying officer in 1947.
2. Hugh Champion de Crespigny had been a Royal Flying Corps pilot who later went on to command British air forces in Iraq in the Second World War. He retired as an air vice-marshal and died in 1969.
3. Apprentice wireless operator/mechanics and electrical and instrument makers were trained at RAF Flowerdown but in 1929, after five entries, the school closed down and re-opened at RAF Cranwell.

CHAPTER TWO

1. The squadron had a bad run of luck when it came to commanding officers. Wing Commander H. A. Smith MC, Lloyd's predecessor, had been killed in a night-flying accident on 14 November 1938.
2. The ORB for 9 Squadron lists LAC Ware as occupying this position without any immediate explanation for the error.
3. Leech had survived a serious accident two years earlier when he had crashed a Heyford he was piloting into some trees and a house on the aerodrome boundary when the squadron had been based in Scampton. Leech and Squadron Leader Lamb died in a collision with another 9 Squadron aircraft on 30 October 1939.

CHAPTER THREE

1. Giles and McKechnie finished 5th and 15th respectively in their entry. First in the order of merit was F. D. Terdery.
2. McKechnie's body was never found but in 2019 a UK-based researcher, Mike McLeod, discovered that his body was not only recovered but also buried and has identified the likely gravesite.
3. Despite Ewing's undoubted bravery, the gunner, William Lansdell, did not survive his injuries. The pilot, Sergeant Edward Hindelang, was also killed.

4.   Six Halton Boys were killed when the *Lancastria* went down.

5.   Among those lost was Flight Lieutenant Bill Simpson who was shot down and badly burned. He went on to write an account of his experiences in three books: *One of Our Pilots is Safe*, *The Way of Recovery* and *I Burned My Fingers*.

6.   Cliff Michelmore served with Gray on 12 Squadron before being commissioned, and the two were great friends. Cliff recalls that Thomas had been drunk on duty a few days before the raid and was awaiting his disciplinary fate. It may have been that his spell as orderly sergeant was part-punishment for his misdemeanour.

7.   Air Marshal Sir Arthur Barratt recounted this incident during the passing out of the 43rd Entry. He said that as one man they all stepped forward and had to toss up to decide who would have the honour of going. "They did their job," he said, "but did not come back."

CHAPTER FIVE

1.   A Q ship was a heavily armed merchant vessel with concealed guns, designed to lure submarines in particular into making surface attacks.

2.   Among the men under his command was Bob Braham, one of the most successful night-fighter and intruder pilots, and Guy Gibson.

CHAPTER SIX

1.   Twinkle sadly did not survive the war. He was killed while serving at a maintenance unit when the Hurricane IIC he was flying dived into the ground near Kemble. More information can be found at http://211squadron.org/rw_pearson_dfc.html.

2.   John Pringle-Wood was later shot down in November 1941 and captured.

3.   Perkins received an immediate DSO and his gunner the Conspicuous Gallantry Medal.

CHAPTER SEVEN

1.   Williams had been awarded the Air Force Medal (AFM) before the war. Later commissioned, he was awarded the DFC in May 1940 and killed in a training accident in 1941 as a squadron leader.

2.   Griffiths was the first RCAF pilot after the First World War to be granted a permanent commission in 1926.

3.   *Target for Tonight* is a famous documentary film following the crew of Wellington 'F' for Freddie. The aircraft was flown by Pickard playing the part of the fictional 'Squadron Leader Dickson'.

4.   Pat Lynch-Blosse was killed with 44 Squadron on the night of 9 May 1942 as a wing commander DFC. John Griffiths-Jones was killed on 3 March 1941 returning from operations to Brest. This was the first loss of a Stirling on operations.

5.   Graham had won a DFM following a tour on Blenheims.

6.   The Messerschmitts were from I/JG52.

CHAPTER EIGHT

1.   Pitcairn-Hill competed with Peter Wykeham for the top honours in their entry. Wykeham went on to become an accomplished and very highly decorated fighter pilot in the western

desert and leader of the audacious raid on the Gestapo headquarters in Aarhus. He retired as an air marshal.

2. Twamley, a regular officer, is credited with flying at least 66 operations.

3. Topping the list in the order of merit was George Witty, killed early in the war as a fighter pilot with 87 Squadron in France.

4. Oboe was a blind bombing device developed by the Telecommunications Research Establishment (TRE) capable of identifying targets with incredible accuracy.

5. John Mitchell went on to become navigator on Ascalon, the personal Avro York allocated to Winston Churchill. He retired as an air commodore LVO, DFC, AFC.

6. Fort, born on 14 January 1912 as one of six brothers, was killed on 15 September 1943 on operations to the Dortmund-Ems canal.

7. The squadron engineering officer was also a former Halton apprentice, Pilot Officer Clifford Caple of the 17th Entry.

CHAPTER NINE

1. From a contemporary interview with John Haslam.

2. 'Speed' Le Good was an experienced former chief flying instructor and flight commander who would later command 35 Squadron and serve on PFF HQ staff. He died in 1992.

3. Taken from *Pathfinders 635 Squadron: Definitive History March 1944 - September 1945* by Chris Coverdale (Pathfinder Publishing, 2009).

CHAPTER TEN

1. Bennett had been the AOC 8 Group, Pathfinder Force during the Second World War and later went on to form British South American Airways.

CHAPTER ELEVEN

1. Born Virginia Cherrill, Lady Jersey had been a Hollywood actress whose most famous role was as the blind flower seller in *City Lights*, starring alongside Charlie Chaplin. Prior to marrying George Child-Villiers, the 9th Earl of Jersey, she had been married to Cary Grant. She later married a Polish airman and settled in California.

2. John Titmas was a veteran of the First World War who flew as an observer with 5 Squadron in France in 1917. He was one of the RAF contingent in South Russia in 1919, later becoming a qualified flying instructor and engineering officer. He transferred to the Technical Branch in 1940.

3. HMS *Centaur* was a light fleet carrier laid down in 1944, launched in 1947 and commissioned in 1953.

CHAPTER TWELVE

1. As quoted in 99 Squadron's operations record book. Hartright was later commissioned and lost with 7 Squadron on 30 June 1941.

2. One online source suggested he was at one time the youngest pilot in the country, gaining a licence at the age of 14.

3. Among its most famous losses was that of its commanding officer Wing Commander Basil Embry, though Embry would evade capture and return to the squadron nine weeks later.

4. His victor was Hans-Joachim Redlich who claimed a 'flak-damaged Halifax'.

5. Cyril Flockhart later succeeded in making a 'home run' and was awarded the Distinguished Conduct Medal.

CHAPTER THIRTEEN

1. One of these pilots was Flight Lieutenant Nigel Maynard, later Air Chief Marshal Sir Nigel Maynard KCB, CBE, DFC, AFC.

2. Squadron Leader McKeand DSO DFC & Bar, AFC died in October 1960 at the age of 38.

3. This turned out to be one of the longest flights ever made by Liberators of Eastern Air Command's Strategic Air Force. The crews were in the air for more than 12 hours, much of it over water.

CHAPTER FOURTEEN

1. Both are now in modern Macedonia.

2. The ship was originally called the *Rondine* but had been renamed the *Enzo Sereni* after a Jewish fighter of that name parachuted into Italy and was captured, tortured and killed by the Nazis.

3. Tuel died in September 2018, during the writing of this book. He was 96.

4. Interview with author July 2019.

5. Interview with H. F. King OBE, the technical editor of *Flight* and published 3 July 1953.

6. Sommerich had been a successful P-38 Lightning pilot against the Japanese.

7. Meier went on to serve in the Vietnam War with the 366th Fighter Wing and retire in the rank of colonel.

CHAPTER FIFTEEN

1. Eeles had the distinction of flying the short-lived Westland Whirlwind as OC 263 Squadron.

2. Spokes was lost in a Canberra T4 WJ871 on 24 February 1956. The aircraft crashed into the ground near Stilton, Huntingdonshire, killing Spokes and Flight Lieutenant Herbert Brice. Spokes was 27.

3. The 12 Squadron ORB mentions various serviceability issues with the aircraft. Equipment failed. Canopies shattered. Mistakes happened. Accidents were not uncommon.

4. Wing Commander Brian Duigan DSO DFC, an Australian who had distinguished himself 15 years earlier in North Africa and the Middle East, is also listed in the ORB as flying that day, though he was not part of 12 Squadron.

5. Blythe won his DFC with 437 Squadron.

6. The unit, which had originally been formed at Woodford, was commanded successively by Wing Commander Shirley Underwood OBE and Wing Commander Terrence Fennell OBE, AFC.

7. Group Captain Leonard Cheshire won the Victoria Cross (to add to three DSOs and a DFC) for sustained bravery over four tours of operations, as opposed to a single act of gallantry. He was also appointed to the Order of Merit (OM).

8. Gerhard Ille learned to fly in Yugoslavia in 1941, eventually becoming a fighter pilot in 5./JG2 in 1944. He was shot down and captured near Bayeux on 24 July 1944. He died in 2007.

CHAPTER SEVENTEEN

1. Charles Turner-Hughes, known as 'T-H', flew in the early years of what was to become Transport Command, and after his commission came to an end, joined Caribbean Airways in Jamaica. He later and more famously became chief test pilot for Armstrong Whitworth and died in 1973.

CHAPTER EIGHTEEN

1. Blyth was one of four RAF pilots selected to fly with 77 Squadron RAAF. He had flown special operations in the Second World War, and evaded being captured after being shot down in September 1942.

2. Other squadron personnel were decorated. Blyth received a Bar to his DFC and there were medals too for the two flight commanders, David Tanner and David Harcourt-Smith. Tanner had learned to fly in Southern Rhodesia and was later CO of 2 Squadron at Leeming. He retired from the RAF in 1976. Harcourt-Smith later went on to become commandant at Cranwell and AOC-in-C of RAF Support Command. He retired in 1989 as Air Chief Marshal Sir David Harcourt-Smith GBE, KCB, DFC.

3. The A300-B4 was the world's first twin-engined wide-bodied airliner.

CHAPTER NINETEEN

1. Alan says that AE could easily be mistaken for air electronics as those were the letters on their brevet. Normally the shortened version of the air engineer was 'eng'. The RAF version was the exact equivalent of the civil flight engineer.

2. Reg Hallam went to the Royal Air Force College Cranwell where he won the Sword of Honour as the best cadet of his year (1957-1960). He had been in contention for the 1956 British team at the Olympics as a pole vaulter but did not compete due to back problems.

CHAPTER TWENTY-TWO

1. The squadron lost the crew of Simon 'Budgie' Burgess and Bob Ankerson on the night of 24 January 1991, both men ejecting and being captured. Their bomb exploded prematurely. Burgess was later killed in a flying accident.

CHAPTER TWENTY-THREE

1. Also spelled Yunis, Younas and Younus in contemporary reports.

CHAPTER TWENTY-FOUR

1. Sadly there are no Halton records surviving for W. S. Reed.

2. *Times of Malta* – review 26 November 2009.

APPENDIX THREE

1.   Mike Evans retired as an air commodore and was one of four apprentices to return as station commander. The other three were Group Captain Ian Blunt (84th), Group Captain Rod Brumpton (106th), and Group Captain Geoff Burton (100th). In addition, Air Commodore Pat Connolly (17th) was commandant of Halton. Under Mike's watch, the association helped establish the Trenchard Museum, create the beautiful series of stained-glass windows in St George's Church, and, most notably, produced the Apprentices' 'Tribute' which was unveiled by HM the Queen on 31 October 1997 and is now the site of the annual apprentices' memorial service held in November each year.

INDEX